The Future
of Religious Minorities in
the Middle East

The Future
of Religious Minorities in
the Middle East

Edited by John Eibner

LEXINGTON BOOKS
Lanham • Boulder • New York • London

Published by Lexington Books
An imprint of The Rowman & Littlefield Publishing Group, Inc.
4501 Forbes Boulevard, Suite 200, Lanham, Maryland 20706
www.rowman.com

Unit A, Whitacre Mews, 26-34 Stannary Street, London SE11 4AB

British Library Cataloguing in Publication Information Available

The hardback edition of this book was previously catalogued by the Library of Congress as follows:

Library of Congress Cataloging-in-Publication Data

Names: Eibner, John, editor.
Title: The future of religious minorities in the Middle East / edited by John Eibner.
Description: Lanham : Lexington, 2017. | Includes index.
Identifiers: LCCN 2017040479 (print) | LCCN 2017042547 (ebook) |
    ISBN 9781498561976 (electronic) | ISBN 9781498561969 (cloth : alk. paper)
Subjects: LCSH: Middle East—Religion. | Religious minorities—Middle East—
    History—21st century.
Classification: LCC BL1060 (ebook) | LCC BL1060 .F88 2017 (print) |
    DDC 305.60956—dc23
LC record available at https://lccn.loc.gov/2017040479

ISBN 978-1-4985-6196-9 (cloth : alk. paper)
ISBN 978-1-4985-6198-3 (pbk. : alk. paper)
ISBN 978-1-4985-6197-6 (electronic)

♾ ™ The paper used in this publication meets the minimum requirements of American National Standard for Information Sciences—Permanence of Paper for Printed Library Materials, ANSI/NISO Z39.48-1992.

Printed in the United States of America

Contents

Introduction

John Eibner

Do religious minorities have a future in the Middle East? If this question had been raised in Constantinople, the traumatized capital of the rump Byzantine Empire, at the end of the AD seventh century, the Greek Orthodox sages would have debated the prospects of survival of the region's newest religious minority. It was composed of Muslim soldiers and colonists who had lately streamed out of the Arabian Peninsula in the course of the earliest Islamic jihads of conquest, and settled initially in military outposts throughout the region. The Arab Muslim invaders had overrun all of Byzantium's possession in the Levant and North Africa, as well as the Mesopotamian and Persian empires of the Zoroastrian Sasanian dynasty. Their conquests were incorporated into a new empire: Dar al-Islam, that is, the territories conquered, subjugated by Islam, and governed according to Islamic law—the shari'a. It was ruled by a Caliph, the successor of Mohammed, the Prophet of Islam. The rest of the world was viewed by the masters of the new Muslim empire as Dar al-Harb—that is, the lands yet to be conquered, subjugated, and integrated into their shari'a-based system of governance.

At the time of the first Islamic jihads, the population of the Levant, North Africa, and Mesopotamia was overwhelmingly Christian. But the Christians did not constitute a monolithic block. They were divided institutionally between Greek Orthodox, Latin Catholics, Coptic Orthodox, Syriac Orthodox and Armenian Orthodox, and the Eastern (Nestorian/Assyrian) traditions, each with roots in a unique historical tradition, language and theological perspective. The Caliphate also contained ancient Jewish communities, heretical Christian-related sects, and pagans, both free thinking and tribal. They were scattered throughout Dar al-Islam. Islamic sects also emerged to challenge the power of the ascendant Caliphs and what eventually became known as the officially recognized schools of orthodox Sunni jurisprudence.

The contemporary rivalry between Sunnis, today representing 85–90 percent of all Muslims globally, and the schismatic Shi'ite minority has its roots in the power struggles between the earliest Caliphs and their rivals. Persia was populated mainly by Zoroastrians, as were parts of southern and eastern Mesopotamia. The Middle East was multicultural, to say the least.

The religious demography of the Middle East has changed dramatically over the past thirteen centuries.[1] The militarily triumphant Muslims, within the institutional framework of shari'a norms, eventually became the majority, and today encompass well over 90 percent of the population. The former majority—the Christians—now make up less than 5 percent and continue to follow a trajectory of demographic decline.[2] The Jewish communities of the region have vanished, apart from within the state of Israel, created in the twentieth century to be a secure homeland for Jews worldwide. Sects like the Alawites, the Yezidis, Druze, Kakais, and Mandaeans, like the Christians, struggle for survival. The Middle East's religious minorities face an existential threat. With the region's post–"Arab Spring" descent into what former CIA Director and US Defense Secretary Leon Panetta has aptly described as a devastating sectarian conflict akin to Europe's sixteenth-century Thirty Years' War,[3] the demographic decline is rapidly accelerating.

The genesis of this volume lies in the grim, prophetic words of one of its contributors, the former President of Lebanon, Amine Gemayel. On January 3, 2011, just as the "Arab Spring" uprisings were beginning to gain momentum, Gemayel delivered a strong message, one that was out of kilter with the prevailing media narratives about developments in the Middle East. "Massacres are taking place for no reason and without any justification against Christians," he declared. "It is only because they are Christians. What is happening to Christians is a genocide."[4] Within a week, Gemayel's concern was echoed by a serving head of state, French President Nicholas Sarkozy. "We cannot accept and thereby facilitate," Sarkozy said, "what looks more and more like a particularly perverse program of cleansing in the Middle East, religious cleansing."[5] Gemayel and Sarkozy detected a deeply disturbing trend of increasing sectarian violence. This phenomenon, if left unchecked, would bring further death, destruction, and displacement to millions of people throughout the region. It would also give additional impetus to a profound civilizational change that is already underway. As the Occident has become more varied culturally, the Orient has become more religiously homogeneous. We see in the post–Cold War era of globalization mosques multiplying in the post-Christian, secularized West, while ever more churches, synagogues, and other non-Islamic temples lie in ruins in the Islamic Orient. These houses of worship, of course, symbolize much more than the private beliefs of those who frequent them. They represent the cultures that have shaped civilizations.

The Gemayel–Sarkozy warnings were a direct response to two high-profile terrorist attacks that reflected this troubling trend. The first took place in October 2010. A dozen well-organized, heavily armed jihadists shouting "Allahu akbar" burst into Baghdad's Our Lady of Deliverance Syriac Catholic Church and shot dead over 50 worshippers with automatic weapons. This sensational mass murder came in the context of a sectarian reign of terror, triggered by the American-led overthrow in 2003 of Saddam Hussein in Operation Iraqi Freedom. The main armed protagonists were Sunni insurgents on the one hand, and a constellation of Shi'ite forces on the other, with the former striving to restore the Sunnis' historic political supremacy, and the latter struggling to consolidate Shi'ite rule. Christians and other non-Muslim minorities were also targeted, especially by the Sunni insurgency. Most attacks against them failed to make headlines. They were mainly individual executions, kidnappings, robberies, extortions and forced conversions to Islam. But they were so widespread that they produced mass migration. Credible estimates suggest that the population of Iraq's Christian community—the country's largest non-Muslim minority—halved from about 800,000 to 400,000 between the onset of Operation Iraqi Freedom in 2003 and the "Arab Spring" uprisings.[6]

Both the Iraqi Prime Minister, Nouri al-Maliki, and the country's Minister for Human Rights, Wijdan Michael, acknowledged that the church massacre in Baghdad was intended as a warning to Christians to leave the country.[7] It was indeed. But Osama bin Laden's al-Qaeda, which took responsibility for the attack, proclaimed an anti-Christian agenda that transcended the borders of Iraq, stating that "all Christian centers, organizations and institutions, leaders and followers, [are] legitimate targets for the mujahideen wherever they can reach them."[8] This global Sunni terror organization furthermore identified Egypt's Christian community, numbering roughly 10 million people, as a special target, claiming that Muslim women were being held by priests and monks in monasteries, so as to incite anti-Christian violence.

The second act of anti-Christian terror that captured the attention of Gemayel and Sarkozy took place just after midnight on New Year's Day 2011. An explosion propelled nails, ball-bearing, and other pieces of shrapnel just outside the Coptic Orthodox Church of St. Mark and Pope Peter in Alexandria. Over 20 were killed and nearly 100 were wounded. Gemayel and Sarkozy sensed that, like the massacre in Baghdad, the Alexandria church bombing was not just a random isolated incident, but was a sign of ripening conditions for the eradication of Christians and other religious minorities from the region. Egypt's newly established National Committee for Combating Sectarian Violence—a civil society group formed mainly of secular Muslims—interpreted the Alexandria church bombing in much the same way. Already twelve months beforehand , the Committee reported that "Egypt has recently witnessed an unprecedented escalation of sectarian violence against peaceful citizens based on their Christian identity."[9] Two days after issuing this statement, confirmation of the Committee's assessment came when six churchgoers were shot dead as they left a Coptic Christmas Eve mass in the village of Naga Hammadi in Upper Egypt.

The local Coptic Orthodox Bishop, H. G. Kirollos, identified the perpetrators as "Muslim radicals," but no evidence emerged pointing to a transnational terror network like al-Qaeda. This anti-Christian act of terror appeared to be the outcome of local sectarian tensions with the murderers apparently encouraged by the incitements of al-Qaeda and by the increasing impunity with which non-Muslims were then being physically attacked. The Naga Hammadi church killings followed days of anti-Christian rioting, prompted by rumors that a young Muslim girl had been raped by a Christian man. Despite the local context, Bishop Kirollos saw that this wave of persecution in his diocese belonged to a broader pattern of such violence: "It is all religious now. This is a religious war about how they can finish off the Christians in Egypt."[10] The anti-Christian violence in Naga Hammadi was "just one in a long list of coordinated attacks against Coptic Christians that have resulted in hundreds of deaths over the last few years without any perpetrators being appropriately convicted in each instance," so stated CNN iReport.[11] By the time of the Alexandria church bombing, one year later, Christian and non-Christian minorities in Egypt and Iraq found themselves caught up in an existential crisis.

Notwithstanding ample evidence in support of their concerns, the Gemayel–Sarkozy warnings were not widely echoed within the international community. In the case of the Baghdad church massacre, the American occupation force claimed that it was a "robbery gone wrong," with no indication of its sectarian nature.[12] The White House declined to issue any statement. In response to the Alexandria bombing, President Obama authorized release of a bland, ritual condemnation and condolences of the sort that nowadays constitutes a kind of secular liturgical response by world leaders to acts of terrorism that capture sufficient media attention.[13] While Pope Benedict had already announced in 2007 the church in the Middle East is "threatened in its very existence," his message was generally muted in Catholic and other church circles.[14] The hushed tones from the side of the church and other quarters were undoubtedly influenced by the stormy—in some cases murderous—reaction in the Muslim world to the Pope's academic lecture the previous year at Regensburg University about the relationship between religion and violence.[15] To say that the violent persecution of Christians and other non-Muslims in the name of Islam is a sensitive issue in both the Occident and the Orient is an understatement indeed. Anxiety about negative reactions profoundly impacts the character of the prevailing narratives produced by Western states and disseminated widely by their organs of public opinion.

In early 2011, as the foundations of long-standing Middle Eastern dictatorships were beginning to tremble against a background of unarmed demonstrators demanding democracy and greater respect for human rights, the narrative of the "Facebook Revolution" was born. Images of young idealistic activists in public places, using the latest social media, created an impression that they were ushering in a new era of Western-style democracy and human rights. Washington played a major role in encouraging this emerging opposition to the Arab dictators and in perpetuating the "Facebook Revolution" narrative in the media.[16] US President Barack Obama announced on May 19, 2011, that the uprisings in the Middle East were American-backed "transitions to democracy," and portrayed them as signs of the fulfillment of his 2009 Cairo speech to the Muslim world, in which he upheld a vision of religious freedom and tolerance.[17] "Across the region," the President proclaimed, "those rights that we take for granted are being claimed with joy by those who are prying loose the grip of an iron fist."[18] At the time the American President spoke these words, his Tunisian and Egyptian counterparts had already been overthrown. Washington's promotion of "transitions to democracy," the President indicated, would henceforth focus on Libya, Syria, and Yemen.

The mass euphoria surrounding the "Arab Spring" eerily resembled the upbeat enthusiasm that accompanied the "Ottoman Spring" just over one hundred years beforehand. In 1908, the "Young Turk" revolt of progressive, secular military officers induced the autocratic, pan-Islamist Sultan-Caliph Abdul Hamid II to reinstate the liberal Constitution of 1876, which had been suspended for the previous three decades. Parliamentary government and civil liberties derived from the European enlightenment were part of the package. So was the principle of equal citizenship regardless of religion. These constitutional changes were revolutionary indeed, and were largely incompatible with the shari'a—the sacrosanct law of Islam. The shari'a had formed the constitutional framework of the Ottoman Caliphate and its imperial predecessors since the AD seventh century. Muslim traditionalists were mortified by the subversion of shari'a principles, especially with regard to the non-Muslim minorities. But the progressive press in Istanbul was jubilant. Christians, Jews, and secular-oriented Muslims danced together in the streets. The religious leaders of these three faith communities openly fraternized with each other. One of the most powerful among the "Young Turk" officers, Enver Bey (subsequently Pasha), issued a public statement, declaring that "henceforth we are all brothers. There are no longer Bulgars, Greeks, Roumans, Jews, Moslems; under the same blue sky we are all equal, we glory in being Ottomans."[19] The celebratory spirit crossed the Atlantic. A

"Grand Mass Meeting" was organized at Carnegie Hall, New York, under the auspices of the Young Turks, the Armenian Revolutionary Federation, and the Hunchakist Society, with the participation of "Turks, Syrians, Greeks, Hebrews, Albanians, etc.," and the reading of a letter of congratulations from President Theodore Roosevelt.[20] It seemed to many, both inside and outside the Middle East, that a new dawn of liberty, equality, and fraternity had arrived for all Ottoman citizens, not least for members of non-Muslim religious minorities.

The exuberance of the "Ottoman Spring" did not last long. Within a decade, the first great genocide of the twentieth century had eradicated more than two million Armenian, Syriac, and Assyrian Christians in Ottoman Anatolia, over one million by death, the remainder by forced migration. Enver Pasha, as Minister for War, jettisoned his "we are all brothers" rhetoric and became one of the principal architects of Ottoman genocide. This precursor of the Holocaust in Central Europe took place in the context of a *jihad* declared by the Ottoman Caliph against World War I adversaries. These grisly events prompted the international community, as then represented by the League of Nations, to grapple with the question of ethnic and religious minorities. But despite the creation of an arsenal of legal instruments designed to guarantee minority rights, religious and ethnic cleansing did not cease. Soon thereafter, most of the remainder of Anatolia's Christians—mainly Greeks—was forced out of the country at the command of the secular regime of Mustafa Kemal Ataturk.

Something similar happened in the aftermath of the heady days of the "Arab Spring." Nearly five years after President Obama presented his vision for the transformation of the dictatorships of the Middle East into democracies, the US government confirmed the veracity of the bleak Gemayel–Sarkozy assessment of trends. In March 2016, US Secretary of State, John Kerry, admitted that a "genocide" against Christians, Yezidis, and Shi'ite Muslims had indeed taken place in Iraq and Syria, and that the Islamic State, referred to as Daesh, was the perpetrator.[21] Secretary Kerry came to this conclusion nearly two years after the Islamic State advanced deep into Iraq from its bases in the Iraqi–Syrian borderlands; conquering the city of Mosul without resistance; driving roughly 400,000 Yezidis, 200,000 Christians, and 200,000 Shi'ites from their homes in Nineveh Province; killing and enslaving tens of thousands; and finally threating to attack US interests in Baghdad and Erbil. American air strikes against the Islamic State in Iraq only began when its advance columns were approaching the outskirts of the Iraqi and Kurdish capitals. President Obama had previously dismissed warnings about the destructive power of the Islamic State, describing it as a mere "jayvee" (junior varsity) player among the jihadists of the Middle East—a judgment he subsequently blamed on faulty American intelligence.[22]

Religious cleansing has not been confined to the Levant and Mesopotamia. In Upper Egypt, Coptic Christians were deported from villages, as anti-Christian violence soared in tandem with the political ascent of the Islamist Muslim Brotherhood following the overthrow of President Hosni Mubarak. Coptic Christians feared that Egypt was sliding fast toward a catastrophe of the sort that had befallen Syria and Iraq. But this process of religious cleansing in Egypt was suspended when the country's armed forces, headed by Gen. Abdel Fattah al-Sisi, seized power in July 2013 against the background of mass demonstrations against the country's new Muslim Brotherhood President, Mohammed Morsi. Egypt's Copts still face discrimination and continue to be targeted by Sunni jihadists, much as they were under President Mubarak and his predecessor Anwar Sadat. But the imminent threat of isolated acts of religious cleansing morphing into full blown genocide has greatly receded—for the time being.

In Yemen, "Arab Spring" protests did not long remain peaceful. The country's President Ali Abdullah Saleh complied with President Obama's demand that he "transfer power."[23] This change of regime has not taken Yemen closer to fulfillment of democracy and religious tolerance. Today, Yemen has become the world's worst humanitarian disaster zone as a sectarian civil war between Sunni and Shi'ite forces ravages the country. Saudi Arabia and its Western allies support militarily the Sunnis, while Iran backs the Shi'ites. Lebanon, a fragile construction of religious minorities, managed to avoid getting caught up in the "Arab Spring." Its senior statesmen and their respective foreign patrons have no interest in disrupting the current balance. But Lebanon could at any moment become a theater of sectarian civil war as it was between 1975 and 1990, especially if outside actors will it.

The territory that has been at the center of most interstate sectarian warfare since the end of World War II, the lands of the old British Mandate of Palestine, has, like Lebanon, been left largely untouched by the "Arab Spring." In PLO- and Hamas-administered territories, the Christian minority continues its long demographical decline and is now in imminent danger of disappearing. In the state of Israel, the Muslim, Christian, and Druze minority communities increase in size. This is attributable largely to the internal stability, social pluralism, and economic prosperity of the Israeli state. But the Israeli Christian population is also boosted by the immigration of Christians from abroad, often members of mixed Jewish-Christian families

The existential threat facing the Middle East's non-Muslim minorities should have come as no surprise. In the immediate post-Holocaust era, the world witnessed the decimation of the Oriental Jewish communities against the background of the mass displacement of Muslim and Christian Arabs from the state of Israel during the War of 1948. But outside of this war zone, the region's Christians sought, and found to a large degree, security in the prevailing ostensibly secular Arab nationalism. The vulnerability of the region's Christians was not so easy for casual observers from the outside to detect. But policy-makers were aware. Already, in the early years of the Cold War, as Washington was striving to replace London and Paris as the dominant power in the region, an American official reminded the United States' Psychological Warfare Program in the Middle East (PWPME) of the limits of religious tolerance. "Orthodox Islam tolerates Christians and Jews," he or she noted, "but only in an inferior position." Referring to the unprecedented tolerance of these minorities in the post-Ottoman French and British Mandates, the agent explained that "the Moslems have had to compromise on this point." But, the official continued, "now . . . that the Arab (Moslem) states have attained full independence, moments of stress can bring this traditional attitude back to the surface." No guarantees of protection were to be found in Arab nationalism, the official claimed, since it "is sometimes a cloak for . . . a xenophobia which is anti-Western and anti-Christian." To drive home his point, the official wrote that "it might not be amiss to recall that Christians of Syria, when sure of their audience, sometimes say in effect: 'Thank God for Israel. If the Moslems ever settle with the Jews, we will be next':"[24] The region has had no shortage of "moments of stress" since this report was filed in Washington, and the region's Christian leadership has discovered that decades of support for the political objectives of Arab nationalism, including the demise of Israel, have not produced long-term protection

The failure of Arab nationalist powers to destroy the state of Israel in the wars of 1967 and 1973, Iran's Islamic Revolution of 1978–1979 and the anti-Russian war in Afghanistan were such "moments of stress," to use borrow the phrase of the PWPME rapporteur These events played a major role in the development of an "Islamic Resurgence" as a powerful factor in global affairs. It was obvious that this development would have a deleterious impact on the human rights of non-Muslim minorities. In 1984, the Directorate of the CIA produced a classified report drawing attention to a strong trend throughout the Middle East toward greater observance of shari'a-based orthodoxy. As a result, the Directorate stated:

All governments of the predominantly Muslim nations in the region, with the exception of Ba'athist Syria and Iraq, have adopted some or all of the following measures in efforts to appease the fundamentalists: 1) Increased consultation with the clergy and religious scholars, 2) Constructed more mosques and Islamic schools, 3) Scheduled more religious programming on television, 4) Sponsored Koranic conferences and trips to Mecca, 5) Cracked down on behavior linked to Western permissiveness, and 6) Established more segregation of the sexes and required more modest dress by women.[25]

The CIA report then went on to announce bad news for Christians and other non-Muslims. "Throughout the region," the Directorate stated,

> the renewal of orthodox Islamic practices has made the position of non-Muslim minorities more precarious. Fundamentalist criticism of other religious and social practices has led to discriminatory government-sanctioned behavior, ranging from minor harassment to persecution. . . . Repressive measures and intolerance of non-Muslim minorities will continue to exacerbate sectarian tension.[26]

No indication was given by the authors of this report that vulnerable non-Muslim minorities of the Middle East were of any strategic or economic interest to the United States, and therefore merited protection, nor did they make any recommendation to combat the negative phenomenon. Instead, Washington perceived its interests to be best served by aligning itself with the religiously intolerant Sunni "Islamic Resurgence," and instrumentalizing it as a weapon against its adversaries, in particular the Soviet Union and Shi'ite Iran. The CIA report acknowledged that principal regional allies adopted more draconian shari'a-based policies as a means of gaining greater legitimacy and of placating "fundamentalists." For example, regarding Saudi Arabia, it confirmed the existence of "rigid rules against [the] public practice of other religions," and noted that "sectarian repression of Shia minority has increased; internal police surveillance and arrests [are] increasing." As for Egypt, it indicated that "constitutionally, Sharia is [the] source of legislation," and that the country experiences "continued government discrimination against Copts." Meanwhile, the US government was then ramping up, in collaboration with the Saudi and Pakistani intelligence services, a policy of empowerment of radical Sunni jihadists to fight as proxies against the Soviet Union in Afghanistan.

Therein lie the roots of the political and military modernization of non-state jihadist movements. They have since developed into the terrorist networks that are now in the forefront of religiously cleansing vulnerable non-Sunnis from their homelands in the Middle East and of committing acts of terrorism in Europe and North America. Since the early days of the "Islamic Resurgence," no coherent policy has been produced by Western powers to address the persecution of religious minorities in Muslim majority countries. Even Nicholas Sarkozy, who proclaimed that "we cannot accept and thereby facilitate . . . religious cleansing," did little more than commission a dust-collecting report on the subject before falling to line with Washington's destabilizing "Arab Spring" regime change policy.[27] Other NATO allies acted much like France.

The Islamic State's crimes against humanity merit designation as "genocide," but Secretary Kerry stopped short of reflecting its full scope. He neglected to identify other perpetrators, many of which had been and continued to be supported by Washington and its network of European and Sunni Islamist regional allies—Saudi Arabia, Qatar, and Turkey. During the previous five years, a huge Sunnistan had been created in Syria and Iraq, virtually devoid of non-Sunnis. This *de facto* entity encompasses the territories conquered not only by the Islamic State, but also those overrun by a host of other radical Islamist militias ranging from the Free Syrian Army to al-Qaeda. The "religious cleansing" we witness today in Syria takes place within a sectarian conflict that has profoundly blighted the lives of all religious backgrounds, having resulted so far in the death of nearly half a million, and the displacement of half the population of 22 million.

The optimists of the "Ottoman and Arab Springs" alike had failed to take an important factor into account. Centuries of institutionalized Sunni supremacism, and its social concomitant—widespread suspicion, if not loathing of non-Muslims—had molded the political culture and the psyche of the Sunni majority of the Middle East. Paper constitutions and secular ideologies imported from the West could not eradicate it, any more than the granting of legal equality of Jews in Central Europe in the nineteenth century could eradicate anti-Semitism, or the emancipation of slaves in the United States and the subsequent repeal of segregation laws could eradicate racism there.

"Habits, more than reason, we find, in everything to be the governing principle of mankind," so wrote David Hume. The Enlightenment philosopher's observation bears recalling when considering contemporary political events, not least in the Middle East. Ancient religious based institutions, such as the *shari'a, jihad, umma, kaffir, dhimmi,* and *mushrikun* to name but a few, produce deep seated habits that are still operative in the political culture of the region.[28] These discriminatory institutions alone do not explain the existential threat facing the region's non-Muslim communities. They are nurtured and instrumentalized by powerful political actors, including external powers. But these dynamic, resilient, and adaptable institutions are important factors that should not be ignored.[29] Whether they are enshrined in law, in prevailing ideology, or simply in the hearts and minds of a multitude, such historic and sacrosanct religious-political institutions are powerful elements of the "Islamic Resurgence." The US intelligence community understood over three decades ago that this phenomenon would endanger non-Muslim minorities in the Middle East. Far from undergoing deconstruction in the face of modernity, these sectarian institutions are making a comeback.

Christian Solidarity International (CSI)—a non-state supported civil society organization whose mandate is drawn from Article 18 of the Universal Declaration of Human Rights[30]—was quicker off the mark than the US State Department to call attention to the festering conditions for "religious cleansing" by issuing a Genocide Alert already in the autumn of 2011. Among the most visible of the conditions was the emergence of an extensive network of armed actors, driven by a supremacist ideology rooted in a religious tradition that collectively defamed defenseless victim groups as inferior and as fundamentally subversive. The dangers flowing from this ideology were compounded by the weakening, and in some cases collapse, of established governments, thereby making resistance to the genocidal impulses of non-state actors more difficult.[31] The credibility of the Gemayel–Sarkozy assessment was not difficult to confirm.

It was at this time, when the "Arab Spring" uprisings were turning into bloody sectarian conflict, that CSI launched the series of talks that are featured in this volume. It was conducted under the title "The Future of Religious Minorities in the Middle East," with the Middle East defined as the Levant, Mesopotamia, Egypt, and Arabia. The series spanned four years and provided a platform in Zurich, Geneva, Bern, and Boston[32] for a host of distinguished scholars, journalists, human rights activists, and political practitioners. The contributors came from a wide variety of political, cultural, and religious backgrounds. This project has been an exercise in diversity of views. Each contributor draws on a deep wellspring of scholarship, experience, sobriety, and passion. Collectively, the presentations make a major contribution to understanding the dynamics of the existential threat confronting the region's religious minorities. They are, on the whole, analytical, not statements of policy.

Some of the contributions were presented in the form of academic papers, while others were delivered as informal observations. Each contribution is dated and stands as a historical document in its own right, representing the views of the contributor at the time of delivery. They have not been updated to reflect current developments. The talks are presented chronologically, with the exception of Taner Akçam's on the anti-Christian genocide in Turkey during the First World War, as it provides important historical context for the presentations that follow.

Do religious minorities have a future in the Middle East? Readers of this volume will not detect many silver linings around the dark clouds. If the institutionalized habits of both the principal regional actors and the Great Powers cannot be broken, the future is grim indeed. This begs another important question, but one not answered here. If social pluralism in the Arab majority Middle East is dying, if the future of religious minorities is doubtful, if acts of genocide and "religious cleansing" persist, with no end in sight, should an international effort be made to help the survivors leave the region and build new lives for themselves and their children in safe and secure locations outside the Middle East? Or, should efforts be redoubled to preserve the region's social pluralism, and thereby enable members of existentially threatened religious minority communities to live in peace and dignity in their own homelands? The answer to these questions will have profound implications for not only the peoples of the Middle East, but for global civilization.

NOTES

1. For in-depth accounts of the historic demographic decline of the largest non-Muslim communities in the Middle East from the time of the Islamic conquests, see Youssef Courbage and Philippe Fargues, *Christians and Jews Under Islam* (trans. Judy Mabro, London: I.B. Tauris, 1998), and Bat Ye'or, *The Decline of Eastern Christianity Under Islam: From Jihad to Dhimmitude, Seventh–Twentieth Century* (trans. Miriam Kochan and David Littman, Madison: Farleigh Dickinson University Press, 1996).

2. Gina A. Zurlo, "A Demographic Profile of Christianity in North Africa and West Asia," in *Christianity in North Africa and West Asia*, eds. Kenneth R. Ross, Mariz Tadros, Todd M. Johnson (Edinburgh: Edinburgh University Press, forthcoming 2018).

3. See Susan Page, "Panetta: '30-Year War' and a Leadership Test for Obama," *USA Today*, October 6, 2014, https://www.usatoday.com/story/news/politics/2014/10/06/leon-panetta-memoir-worthy-fights/16737615/. Franck Salameh forecast in March 2011 that a "30-Year War" would be the likely outcome of the "Arab Spring" uprisings, unless the artificial Arab edifice of the region were to be replaced by existing ethno-religious nations. See Franck Salameh, "The Arab Westphalia," *The National Interest*, March 7, 2011, http://nationalinterest.org/commentary/the-arab-westphalia-4949.

4. Quoted after CBS News, "Ex-Lebanon Leader: Christians Target of Genocide," *CBS News*, January 3, 2011, http://www.cbsnews.com/news/ex-lebanon-leader-christians-target-of-genocide/.

5. Quoted after Henry Samuel, "Nicolas Sarkozy Says Christians in Middle East are Victim of 'Religious Cleansing,'" *The Telegraph*, January 7, 2011, http://www.telegraph.co.uk/ news/worldnews/europe/france/8246278/Nicolas-Sarkozy-says-Christians-in-Middle-East-are-victim-of-religious-cleansing.html.

6. See BBC, "Iraqi Christians' Long History," *BBC*, November 1, 2010, http://www.bbc.com/news/world-middle-east-11669994, and Todd M. Johnson and Gina A. Zurlo, "Ongoing Exodus: Tracking the Migration of Christians for the Middle East," *Harvard Journal of Middle Eastern Politics and Policy* 3 (2013–2014): 44.

7. See Tehran Times, "Grand Ayatollah Sistani Condemns Attack on Baghdad Church," *Tehran Times*, November 3, 2010, http://archive.li/bB8Fj#selection-517.12-517.126, and Muhanad Mohammed, "Iraq Church Raid Ends with 52 Dead," *Reuters*, November 1, 2010, http://www.reuters.com/article/us-iraq-violence-idUSTRE69U1YE20101101.

8. Quoted after CNN, "All Christians 'Targets,' Iraqi Militant Group Says," *CNN*, November 3, 2010, http://edition.cnn.com/2010/WORLD/meast/11/03/iraq.christians.threat/, and "Al-Qaeda Threatens Christians," *Al-Manar TV*, November 3, 2010.

9. Quoted after Saif Nasrawi, "Sectarian Violence: What Can Be Done?" *Egypt Independent*, January 5, 2010, http://www.egyptindependent.com/sectarian-violence-what-can-be-done/.

10. Quoted after Jack Shenker, "Egyptian Christians Riot after Fatal Shooting," *The Guardian*, January 7, 2010, https://www.theguardian.com/world/2010/jan/07/egypt-gunmen-kill-coptic-christmas.

11. CNN iReport, "Violence against the Christian Population of Egypt," *CNN iReport*, January 16, 2010, http://ireport.cnn.com/docs/DOC-392091.

12. Al Jazeera, "Iraq church hostages rescued," *Al Jazeera*, November 1, 2010, http://www.aljazeera.com/news/middleeast/2010/10/20101031155653449733.html.

13. See Barack Obama, "Statement by the President on the terrorist attacks in Egypt and Nigeria," *The White House*, January 1, 2011, https://obamawhitehouse.archives.gov/the-press-office/2011/01/01/statement-president-terrorist-attacks-egypt-and-nigeria.

14. Quoted after Zenit, "Iraqi Christians Searching for Signs of Hope," *Zenit*, June 9, 2011, https://zenit.org/articles/iraqi-christians-searching-for-signs-of-hope/.

15. His Holiness Benedict XVI, "Faith, Reason and the University. Memories and Reflections," Regensburg, September 12, 2006, http://w2.vatican.va/content/benedict-xvi/en/speeches/2006/september/documents/hf_ben-xvi_spe_20060912_university-regensburg.html. The Pope, while appealing for the inclusion of rationality as an essential aspect of religious dialogue, cited passages from a fourteenth-century dialogue with the Byzantine emperor, among them the sentence, "Show me just what Mohammed brought that was new, and there you will find things only evil and inhuman, such as his command to spread by the sword the faith he preached."

16. See Scott Ritter, "'Digital Democracy' and the 'January 25 Revolution' in Egypt," *HuffPost,* January 26, 2016, http://www.huffingtonpost.com/scott-ritter/digital-democracy-and-the_b_9077082.html.

17. See Barack Obama, "Remarks by the President on a New Beginning," *The White House*, June 4, 2009, https://obamawhitehouse.archives.gov/blog/2009/06/04/presidentrsquos-speech-cairo-a-new-beginning.

18. This speech was portrayed by the White House as a presentation of the President's "vision for a new chapter in American diplomacy as calls for reform and democracy spread across the Middle East and North Africa." Barack Obama, "Remarks by the President on the Middle East and North Africa," *The White House*, May 19, 2011, https://obamawhitehouse .archives.gov/realitycheck/photos-and-video/video/2011/05/19/moment-opportunity-american-diplomacy-middle-east-north-africa?page=26#transcript.

19. Lord Kinross, *The Ottoman Centuries: The Rise and Fall of the Turkish Empire* (New York: Morrow, 1977), 574.

20. Bedross Der Matossian, "Revolutionary Fallout: How the Young Turks went from Carnegie Hall to the Collapse of the Ottoman Empire," Stanford University Press Blog Series on *Remembering the Armenian Genocide*, May 20, 2015, http://stanfordpress.typepad .com/blog/2015/04/revolutionary-fallout-.html. (Author of *Shattered Dreams of Revolution: From Liberty to Violence in the Late Ottoman Empire* [Stanford: Stanford University Press, 2014].)

21. See John Kerry, "Remarks on Daesh and Genocide," US Department of State, March 17, 2016.

22. See David Remmick, "Going the Distance: On and Off the Road with Barack Obama," *The New Yorker*, January 27, 2014, http://www.newyorker.com/magazine/2014/01/27/going-the-distance-david-remnick, and CBS News, "Obama: US Underestimated Rise of ISIS in Iraq and Syria," *CBS News*, September 28, 2014, http://www.cbsnews.com/news/obama-u-s-underestimated-rise-of-isis-in-iraq-and-syria/.

23. Barack Obama, "Remarks by the President on the Middle East and North Africa," The While House, May 19, 2011, https://obamawhitehouse .archives.gov/realitycheck/photos-and-video/video/2011/05/19/moment-opportunity-american-diplomacy-middle-east-north-africa?page=26#transcript. Karim Fahim and Laura Kasinof, "Yemen's Leader Agrees to End 3-Decade Rule," *New York Times*, November 23, 2011, http://www.nytimes.com/2011/11/24/world/middleeast/yemen-saleh-transfer-power-deal-saudi-arabia.html.

24. United States Psychological Warfare Program in the Middle East: Study and Recommendations for Improvements, December 10, 1957, Secret (Inter Agency Report), Folder Near and Middle East 1957, Box, 154, Lot 167D548, State Department, Lot Files, Records of PPS 1957–1961 RG 59, National Archives.

25. Central Intelligence Agency (CIA), Directorate of Intelligence, "Near East–South Asia: Regime Responses to Islamic Fundamentalist Demands," July 23, 1984. https://www.cia.gov/library/readingroom/docs/CIA-RDP85T00287R001301870001-3.pdf.

26. Ibid.

27. Sénateur Adrian Gouteyron, *Rapport sur la Situation des Communautés Chrétiennes d'Orient*, Paris, 2011.

28. *Shari'a*—The sacrosanct, universal law of Islam, whose principles should govern all aspects of human endeavour, including the organization of society and the state. Shari'a principles are drawn from the Kur'an, and from the words and deeds of the Prophet Mohammed. *Jihad*—The sacred endeavour to expand the bounds of *Dar al-Islam*, using shari'a sanctioned means, ranging from violence to personal piety. *Umma*—The universal community of Muslims. Within *Dar al-Islam*, members of the *umma* constitute a privileged caste. *Kafir*—One who do not accept the basic tenets of Islam. *Dhimmi*—A Christian, Jew, or a Persian Zoroastrians who accepts the rule of Muslims and the lower caste assigned to them by the Shari'a. The spirit, if not the letter of the disabilities imposed this caste is embodied in the *'ahd Umar* (the 'Pact of Umar'), which, according to tradition, fixed the terms of surrender imposed by the 'Rightly Guided Caliph' Umar I on conquered Christians and Jews. In return for accepting this status, protection is to be afforded *dhimmis*, so as to guarantee physical security and the right to worship and to live according to the tenets of their faith community. *Dhimmis* who are deemed individually or collectively to have violated the disabilities on which protection depends run the risk of being regarded by their Muslim overlords as outside the protection of the law. Mushrikun—Non-Muslims who do not belong to the protected caste of the *dhimmis*. They remain outside the law, and can therefore be killed, enslaved, or otherwise abuse with impunity. The most authoritative source in English on these institutions is the *Encyclopaedia of Islam*, New Edition, 12 vols., Leiden: Brill, 1986–2004.

29. These ancient institutions are often ignored in contemporary analyses of sectarian issues in the Middle East. Nader Hashemi and Danny Postel, the editors of

Sectarianization: Mapping the New Politics of the Middle East, Oxford University Press, Oxford, 2017, have done so in their ambitious effort to "explain the explosion of sectarian conflicts in the Arab Islamic world today." This complex phenomenon cannot be comprehensively understood by viewing it through the prism of the "machinations of dictators and tyrants," while obfuscating the history of the religiously based political institutions that have provided so much character to the region's sectarian conflicts from the 7th century A.D. until the present day.

30. Universal Declaration of Human Rights, Article 18: "Everyone has the right to freedom of thought, conscience and religion; this right includes freedom to change his religion or belief, and freedom, either alone or in community with others and in public or private, to manifest his religion or belief in teaching, practice, worship and observance."

31. See Helen Fein, "What are the Conditions for Genocide?" Center on Law and Globalization, no date, based on Helen Fein, "Genocide: A Sociological Perspective," *Current Sociology* 38, no. 1 (1990): 1–126.

32. Events in Boston were co-sponsored with the Departments of Slavic and Eastern Languages and Literatures and Political Science, and the Boise Center for Religion and American Public Life at Boston College. The contribution entitled "Social Pluralism, 'Religious Cleansing' and Hybrid Warfare in Contemporary Syria" is based on a talk given at the Changing Character of Modern Warfare Seminar, Pembroke College, Oxford.

WORKS CITED

Al Jazeera. "Iraq church hostages rescued." *Al Jazeera.* November 1, 2010. http://www.aljazeera.com/news/middleeast/2010/10/20101031155653449733.html.

Al-Manar TV. "Al-Qaeda Threatens Christians." *Al-Manar TV.* November 3, 2010.

Bat Ye'or. *The Decline of Eastern Christianity Under Islam: From Jihad to Dhimmitude, Seventh–Twentieth Century.* Translated by Miriam Kochan and David Littman. Madison: Farleigh Dickinson University Press, 1996.

BBC. "Iraqi Christians' Long History." *BBC.* November 1, 2010. http://www.bbc.com/news/world-middle-east-11669994.

Benedict XVI. "Faith, Reason and the University. Memories and Reflections." Lecture. Regensburg, September 12, 2006. http://w2.vatican.va/content/benedict-xvi/en/speeches/2006/september/documents/hf_ben-xvi_spe_20060912_university-regensburg.html.

CBS News. "Obama: US Underestimated Rise of ISIS in Iraq and Syria." *CBS News.* September 28, 2014. http://www.cbsnews.com/news/obama-u-s-underestimated-rise-of-isis-in-iraq-and-syria/.

———. "Ex-Lebanon Leader: Christians Target of Genocide." *CBS News.* January 3, 2011. http://www.cbsnews.com/news/ex-lebanon-leader-christians-target-of-genocide/.

Central Intelligence Agency (CIA), Directorate of Intelligence. "Near East—South Asia: Regime Responses to Islamic Fundamentalist Demands." July 23, 1984.

CNN. "All Christians 'Targets,' Iraqi Militant Group Says." *CNN*. November 3, 2010. http://edition.cnn.com/2010/WORLD/meast/11/03/iraq.christians.threat/.

CNN iReport. "Violence against the Christian Population of Egypt." *CNN iReport*. January 16, 2010. http://ireport.cnn.com/docs/DOC-392091.

Cohen, Jared and Ben Rhodes (NYT).

Courbage, Youssef, and Philippe Fargues. *Christians and Jews Under Islam*. Translated by Judy Mabro. London: I.B. Tauris, 1998.

Fein, Helen. "What are the Conditions for Genocide?" Center on Law and Globalization, no date, based on Helen Fein, "Genocide: A Sociological Perspective," *Current Sociology* 38 no. 1 (1990): 1–126.

Gouteyron, Adrian (Sénateur). *Rapport sur la Situation des Communautés Chrétiennes d'Orient*. Paris 2011.

Hashemi , Nader and Danny Postel. *Sectarianization: Mapping the New Politics of the Middle East*. Oxford: Oxford University Press. 2017.

Johnson, Todd M., and Gina A. Zurlo. "Ongoing Exodus: Tracking the Migration of Christians for the Middle East." *Harvard Journal of Middle Eastern Politics and Policy* 3 (2013–2014).

Kerry, John. "Remarks on Daesh and Genocide." US Department of State. March 17, 2016.

Lord Kinross. *The Ottoman Centuries: The Rise and Fall of the Turkish Empire*. New York: Morrow, 1977.

Matossian, Bedross Der. *Shattered Dreams of Revolution: From Liberty to Violence in the Late Ottoman Empire*. Stanford: Stanford University Press, 2014.

———. "Revolutionary Fallout: How the Young Turks went from Carnegie Hall to the Collapse of the Ottoman Empire." Stanford University Press Blog Series on *Remembering the Armenian Genocide*. May 20, 2015. http://stanfordpress.typepad .com/blog/2015 /04/revolutionary-fallout-.html.

Mohammed, Muhanad. "Iraq Church Raid Ends with 52 Dead." *Reuters*. November 1, 2010. http://www.reuters.com/article/us-iraq-violence-idUSTRE69U1YE20101101.

Nasrawi, Saif. "Sectarian Violence: What Can Be Done?" *Egypt Independent*, January 5, 2010, http://www.egyptindependent.com/sectarian-violence-what-can-be-done/.

Obama, Barack. "Remarks by the President on a New Beginning," *The White House*, June 4, 2009, https://obamawhitehouse.archives.gov/blog/2009/06/04/ presidentrsquos-speech-cairo-a-new-beginning.

———. "Statement by the President on the terrorist attacks in Egypt and Nigeria." *The White House*. January 1, 2011. https://obamawhitehouse.archives.gov/the-press-office/ 2011/01/01/statement-president-terrorist-attacks-egypt-and-nigeria.

———. "Remarks by the President on the Middle East and North Africa." *The White House*. May 19, 2011. https://obamawhitehouse .archives.gov/realitycheck/photos-and-video /video/2011/05/19/moment-opportunity-american-diplomacy-middle-east-north-africa? page=26#transcript.

Page, Susan. "Panetta: '30-Year War' and a Leadership Test for Obama." *USA Today*. October 6, 2014. https://www.usatoday.com/story/news/politics/2014/10/06/ leon-panetta-memoir-worthy-fights/16737615/.

Remmick, David. "Going the Distance: On and Off the Road with Barack Obama." *The New Yorker*. January 27, 2014. http://www.newyorker.com/magazine/2014/01/27/going-the-distance-david-remnick.

Ritter, Scott. "'Digital Democracy' and the 'January 25 Revolution' in Egypt." *HuffPost*. January 26, 2016. http://www.huffingtonpost.com/scott-ritter/digital-democracy-and-the_b_9077082.html.

Salameh, Franck. "The Arab Westphalia." *The National Interest*. March 7, 2011. http://nationalinterest.org/commentary/the-arab-westphalia-4949.

Samuel, Henry. "Nicolas Sarkozy Says Christians in Middle East are Victim of 'Religious Cleansing.'" *The Telegraph*. January 7, 2011. http://www.telegraph.co.uk/news/worldnews /Europe/france/8246278/Nicolas-Sarkozy-says-Christians-in-Middle-East-are-victim-of-religious-cleansing.html.

Shenker, Jack. "Egyptian Christians Riot after Fatal Shooting." *The Guardian*. January 7, 2010. https://www.theguardian.com/world/2010/jan/07/egypt-gunmen-kill-coptic-christmas.

Tehran Times. "Grand Ayatollah Sistani Condemns Attack on Baghdad Church." *Tehran Times*. November 3, 2010. http://archive.li/bB8Fj#selection-517.12-517.126.

Zenit. "Iraqi Christians Searching for Signs of Hope." *Zenit*. June 9, 2011. https://zenit.org/articles/iraqi-christians-searching-for-signs-of-hope/.

Zurlo, Gina A. "A Demographic Profile of Christianity in North Africa and West Asia." In *Christianity in North Africa and West Asia*, edited by Kenneth R. Ross, Mariz Tadros, and Todd M. Johnson. Edinburgh: Edinburgh University Press, forthcoming 2018.

Chapter 1

The Anatomy of Religious Cleansing: Non-Muslims in the Ottoman Empire (1914–1918)

(Boston, October 22, 2014)

Taner Akçam

The last century of the Ottoman Empire, especially the period between 1878 and 1924, was characterized by a series of forced mass deportations, expulsions, and ethnic cleansing, which included mass killings. The Armenian Genocide might represent the pinnacle of this period; however, there was also the ethnic cleansing of Greeks in the Ottoman Balkans and western Anatolia in 1913 and 1914, the genocide against the Assyrians during the First World War, and the genocide against Pontus Greeks—that is, the Greeks that were living on Anatolia's Black Sea Coast—who were victims of genocidal massacres in 1921 and 1922. The genocide against the Greeks was as important as the Armenian Genocide, and it occurred as part of the same process.

I think it is fair for us to use the term "Ottoman genocide," and to talk about a genocidal process to describe the period between 1878 and 1924. Here, I distinguish between the genocidal process and moments of genocide: one covers the long-term process between 1878 and 1924, the other consists of the moments when genocide occurred. All of the mass deportations, massacres, and genocides were carried out by one state. As such, they represented the policy of the Ottoman administration, and each event was interrelated with the others; but until recently, with some exceptions, all of these events have been analyzed and discussed as separate social phenomena, without much contextualization. Each ethnic group—Assyrians, Armenians, Greeks, and all the others—developed a historiography confined to its own history, rarely in connection with other mass crimes in the same area and region.

There have been some limited attempts, in recent years, to explain the entire process within the broader context of Ottoman demographic policy, but for the most part, scholars working in these areas have stayed within their own national field of inquiry. To formulate this another way, even in cases where there were attempts to contextualize or put the different cases together, this has been done, for the most part, by placing these different events next to each other as separate entities in what we call, in our field, a comparative perspective, rather than trying to explain them as evidence of one interconnected process, or one history.

My suggestion is that we develop a new understanding of the period and start talking about the Ottoman genocide of the Christians. I will present a short glimpse of the period 1913–1918, and show how Ottoman policies against the Greeks, Assyrians, and Armenians were strongly interrelated—not isolated acts, but part of a comprehensive policy implemented by one government. These actions were carried out as part of a general plan under the heading of demographic policy, which amounted to the ethnic cleansing of Anatolia, or what I occasionally call the homogenization of Anatolia on Turkish-Muslim grounds. It involved the expulsion of all or most of the Christian population of Anatolia. The policy was implemented as a general resettlement plan between 1913 and 1918, continued against the Pontus Greeks in the years 1921 and 1922, and ended with a population-exchange agreement between Greece and Turkey in 1924. The main goal of the policy was to ensure the formation of a homogeneous Anatolia, an Anatolia with a majority Turkish-Muslim population. The elimination of the Christian population was central to this plan, but it was not the only component.

The demographic plan had two primary components. One was focused on the Muslim population of non-Turkish origin, such as Kurds, Arabs, and immigrants from the Balkans. They were relocated and dispersed among the Turkish majority to ensure assimilation. The other component was the elimination of non-Muslim people from Anatolia, the result of which was that over two million Armenians, Assyrians, and Greeks were either forcibly expelled or massacred between 1914 and 1918. This resulted in the complete reconfiguration of Anatolia. Of the estimated 17 million people who lived in Anatolia at the time, at least one-third were either resettled somewhere else, deported, or annihilated. Expulsion, extermination, and assimilation were the three essential elements of the policy, which was applied against all Christian groups, with no exception.

My research has led me to some very interesting sources. I have made extensive use of the Ottoman language documents in the Prime Ministerial Ottoman archive in Istanbul; they include the crucial papers of the Interior Ministry (*Dahiliye Nezareti Evrakı*), which contain a great deal of information directly relevant to the subject. I have also made extensive use of the papers from the Interior Ministry's Cipher Office. The Cipher Office was established in 1913, just one year before World War I started, for the purpose of telegraphic communication between the central Ottoman administration and its various provincial functionaries. Communication was in the form of short telegraphic messages that included the orders of the central government; they were encoded—that is, ciphered—and the ciphers were regularly modified.

The Cipher Office profoundly changed the relationship between the central administration and the provinces. In those days, traveling from Istanbul to any province in eastern Anatolia or sending a circular or any written document usually took three to four weeks. Then, just before the war started, the central administration set up this institution within the Interior Ministry to quickly send short orders of only a couple of sentences, which sometimes included the message, "The main document is on its way." The local individual in the telegram office would take the cipher document to the government office, where another individual who knew these ciphers would translate the message into modern Ottoman. The officers would write the meaning on top of the telegrams, which is how we can read them today. These cipher documents are crucial for us to understand the Armenian Genocide, because throughout the deportation period the central authorities used these telegrams to communicate with the regions on a daily basis.

It was not only the Interior Ministry that used the Cipher Office. All the other ministries did so as well. For example, I found an important telegram from the Ministry of Education on the assimilation of Armenian children. It was sent to certain eastern provinces before the Armenians had even been sent there, and it says, "There will need to be some orphanages for children; give us the numbers [for how many you can accommodate]." Clearly, they were preparing for the presence of Armenian orphans. These may seem like very fine details, but they are important for understanding the bigger picture. In this case, there must have been a cabinet meeting which took a decision about the education of Armenian orphans and the need for orphanages. After this decision, the Education Ministry took the matter in hand and used the Cipher Office to send a short telegram to the regions, which says, "Consideration has been given to the idea of the education and upbringing of the children." This is noteworthy, because the deportations had not started yet. But the Ottoman government was already preparing for the education and upbringing of children under the age of 10 of those Armenians who would be relocated or deported—either through the establishment of an orphanage, or gathering the children into an already existing orphanage. "Report back with all haste," the telegram says, because they wanted to know how many such orphan children could be accommodated within the provinces, so they could estimate how many would need to go to other places. The Turkish government commonly argues that the Armenian Genocide and its policy toward Christians need to be understood within the framework of "war measures." But the Ministry of Education telegram proves that this had nothing to do with the war: this was planned population policy, planned demographic policy.

It is always difficult to pinpoint a historical beginning date in any social process, because any event that might designate such a beginning is always the result of the events that preceded it. Nevertheless, let us open the scene in the Ottoman Empire in 1912–1913, with the end of the Balkan Wars, as the Empire was confronting its greatest loss. During the nineteenth century, the Ottoman Empire lost around 60 percent of its territory, but in just one month of the Balkan War, in October 1912, the Empire lost about 80 percent of its European lands. For the Committee of Union and Progress, the ruling party of that period, it was clear that the collapse of the Empire was imminent. During 1913, the newspaper *Tanin,* which was the central organ of the Committee of Union and Progress, featured menacing headlines like this: "It is impossible to save Anatolia from the destiny awaiting Rumelia."[1] (*Rumelia* is the Ottoman name for the Balkans.)

After losing the Balkans, they believed now the time was ripe for the same thing to occur in Anatolia, which was home to a large Christian population. In 1913–1914, Christians made up approximately 25–30 percent of the Ottoman population in Anatolia. It was not a small minority; there were some cities in eastern Anatolia, like Van, which were majority Armenian, and then also some cities in the west, like Smyrna, where Greeks were in the majority.

However, fear of the imminent demise of the Empire was in fact nothing new; it was part of the history of the nineteenth century, which witnessed the process of decline. It had once been a magnificent empire ruling over three continents, and had successfully held together all of the various religious and ethnic groups within its territory. Islamic culture and the Ottoman legal system were once progressive by comparison with the European systems, exercising a high degree of tolerance—this is what Muslims today are very proud of. Nevertheless, this tolerance never encompassed an inherent notion of equality, because Christians were not the equals of Muslims.

As the Empire decayed, it was unable to respond appropriately to the growing call from Christians for equality and freedom, which was the basic demand from Ottoman Christians who wanted reform. What happened in the Balkans in 1912–1913 had already played out during the nineteenth century, beginning with the Serbian uprisings in 1804 and 1815–1817, and then in Greece, Bulgaria, Romania, and so on. Christians within the Empire, particularly those living in Europe, demanded equality and freedom—yet it was impossible to respond to those demands while remaining within the Islamic legal system and culture. The mindset of state bureaucrats and Islamic jurisprudence opposed any idea of equality between Muslims and Christians, and demands for equality and social justice were often violently suppressed by the Ottoman rulers. In the nineteenth century, the Great Powers of the time (Britain, France, Russia, Prussia, and Austria-Hungary), whose self-interest lay in the preservation of a weak Ottoman Empire, began intervening ever more directly in its internal affairs, demanding reforms.

Under pressure from the Great Powers, some concessions were made by the Ottomans, but when the pressure eased, the concessions would be forgotten, so none of them was ever enacted.[2] This led to more uprisings by Christians demanding reform. Each uprising was suppressed ever more violently, and this in turn led to more interference from outside. This vicious circle, a catch-22 situation for the Ottomans, became a self-fulfilling prophecy: the Ottomans perceived the growing demands for freedom and equality from segments of their internal population as a national security threat, while it was the failure to heed those demands that ended up creating a national security threat. (It is interesting that today the Turkish government reacts to Kurdish demands in the same way. For reasons of national security, it never acknowledges Kurdish demands for equality and freedom, but ignoring Kurdish demands has created real security concerns for the state.) The authorities were increasingly convinced that tolerating the Ottoman Christians in Anatolia would lead to a national collapse, and they made a series of policy decisions aimed at the ethnoreligious homogenization of Anatolia.

Available Ottoman documents show that the planned demographic policy began to be implemented in the Aegean region against the Greeks, first in 1913, and then in the spring of 1914. Ottoman losses during the Balkan War of 1912 were a major trigger. The Ottomans lost approximately 80 percent of their European landholdings, and 69 percent of their population in Europe in the space of a month: a big shock for the Ottoman rulers. Not only did they lose their land; they lost their homeland—almost the entire ruling elite of the Union and Progress Party was from Macedonia, Albania, and the Balkans. As a result of the war, the Ottoman government agreed to exchange populations with Greece, Bulgaria, and Serbia. Indeed, the first internationally known population-exchange agreements were signed between Serbia, Greece, and Bulgaria in 1913. As a result of these agreements, populations mostly around the border areas were transferred. The Ottomans then used the same strategy of exchange to extend the policy against Greeks in western Anatolia, on security grounds; in their own words, "The policy against the Greeks aimed to liquidate the concentration of the non-Turkish population that had accumulated at strategic points, and was susceptible to negative foreign influence."

The first measures against the Greeks on the Aegean coast followed a two-track communication and operational system. On the surface, the government had an official agreement with Greece, according to which Muslims and Christians would be exchanged and resettled. The first population-exchange agreement between Turkey and Greece was signed around November 1913, and the negotiations continued for further exchanges in May 1914; a special commission was set up for this purpose. But during that period, especially when they were negotiating with the Greeks about the population exchange, they were in fact implementing a policy of forcible expulsion, which was the second track. On the one hand, two states were sitting and negotiating, making some agreement on population exchange that made it a legal act. On the other hand, they were proceeding with an illegal process of "emptying out" Anatolia.

For this purpose, the Ottoman authorities used the Special Organization, a paramilitary operation unit within the Turkish Defense Ministry that was established toward the end of 1913, after the Balkan Wars. Like the Nazi SS, the Special Organization carried out illegal operations, which included forcibly emptying Greek villages by way of attacks on villagers, massacres, and plundering. The overall purpose was not extermination, although there were occasional massacres, for example in Foça (Phocaea), a small town close to Smyrna,[3] where around 200 Greek villagers were killed because they refused to leave. These operations pushed the Greeks to the coast of Anatolia, and eventually to Greece. The official explanation was, "They escaped. This has nothing to do with government policy." In reality, the Ottoman government itself hired special trading ships which took the refugees to Greece. Concrete preparations for this plan started in 1913.

The policies that were set in motion against the Greeks between 1913 and 1914 were forerunners of the subsequent wartime deportation of the Armenian and Assyrian populations. We can say that the policies against the Greeks in 1913 and 1914 were a trial run for the deportation and killing of Armenians and Assyrians from 1915–1917.

The interesting part is that the forcible expulsion of the Greek population from that area stopped suddenly, in November 1914, with the beginning of the First World War. The reason for this was that Germany was negotiating with Greece for the possible participation of Greece in the war alongside Germany. Germany pressured the Ottoman government in Istanbul to stop the deportations from the Aegean coast. This shows that pressure from the Great Powers can stop certain policies. I published the related documents in my book *The Young Turks' Crime against Humanity: The Armenian Genocide and Ethnic Cleansing in the Ottoman Empire* (Princeton: Princeton University Press, 2012). The Ottoman Interior Minister Talaat Pasha sent a telegram to all the provinces on November 2, 1914, saying in effect, "Stop forcibly removing Greeks from their villages. Our new policy is: we have an agreement with Germany; we should not touch the Greek population." And indeed, they did not touch the Greek population again until 1917, when, because of the Russian invasion, they started to move the Greeks from the coastal areas, not to Greece, but within Anatolia. They justified this as a military measure.

The American ambassador in Istanbul, Henry Morgenthau, drew attention to the fact that the methods used during the Armenian Genocide were similar to those used throughout the Greek expulsions. In a report to Washington, he wrote:

"The Turks adopted almost identically the same procedure against the Greeks as that which they had adopted against the Armenians. They began by incorporating the Greeks into the Ottoman army and then transforming them into labour battalions. . . . These Greek soldiers, just like the Armenians, died by the thousands from cold, hunger, and other deprivations. . . . Everywhere the Greeks were gathered into groups, and, under the so-called protection of the Turkish gendarmes, they were transported, the larger part on foot, into the interior [regions of Anatolia]."[4]

What Morgenthau could not know, of course, was that in 1921 and 1922, the new nationalist government in Ankara, under the leadership of Mustafa Kemal, would use exactly the same methods against the Pontus Greeks: arrest of community leaders, who were then put on trial and hanged; separation of the able-bodied men, who were placed into labor battalions or killed directly; and then the forcing of women and children into marches that became death marches. Exactly the same tactics had been used against the Greeks in 1913–1914 and the Armenians in 1915–1917.

Based on Ottoman archival materials, we can discern four different factors that drove the deportation and resettlement of the entire Anatolian population during the period 1913–1918. Firstly, the Christians of Anatolia were perceived as an existential threat to the nation. Secondly, areas vacated by the Christians could be filled with Muslims expelled from the Balkans and the Caucasus. These two factors were part of long-term demographic planning. Thirdly, military reasons were invoked. For instance, some Assyrians were expelled in December 1914 from the Van–Hakkari region to an area in the west of Anatolia; and before the genocide started, Armenians were deported from an area of Cilicia called Dörtyol. Fourthly, there was the need to resettle Muslims displaced as a result of the First World War. The Kurds, for example, had escaped the Russian army in the eastern war zones. This unexpected escape became an important part of Ottoman demographic policy. The number of Muslims who had to be resettled in new areas was approximately one million.

Already in May 1913, the Ottoman government had established a special Department on Immigration and Resettlement within the Interior Ministry, part of whose responsibility it was to rename Christian villages under a policy of Turkification. After the expulsion of Armenians and Assyrians in 1915, the renaming process was accelerated, but the provincial administrative commissions that were responsible were not well-organized. In order to stabilize the process, the Defense Ministry issued an instruction on January 15, 1916, that all towns, villages, mountains, and rivers that had non-Islamic names had to be given Turkish names. This process created an enormous problem during the war years, because no one was familiar with the new names. In a second decree, they suspended the process because the military could not communicate with each other using the new place names.[5]

In implementing the general population resettlement plan, the Ottoman authorities drew up maps that showed the ethnic demography of each region. They also detailed the education, languages, and economic conditions of the different ethnic groups, and the relationships between them. A telegram from 1915 to the provinces said, "There is a need for the procurement of two logs, in which the national identities of the population for each administrative unit, from counties to villages, are known: [the provinces] should prepare this map and send it to the central Government." Another telegram said, "The national identities of the population must be written down, from past and present, all the changes. And even at the village level, these changes and the numbers should be sent to Istanbul." There are dozens of similar documents requesting information from every region. Just one more example: in 1916, the Interior Ministry was requesting the procurement and dispatch of a log of the names of vacated villages, on the Marmara coast, along with numbers of the Greek deportees from that region. As part of this demographic policy the priests, the religious leaders of the Christians, were required to share information about the fluctuation of the population in their communities; when they sent incorrect information or tried to withhold information, they were penalized.

In the case of the Greeks, it was easy to dispose of people; you could put them on ships and send them to Greece. But where are you going to send the Armenians? Did they have a state? At the beginning, the Ottoman government seriously considered sending the Armenians to Russia, but they abandoned this idea for fear of retaliation. In their communications we read them saying, "If we send the Armenians to Russia, they will join the Russian army and come back again." This is the primary reason why the policy against the Armenians had to be genocide—because there was no place to send them where they would not be a threat.

The second reason was also important: in February 1914, the Ottoman government signed an agreement with Russia, according to the terms of which there would be two autonomous Armenian provinces in eastern Anatolia, with foreigners as governors—one Norwegian and one Dutch. Half the police and half the gendarmerie were to be Armenian, and Armenians should be part of the civil administration if their number exceeded 10 percent of the local Muslim population. Not only the Ottomans, but the French, Russians, and all the other powers understood that this was the beginning of an independent Armenian state, because this was how the Ottomans had lost Serbia, Bosnia and Herzegovina, Bulgaria, and Romania. The Ottoman government wanted to prevent this at any cost. When they entered the war in November 1914, the first thing they did was to annul the agreement. Then in January/

February 1915, they lost a major battle in the Caucasus against the Russians at Sarıkamış. Almost 80,000 Ottoman soldiers were destroyed by cold weather and by the Russian army. This opened the door for the Russians, and the Ottoman government expected that Russia would then take steps to implement the reform agreement. It was no coincidence that the decision to deport the Armenians followed the Battle of Sarıkamış. War in the Dardanelles further threatened the Empire, and provided another reason for the decision to exterminate the Armenian population. This process began in April 1915.

The resettlement of Muslims in villages vacated by Christians began immediately after the expulsion of the Christians. We can read in the Ottoman documents the time difference between emptying the Armenian villages and relocating and resettling Muslims in those villages: in some areas, it was not more than two to three weeks. This shows how well prepared the authorities were. I make this point to emphasize that the expulsions were not the result of simple Islamic fanaticism. It is clear that religion played an important role, but social engineering was also an important part of the government's thinking.

One of the main aims of the resettlement policy was the speedy assimilation of the different Muslim ethnic groups. In the Ottoman documents, the Arabic words *temsil* and *temessül* (plural), which signify "assimilation," were used openly. In order to achieve assimilation, Muslim groups were separated from their religious leaders; for example, Kurdish tribal leaders had to be separated from their tribes and settled in different areas. Furthermore, the groups themselves were dispersed throughout Anatolia.

A telegram dated May 2, 1916, stated that the intention of the resettlement policy was to make the Kurds forget their ethnic and cultural identity. They would not be resettled in areas that would allow them to retain their national identity. For instance, the local authorities had relocated certain Kurds in Urfa Province in the southeast, but this could not be allowed, because the Kurds had a very good relationship with the neighboring Arabs, and in these circumstances would never forget their culture and their language. They had to be sent further into the Turkish heartland of Anatolia, to Konya. The goal was that Kurds and other non-Turkish-Muslim groups should forget their culture and non-Turkish languages. The documents show that the government explicitly ordered the regional authorities to ensure that any relocated group did not constitute more than 5–10 percent of the original population.

In each region, the government and the local authorities kept continual track of population percentages. The central government constantly asked for numbers both of the expelled groups and the remaining and relocated groups: percentages of Orthodox Armenians, Protestant Armenians, and Catholic Armenians; their percentages in relation to each other and to the Muslim population, and so on. And they requested this information almost on a weekly basis.

Who was in charge of the Armenian deportations throughout this period? It was the Office of Statistics, in the Interior Ministry. The Office of Statistics was in charge of the entire deportation process, and kept close track of the numbers. According to Ottoman statistics, the number of deported Armenians was around 1.2 million. The Muslim population in Syria and Iraq, where the Armenians were supposed to be resettled, was around 2 million. The authorities said 1.2 million Armenians from throughout Anatolia were deported to desert areas, today's Syria, mainly Aleppo and the surrounding areas. Concentration camps were established along the rivers to hold them. But in the telegrams they were sending to Aleppo, Mosul, and the other governorates, the authorities were saying that the Armenians should not exceed 10 percent of the local population. The Muslim population of the entire area, including Mosul, was around 2 million, so if you wanted to settle Armenians as 10 percent of the Muslim population, what would you do with 1.2 million Armenians? Only between 150,000 and 200,000 survived the process that followed; that figure corresponded perfectly with the requirement of restricting the Armenian population to 10 percent of these predominantly Arab areas.

Because the Ottomans were taking a population census almost on a weekly basis, they got information toward the end of 1915 that the number of Armenians who arrived in the new settlement areas in today's Syria was around 500,000. This was why they organized the mass killings of the summer of 1916. More than 200,000 Armenians were exterminated in the area surrounding Deir ez-Zor within 2 months. This is the place we call the Auschwitz of the Armenian Genocide. It was home to the Armenian Genocide Memorial, which Islamic State of Iraq and Syria recently attacked and destroyed.

I think that, if one compares their plans and the implementation of their plans, the Ottoman Committee of Union and Progress was more successful than the Nazis. Some Holocaust scholars argue that there was a discrepancy between what the Nazis planned—the creation of a racial empire in all of Eastern Europe—and what they achieved. Götz Aly, for instance, argues that only 20–30 percent of the entire Nazi plan could be implemented. In the case of the Ottomans, I would say they really successfully implemented their genocidal policy.

Finally, one of the purposes behind removing the Christian population from Anatolia was to develop a new Turkish-Muslim bourgeois class, a dimension that has mostly been ignored by scholars. In furtherance of this purpose, the properties of Greeks, Assyrians, and Armenians were either sold at bargain-basement prices or distributed free to Muslims. The Ottoman authorities issued different laws and regulations in this regard. In a nutshell, these laws and regulations mandated that a special commission be established in each of the provinces in order to sell some of the Armenian and Greek properties by auction. Crops and livestock were to be treated in the same way. Fields were to be harvested and the crops sold, with the proceeds recorded. But today, we do not know where the property registers are. They have vanished; we cannot find them in the Ottoman archives.

So what actually happened to the properties that were confiscated during the war years? They were distributed among Muslim immigrants in the regions, and those who were resettled in the previously Greek and Armenian villages, in order to create a Muslim bourgeois class with enough capital to rival and replace what had been lost with the expulsion of the Christian bourgeoisie. They were sold off to cover military expenses. Ottoman participation in the First World War was partly financed by the revenue from Christian properties. Some of the substantial buildings were repurposed for government use, such as prisons, schools, and hospitals. If you travel through Anatolia, in almost all major cities there is a handsome building, called, for example, the House of Ataturk. Mostly these houses belonged previously to a Greek or an Armenian. The entire ruling elite took part in this economic plundering.

In conclusion, while there was some occasional disruption in the procedures that were followed regarding Christians in the Ottoman Empire between 1878 and 1924, the Ottomans overall exhibited consistency of policy. Particularly after Ottoman losses in the Balkan War of 1912, the elimination of all Christians—Greeks, Assyrians, and Armenians—from Anatolia was bedrock Ottoman policy. The Pontus genocide of 1921 and 1922 and the population exchange in 1924 were the last chapters in a process of ethnic cleansing—genocide, in fact—against the Ottoman Christians. Today's Turkish Republic, established in 1923, owes its existence to the elimination of Christians from Anatolia. Christians accounted for approximately 25–30 percent of the entire Ottoman population in 1914. Today, Christians are not even 1 percent of the Turkish population.

We say we are proud to be a Muslim country, with a population that is 99.5 percent Muslim. But this pride is possible only because of an extermination policy against Christians. If the genocide of Pontus Greeks and Assyrians, not to mention of Armenians, continues to be denied in the face of mountains of contrary evidence, the reason must be the fact that modern Turkey was constructed on top of this annihilation and denial, which permit the Turkish government to perpetuate the myth of an exclusive legacy over their lands. It could be argued that there are a lot of nation-states in the world that were built upon genocide or similar atrocities; however, most of these nations are not afraid to face their dark past. If Turkey cares about its reputation, and wants to be considered a respected member of Europe, it must first and foremost confront this dark chapter in its founding, and make honesty and integrity principles of its government. Turkey should also see and understand that an acknowledgment of historic wrongdoing is the beginning of good neighborly relations in the region. Thus, peace, security, and stability in the Middle East can only be achieved if Turkey starts acknowledging its wrongdoings to other nations in the past.

NOTES

1. Aram Andonian, *Balkan Savaşı* (Istanbul: Aras Yayıncılık, 1999), 227.

2. For more details on Russian and Great Power policies in connection with Armenian reform see Roderic H. Davidson, "The Armenian Crisis, 1912–1914," *American Historical Review* 53, no. 3 (April 1948): 481–505.

3. This became known as the Massacre of Phocaea.

4. Henry Morgenthau, *Ambassador Morgenthau's Story* (Garden City, NY: Doubleday, Page & Co., 1918), 324–25.

5. I was born in Ardahan, and the villages around my city have mostly Armenian, Greek, or Georgian names. I remember that in the 1970s, the authorities were still trying to change these names; this is an ongoing process in Turkey—maybe we should call it part of a cultural genocide.

WORKS CITED

Akçam, Taner. *The Young Turks' Crime against Humanity: The Armenian Genocide and Ethnic Cleansing in the Ottoman Empire*. Princeton: Princeton University Press, 2012.

Andonian, Aram. *Balkan Savaşı*. Istanbul: Aras Yayıncılık, 1999.

Davidson, Roderic H. "The Armenian Crisis, 1912–1914." *American Historical Review* 53 no. 3 (April 1948): 481–505.

Morgenthau, Henry. *Ambassador Morgenthau's Story*. Garden City, NY: Doubleday, Page & Co., 1918.

Chapter 2

Dhimmis No More: Christians' Trauma in the Middle East

(Bern, March 7, 2012)

Daniel Pipes

A new strain has developed in Sunni Muslim thinking: ethnic cleansing. It is not genocide, but it involves expelling non-Sunni populations. Its spread means that non-Muslim minorities have a grim future in Muslim-majority countries; and some may have no future there at all. I shall trace the origins of ethnic cleansing in the Middle East, note its impact, especially on Christians, and consider responses to it.

To begin, let us look at the standing of non-Muslims in Muslim-majority countries before 1800. Muslims viewed non-Muslims in two categories: monotheists recognized by Islam as adhering to a valid faith (this being mostly Jews and Christians), and polytheists (especially Hindus) lacking that recognition. The former category, our topic here, are known as People of the Book (*Ahl al-Kitab*).

Muslims were relatively tolerant of People of the Book—but only if they accepted becoming *dhimmis* (i.e., protected persons) who acknowledged the rule of Muslims and the superiority of Islam; in other words, if they accepted an inferior status. They had to pay special taxes (called *jizya*), and could not serve in the military or the police or, more generally, exercise authority over Muslims. Sumptuary laws abounded; a Christian or Jew should walk or go by mule but not ride a horse and should defer to a Muslim on the street. (Of course, actual practice differed from one country to another and from one era to another.)

The recognized place granted to religious minorities made Muslim-ruled countries quite unlike premodern Christendom. Christians under Muslim rule enjoyed better conditions than Muslims under Christian rule; in 1200 or so, one would much rather be a Christian living in Muslim Spain than a Muslim living in Christian Spain. Likewise for Jews: Mark R. Cohen observes that "the Jews of Islam, especially during the formative and classical centuries (up to the thirteenth century), experienced much less persecution than did the Jews of Christendom."[1]

But we must not romanticize the *dhimmi* status. Yes, it offered a degree of tolerance, cohabitation, and deference—but these were premised on the assumption of Muslim superiority and non-Muslim inferiority. It could also be abused at whim by Muslims. No modern citizen would accept the disabilities that accompanied living as a *dhimmi*.

Indeed, the *dhimmi* status came crashing down in modern times, which is to say after 1800, as European powers (British, French, Dutch, Spanish, Italian, Russian, and others) overwhelmed nearly the whole Muslim world. Even those few countries—Yemen, Arabia, Turkey, Iran—that escaped direct European control felt Europe's predominance.

Christian imperialists flipped the *dhimmi* status on its head, favoring Christians and also Jews, both of whom showed greater willingness to accept the new rulers, learn their languages and skills, work for them, and serve as intermediaries to the Muslim-majority population. Naturally, majority Muslim populations resented this heightened status of Christians and Jews.

When European rule came to its inevitable end, Muslims on returning to power put the minorities roughly back in their place—and worse, for the *dhimmi* status had earlier been discarded and was not to be revived. Unsure of themselves, the new rulers generally looked darkly at Peoples of the Book, angry at their having serviced the imperialists and suspicious of their abiding connections to Europe (and in the Jewish case, their new connections to Israel).

One could say that the second-class *dhimmi* status now became a third- or fourth-class post-*dhimmi* status. The breakup of the Ottoman Empire witnessed more persecution of Christians and Jews than perhaps ever before, starting with the Armenians of Turkey in the 1910s and culminating with recent Christian traumas in Iraq and Syria.

Before continuing with the Christian experience, a few side words on the Jewish one. Ancient Jewish communities disappeared as a result of the collapse of the *dhimmi* status and the creation of Israel in 1948. Jews decamped or were pushed out, especially out in the 20-year period after World War II. The small but lively Jewish community of Algeria offers perhaps the most dramatic illustration of the post-imperial changes. The Jews there had so connected themselves to French rule that the entire Jewish community fled the country along with the French rulers in July 1962.[2] In 1945, the Jewish population in Muslim-majority countries numbered about a million; today, it hovers between 30,000 and 40,000, nearly all of whom live in Iran, Turkey, and Morocco. No more than a handful live elsewhere: maybe 60 Jews in Egypt, 9 in Iraq, and even fewer in Afghanistan; these nearly defunct communities of the elderly will no longer exist within a few years.

As the expression goes, "First the Saturday people, then the Sunday people." And now is the Christian turn. Christians are now recapitulating the Jewish exodus. From 1500 to 1900, Christians made up a consistent 15 percent of the Middle East's population, according to David B. Barrett and Todd M. Johnson.[3] In 1910, that number had dipped to 13.6 percent, according to Todd M. Johnson and Gina A. Zurlo;[4] and in 2010, Christians had been reduced to a meager 4.2 percent, or less than a third as large as a century earlier. The downward trend, of course, is steeply continuing. *(handwritten margin note: Christian trend)*

As the journalist Lee Smith puts it: "Being Christian in the Middle East has never been easy, but the wave of uprisings that has swept the region over the past year has made the situation for the region's Christian minority almost unbearable."[5] The examples are alarming, and in many ways unprecedented in the long history of Muslim–Christian relations. Here are some of them (with thanks to Raymond Ibrahim):[6]

1. In Nigeria, the Islamist group Boko Haram in 2011 killed at least 510 people, mainly Christians, and burned down or destroyed more than 350 churches in 10 northern states.
2. In Uganda on Christmas Eve 2011, Muslims threw acid on a church leader, leaving him with severe burns.
3. In Iran, a church celebrating Christmas was raided by security, and all those present, including Sunday school children, were arrested and interrogated.
4. In Tajikistan, a young man dressed as Father Frost (i.e., Santa Claus) was stabbed to death while visiting relatives and bringing gifts.
5. In Malaysia, parish priests and church youth leaders had to get caroling permits, requiring them to submit full names and ID numbers at police stations.
6. In Indonesia, "vandals" decapitated a statue of the Virgin Mary.

The message is clear: "Christians, you are unwelcome. Go."

Christians have responded by rapidly exiting the Middle East, to the point that the faith is dying in its birthplace. In Turkey, the Christian population numbered 2 million in 1920, but now only numbers some thousands. In Iraq, CSI found in 2007 that close to half of the roughly one million Christians who had been living there in 2003 had fled the country. The Iraqi Christian Relief Council cried out, "We're on the verge of extinction."[7] In Syria, Christians represented about one-third of the population at the beginning of the last century, today they count for less than 10 percent. In Lebanon the number went from about 55 percent 70 years ago to under 30 percent today. Copts are leaving as never before in their long history.

In the Holy Land, Christians made up 10 percent of the population in the Ottoman period; that figure is now down to about 2 percent. Bethlehem and

Nazareth, the most identifiable of all Christian towns, enjoyed Christian majorities for nearly two millennia, but no more: they are now majority Muslim towns. In Jerusalem, Christians outnumbered Muslims in 1922; today the Christian population of Jerusalem is a mere 2 percent. Despite this emigration, Khaled Abu Toameh, a Muslim Palestinian journalist, notes that "Israel remains the only place in the Middle East where Arab Christians feel protected and safe."[8] More Arab Christians live outside the Middle East than in their homelands.

Eastern Christians are dealing with this crisis in various ways. I will review three of them. Melkite Catholics (who live primarily in Lebanon and Syria) have tried to avoid trouble by telling Muslims exactly what they want to hear. Patriarch Gregory III Laham of Antioch memorably announced in 2005: "We are the Church of Islam. . . . Islam is our milieu, the context in which we live and with which we are historically associated. . . . We understand Islam from the inside. When I hear a verse of the Koran, it's not something foreign to me. It's an expression of the civilization to which I belong."[9] Gregory blamed Islamism entirely on the West: "Fundamentalism is a sickness that gets loose and takes root because of the void of the Western modernity."[10]

In the same spirit, Gregory in 2010 blamed Israel for jihadi attacks on Eastern Christians: The violence, he said, "has nothing to do with Islam. . . . But it is actually a conspiracy planned by Zionism and some Christians with Zionist orientations and it aims at undermining and giving a bad image of Islam. . . . It is also a conspiracy against Arabs . . . to deny them their rights and especially those of the Palestinians.[11] He added in 2011 that the Palestinian–Israel conflict is the "sole" reason for the migration of Eastern Christians from the Middle East, and this is causing them to face "demographic extinction."[12] Gregory's approach amounts to: Muslims, please do not hurt us; we will say anything that you wish. We have no identity of our own. We are, in fact, a kind of Muslim. It is full-*dhimmi* supplication for the post-*dhimmi* era.

Maronites historically offered the most dramatic contrast to this self-denigration. For theological (the Catholic Church) and geographical (the mountains) reasons, they represented the most assertive and free Christian community in the Middle East. Armed and autonomous, they kept Muslim overlords at a distance. In 1926, they uniquely induced an imperial power, France, to create a state, Lebanon, for them. But the Maronites were greedy: rather than accept a *Petit Liban* where they made up 80 percent of the population, they demanded and won a *Grand Liban* where they made up lesser than 40 percent of the population. Fifty years later, in 1976, the Maronites paid the price for this overreach when the Muslims mounted a fifteen-year civil war which broke Maronite power.

Maronites responded by turning on each other. While some remain defiant, the most important faction has become akin to the Melkites. Former General

Michel Aoun stood up to the Syrians in 1991; today he toadies to Hezbollah and serves the jihad. Lee Smith put it like this: "The Maronites had always distinguished themselves as among the region's most stubbornly independent of confessional sects. But fear, resentment, and short-sided political calculation have led them today to seek protection and patronage from the Middle East's most dangerous and retrograde elements: Syria, Iran, and Hezbollah."[13] In brief, the Maronites have gone from being free Christians to partial *dhimmis*.

Since the Islamic conquest of Egypt nearly fourteen centuries ago, Egypt's Copts pursued a path nearly opposite that of the Maronites. Their geography (flat), history (strong central government), and society (interspersed among Muslims), were all unfavorable to independent power, forcing Copts to bow their heads. Fully accepting the *dhimmi* status, Copts survived and withstood Islamization more successfully than most other Middle Eastern Christians, as their relatively large numbers attest. The colonial era offered them a bigger role and they readily took it, as symbolized by the grandfather of former UN Secretary General Boutros Boutros-Ghali, who served as the prime minister of Egypt in 1908–1910. That interlude of power shuddered to a close with the British departure in the 1950s.

Starting about 1980, two parallel developments have taken place. On the one hand, Islamists have systematically targeted Copts, engaging in various forms of coercion and violence against them, abetted by the government of Egypt—which generally places higher priority on maintaining good relations with the Islamists than on protecting its Christian minority. Christians became a political football; for example, Hosni Mubarak played a double game, pretending to be the protector of the Copts while he was anything but. On the other hand, after centuries of near-silence, the Copts found their collective voice. They have organized to defend themselves, become vocal about their plight, and led the protests when a visiting Egyptian president visited Washington. Despite a very long tradition of quiescence, Copts are becoming the new Maronites.

Notwithstanding these disparate methods of coping—super-*dhimmi*, *dhimmi*, and assertive—the general future of Christianity in the Middle East looks bleak. The *dhimmi*'s accepted place gave way to fleeting improvement followed by a mentality of ethnic cleansing.

One hears a great deal about the hatred and fear of Islam, now called "Islamophobia." But Ayaan Hirsi Ali, the ex-Muslim and former Dutch parliamentarian, finds the real problem to be something quite else—namely, Christophobia:

A fair-minded assessment of recent events and trends leads to the conclusion that the scale and the severity of Islamophobia pales in comparison with the bloody Christophobia currently coursing through Muslim-majority nations from one end of the globe to the other. The conspiracy of silence surrounding this violent expression of religious intolerance has to stop. Nothing less than the fate of Christianity—and ultimately of all religious minorities [among Muslims]—is at stake.[14]

In combination, the ethnic cleansings of Jews and Christians mark the end of an era. The attractive multiplicity of Middle Eastern life is being reduced to the flat monotony of a single religion and a handful of beleaguered minorities. The entire region, not just the minorities, is impoverished by this trend.

What can Western advocates—including Christian Solidarity International—do about this problem? Only two options exist: to protect non-Muslims—Christians and others—to enable them to continue living in Muslim-majority countries, or to help them leave, giving up on their historic homelands.

The first option is obviously preferable; Christians have an inalienable right to stay put. But how do Westerners help them achieve this? That requires both acts of will on their part and a willingness on the part of Muslims to change. But neither of these looks in the least like a realistic prospect. Especially when the human rights of others are at stake, democratic governments alone cannot simply make decisions; they need popular support. At present, Westerners appear unwilling to take the steps required—such as economic and military pressure—to ensure the survival in place of Middle Eastern Christianity.

Which leaves the less attractive alternative: helping Christians to leave and then opening doors to let them in. Emigration is an inherently painful experience and democracies will have difficulty formulating policies to give priority to adherents of certain faiths. These and other negatives notwithstanding, migration is a real option, and one that is daily being acted on. And so, Middle Eastern Christians, tragically, are disappearing before our eyes from their ancient homes.

NOTES

1. Mark Cohen, *Under Crescent and Cross—The Jews of the Middle Ages* (Princeton: Princeton University Press, 2008), xxiii.

2. See Lloyd C. Briggs and Norina Lami Guède, *No More For Ever: A Saharan Jewish Town* (Cambridge: Papers of the Peabody Museum of Archaeology and Ethnology, 1964).

3. See David B. Barrett and Todd M. Johnson, *World Christian Trends AD 30–AD 2200: Interpreting the annual Christian megacensus* (Pasadena: William Carey Library, 2001).

4. See Todd M. Johnson and Gina A. Zurlo, "Ongoing Exodus: Tracking the Emigration of Christians from the Middle East," *Harvard Journal of Middle Eastern Politics and Policy*, vol. III (2013–2014): 39–49.

5. Lee Smith, "Agents of Influence," *Tablet*, January 4, 2012, http://www.tablet-mag.com/jewish-news-and-politics/87240/minority-interest.

6. See Raymond Ibrahim, "Christmas Under Islam. Hardly a Season to be Jolly," *PJ Media*, January 17, 2012, http://www.meforum.org/3157/christmas-under-islam.

7. Quoted after Raymond Ibrahim, "Iraq's Christians Near Extinction," *Front-PageMagazine .com*, December 21, 2011, http://www.meforum.org/3135/iraq-christians-extinction.

8. Khaled Abu Toameh, "Arab Spring Sending Shudders Through Christians in the Middle East," *Gatestone Institute*, December 20, 2011, https://www.gatestonein-stitute.org/2685/arab-spring-christians.

9. Quoted after Gianni Valente, "We are the Church of Islam. Interview with the patriarch of Antioch Grégoire III Laham," *Synod of Bishops* no. 10 (2005), http://www.30giorni.it/articoli_id_9596_l3.htm.

10. Ibid.

11. Quoted after Mohammed Zaatari, "Sidon archdiocese reopens following refurbishment," *The Daily Star*, December 6, 2010, http://www.dailystar.com.lb//News/Lebanon-News/2010/Dec-06/60969-sidon-archdiocese-reopens-following-refurbishment.ashx#ixzz1817 rlDqU.

12. Quoted after Aymenn Jawad, "Middle Eastern Christians and anti-Semitism," *The Jerusalem Post*, August 1, 2011, http://www.jpost.com/printarticle.aspx?id=231998.

13. Lee Smith, "Agents of Influence," *Tablet*, January 4, 2012, http://www.tablet-mag.com/jewish-news-and-politics/87240/minority-interest.

14. Ayaan Hirsi Ali, "The Global War on Christians in the Muslim World," *Newsweek*, February 6, 2012, http://europe.newsweek.com/ayaan-hirsi-alithe-global-war-christians-muslim-world-65817?rm=eu.

WORKS CITED

Abi-Habib, Maria. "Christians, in an Epochal Shift, Are Leaving the Middle East." *The Wall Street Journal*. May 12, 2017. https://www.wsj.com/articles/christians-in-an-epochal-shift-are-leaving-the-middle-east-1494597848.

Ali, Ayaan Hirsi. "The Global War on Christians in the Muslim World." *Newsweek*. February 6, 2012. http://europe.newsweek.com/ayaan-hirsi-alithe-global-war-christians-muslim -world-65817?rm=eu.

Barrett, David B., and Todd M. Johnson. *World Christian Trends AD 30–AD 2200: Interpreting the annual Christian megacensus*. Pasadena: William Carey Library, 2001.

Briggs, Lloyd C. and Norina Lami Guède. *No More For Ever: A Saharan Jewish Town*. Cambridge: Papers of the Peabody Museum of Archaeology and Ethnology, 1964.

Cohen, Mark. *Under Crescent and Cross—The Jews of the Middle Ages*. Princeton: Princeton University Press, 2008.

Ibrahim, Raymond. "Iraq's Christians Near Extinction." *FrontPageMagazine.com*. December 21, 2011. http://www.meforum.org/3135/iraq-christians-extinction.

———. "Christmas Under Islam. Hardly a Season to be Jolly." *PJ Media*. January 17, 2012. http://www.meforum.org/3157/christmas-under-islam.

Jawad, Aymenn. "Middle Eastern Christians and anti-Semitism." *The Jerusalem Post*. August 1, 2011. http://www.jpost.com/printarticle.aspx?id=231998.

Johnson, Todd M., and Gina A. Zurlo. "Ongoing Exodus: Tracking the Emigration of Christians from the Middle East." *Harvard Journal of Middle Eastern Politics and Policy* vol. III (2013–2014): 39–49.

Smith, Lee. "Agents of Influence." *Tablet*. January 4, 2012. http://www.tabletmag.com/jewish-news-and-politics/87240/minority-interest.

Toameh, Khaled Abu. "Arab Spring Sending Shudders Through Christians in the Middle East." *Gatestone Institute*. December 20, 2011. https://www.gatestonein-stitute.org /2685/arab-spring-christians.

Valente, Gianni. "We are the Church of Islam. Interview with the patriarch of Antioch Grégoire III Laham." *Synod of Bishops* no. 10 (2005). http://www.30giorni.it / articoli_id_9596_l3.htm.

Zaatari, Mohammed. "Sidon archdiocese reopens following refurbishment." *The Daily Star*. December 6, 2010. http://www.dailystar.com.lb//News/Lebanon-News/2010/Dec-06/60969-sidon-archdiocese-reopens-following-refurbishment.ashx#ixzz1817rlDqU.

Chapter 3

Syria, the "Arab Spring," and the Future of Christians and other Religious Minorities

(Zurich, June 12, 2012)

Habib Malik

Since the middle years of the last century, the persistent plague afflicting the Middle East region as a whole has been repressive dictatorial regimes run by despots with a stranglehold on their societies and peoples. But for over a year now, one after the other, they have been collapsing. No one with a modicum of moral sensibility could condone what these regimes have done to their people, or how some, like the Assad regime in Damascus, continue to massacre innocents. I come from Lebanon, where few have forgotten the misery inflicted on the Lebanese by the nearly three decade-long Syrian occupation of their country.

Hence it is understandable that the initial euphoria when uprisings occurred in a number of Arab countries would lead enthusiasts to call the phenomenon the "Arab Spring." There were high hopes that these revolutions would usher in a bright new era of freedoms, rights, and participatory politics for the Arab region. Eighteen months later, what remains is a jumble of disturbing outcomes and ominous tendencies that resembles anything but a democratic spring. The two overriding questions today are, firstly, what will replace these repressive regimes, and secondly, at what cost to their peoples and to the region as a whole will their elimination come.

In the early days, the hype in the Western media—that quickly infected Arab media—spoke of the Facebook generation of Arab youth, the power of social media to bring swift political transformation to Arab societies, the voice of Arab liberals finally making itself heard, and other exclamations of this kind. What transpired on the ground, however, is something very different. Facebook and social media had the ephemeral impact of igniting the protests, but achieved nothing close to the serious and sustained political organization and institutionalization that would see them through to concrete and lasting gains. Networking is not the same as organization-building. And the "voices of Arab liberals" soon gave way to chants of "Allahu akbar." Effectively, the revolutions were either stunted or hijacked by the better organized and better funded illiberal forces of Islamism, thereby plunging the region into an uncertain future fraught with perils.

Most vulnerable throughout the Middle East are the native non-Sunni Muslim and non-Muslim, specifically Christian, minority communities. Also vulnerable are many Muslims, especially women, who do not wish to live under strict versions of shari'a or Islamic law. But this is precisely where the region is headed if present trends continue. Women will have it especially hard. They will have to cover up because their nakedness invites abuse—a classic example of blaming the victim. And the open approval of honor killings, if you add that to this notion of covering up, means a grotesquely savage new reality will have set in.

The overthrow of Ben Ali in Tunisia did eventually bring in Moncef Marzouki, a moderate, as leader. But the Islamists have been strengthened, and the ongoing challenge is by no means a settled matter. Shortly after Gaddafi's death in Libya, Mustafa Abdul Jalil, then head of the National Transitional Council, declared that henceforth polygamy would be accepted on a wide scale, and the country would be ruled on the basis of the shari'a. It took a subsequent uproar, mainly from abroad, for him to backtrack. Yet Libya is still far from being on the road to democracy. And Egypt, a year and a half after the revolution that ousted Mubarak, has produced two presidential candidates for the run-off elections, neither of them a liberal: Ahmed Shafik of the old regime, Mubarak's last prime minister, and Mohammed Morsi of the Muslim Brotherhood. We cannot but repeat Francis Fukuyama's recent frustrated exclamation in *Newsweek*: "How did we come to this pass, where the two most powerful forces in the new Egypt either represent its authoritarian past, or else are Islamist of suspect liberal credentials?"[1] Can anyone therefore accuse the Copts, Egypt's eight or so million Christians, of exaggerated or even unfounded fears when we know full well the sort of recurring bloody attacks their community has suffered at the hands of both politically ascendant groups in Egypt today?

The disconnect between the optimistic Western rhetoric of a new democratic dawn for the Arab East and the depressing realities on the ground is only surpassed in absurdity by the identity of the regional allies the West has chosen to spearhead this movement of liberation from tyranny—namely, Saudi Arabia and Qatar. Nothing highlights this bizarre situation more than what is going on in Syria. Are we to believe that fanatical states like Saudi Arabia and Qatar, enjoying unwavering Western backing, are actually championing a liberal alternative to the Assad dictatorship in Syria? Of course not. They are financing and supporting a militant Sunni, Salafi, or Wahhabi replacement there (and indeed anywhere else in the region they can manage it). Grasping this single stark fact allows so many pieces of both the Syrian and the wider regional puzzles to fall into place. It exposes the short-sighted policies of the Western powers. It also explains the deep ambivalence felt by Syria's Christians and other targeted minorities there and in neighboring countries with regard to regime change in Damascus. The tragic choice of these minorities is sadly what I would call between the frying pan and the fire, that is, between bad and worse. These vulnerable minorities, which are ambivalent about regime change, are not blind supporters of the bloody regimes in power, nor are they gratuitous Islamophobes, as they are sometimes unjustly accused of being.

Moreover, Saudi–Qatari promotion of Sunni militancy shatters the illusion nurtured by a beguiled Western media that the Syrian opposition to Assad's brutal rule comprises merely benign and moderate Sunni Islam. The first wave of opposition leaders who ignited the anti-regime protests 18 months ago have nearly all vanished, and given way to the so-called Free Syrian Army, a militant Islamist grouping with long beards that practices kidnappings and beheadings on a regular basis, and incessantly chants "Allahu akbar" in al-Qaeda-style when it films military attacks against regime forces. There is basically no difference between the Syrian regime kidnapping people for political reasons in Lebanon during that country's 1975–1990 war, and the Syrian opposition today kidnapping Lebanese for sectarian reasons—most recently, eleven Shi'ite pilgrims returning from Iran were abducted inside Syria just next to the Turkish border. These are two faces of the same ugly coin. There is plenty to worry about if the Syrian opposition has already started to kidnap religious pilgrims. Once in power, how will this opposition treat minorities?

Given these disturbing developments, how is one to take seriously the reassurance to Christians, Alawites, and other minorities in Syria issued recently by Abdul Basit Sida, the new president of the Syrian National Council, that they will be well-treated and allowed to participate in politics once the Assad regime is gone?[2] To their credit, some weeks previously the US Secretary of State Hillary Clinton, Secretary of Defense Leon Panetta, and Chairman of the Joint Chiefs of Staff General Martin Dempsey expressed doubts about the immunity of the Syrian opposition to Salafi infiltration, and showed a prudent reluctance to support an all-out arming of this suspect opposition. Saudi–Qatari stoking of the fires of Sunni extremism in Syria and elsewhere justifies the apprehensions of many nations, including Russia and China, that what will follow Assad will be a far worse scenario, not only for Syria but also for the entire Middle East.

What is likely to replace the repressive and faltering Assad regime in Syria, the fallen Mubarak regime in Egypt, and other similar dictatorships throughout the region? Most likely, if present trends continue, the better funded, better motivated, and better organized Islamists of these various countries. And at what price will this change of dictatorships come? Well, if Kofi Annan's recent warning is true—and, sadly, I believe it is—Syria, unlike Libya, will not implode, but will rather explode,[3] with catastrophic consequences for the entire region. The outcome will either be bloody, open-ended chaos featuring Sunni–Shi'ite carnage, with Christians and other minorities trampled underfoot, or the emergence of a far worse dictatorship of the Salafi–Jihadi–Takfiri variety—what some sources have termed "Islamofascism."

My main concern is the adverse impact all of this will have on native minority communities, especially the Christians. This is not to suggest that these communities are the only ones suffering. But they, more than all others, are in danger of being overlooked, bypassed, and ignored until it is too late. Christian suffering has a way of being chronically underreported. And when finally it receives attention, the damage has usually already been done, and there is very little follow-up.

Without these Christian communities, pluralism in the Middle East is all but dead, and along with it any real chance for genuine freedoms and democracy. Indigenous Middle Eastern Christians, whether in Syria, Lebanon, Egypt, Jordan, among the Palestinians, and whatever remains of them in Iraq, do not see a "spring" anywhere in sight. To them, the term "Arab Spring" sounds increasingly like black humor or a bad joke. They see instead the makings of an Arab nightmare, one with the possibility of bringing death and destruction not only to them, but also to people and cultures far beyond the Middle East.

Historically, Christians did not participate in the creation of these repressive regimes, except individually and intellectually in the persons of certain Greek Orthodox theoreticians of Ba'athism and Arabism.[4] On the other hand, Christians did help to usher in modernity to the Arab region during the Arab cultural renaissance beginning in the late nineteenth century, and ever since. They also led in the defense of the great Arab national causes, including that of Palestine. Christians therefore do not need a certificate of good behavior, a seal of approval, from anyone.

Today these same Christians of the Arab world are basically afraid of the unknown, in the absence of any Arab model for democracy. Their region is historically freedom-starved. The vast majority of them have lived for centuries as *dhimmis*—that is, second-class subjugated individuals and communities deprived of basic freedoms. Now, under mainly Sunni rule, Islamism is everywhere on the rise. There is no real pluralism or acceptance of minorities, and there is no reliable roadmap to guide this transition to democracy. And no power offers them any reassurance: not Muslim moderates—minority communities, especially the Christians, have little confidence in the ability of Sunni moderation specifically to stand on its own two feet—not the West, and not Russia, although the latter has been vocal in its concern for their plight through the words and regional visits of Moscow Patriarch Kirill.

In addition, native Christian communities suffer chronic demographic shrinkage and mounting emigration. Witness the battering endured by Lebanon's Christians since 1975, the decimation of Iraq's Christians since 2003, the continuing harassment of Egypt's Copts, and now the fear of Syria's Christian communities. Middle East Christians are not enamored of political adventurism nor of repressive regimes. Their aims are modest: not to have their churches and communities targeted in Iraq and Egypt; to try and retain even a token presence in the Holy Land; to enjoy equality and freedom in a pluralist system; not to be singled out as scapegoats or revenge objects in the mayhem in Syria; and not to revisit any of Lebanon's recent sectarian and religious horrors. It is not the specialty of Christians to address the crucial question now being historically posed; that is, the place of political Islam in the running of the Arab state and the prosecution of political power. It is not the Christians who should give answers to this question. What Christians want for themselves, they also want for their fellow Muslims and for the other minorities: freedom, mutual respect, and no maltreatment.

How this question of the place of Islam in the new emerging Arab state order will be addressed will profoundly affect the future of all minority communities native to the region, including Christians. The underlying issue, of concern to all, is the endemic weakness of liberalism in an Arab and predominantly Islamic context. As I hinted earlier, Sunni moderation has revealed itself to be weak, short-lived, disorganized, and easily intimidated into silence or submission. I am not denying there are Sunni moderates; of course there are Sunni moderates. Probably the vast majority of them are just ordinary people who want to get by and basically live and let live. But it only takes a handful of violent extremists for everyone to feel intimidated. The fear lurking in the present situation for Christians and other minorities—Alawites, Druze, and Kurds (the Kurds are Sunnis, but they are not Arabs, so they are an ethnic minority)—is fear of the slippery slope: the gradual but incremental slide toward greater and more violent Islamist extremism. These fears should not be made light of; they are not hallucinations born of a fertile imagination, nor are they, as some have claimed, the result of a trap, the sectarian bogeyman set by the Assad regime. Of course such regimes do cynically exploit sectarianism for their own purposes, but they do not fabricate sectarianism. It exists as an independent reality throughout the region, and it always has.

There is a spurious argument, currently popular mainly in American think tank circles, that goes something like this: As a matter of principle, we are obliged to support the overthrow of repressive dictatorships. And since we cannot always control who or what replaces them, despite all the rhetoric of democracy, freedom, and human rights, we will deal with the replacement later on, on the basis of our same principles, even if the replacement turns out to be as bad as, or even worse than, the toppled tyrant. This line of reasoning is disingenuous and hypocritical. Where were these voices when the US policy was centered on propping up these now hateful regimes? The argument is also fundamentally immoral and irresponsible. Looking the other way as Islamists come to power, not to mention aiding and abetting them to reach their objective, is to know that a worse situation is developing, but to ignore this rather than actively try to pre-empt it. One certain casualty of this form of irresponsible neglect, if not of callous experimentation—a favorite pastime of some think tank analysts—are the vulnerable minorities and moderates, all but designated beforehand as expendable, or as affordable collateral damage.

Instead of doing everything to try to strengthen the admittedly weak forces of moderation within any opposition movement, we see a resigned and lazy attitude that readily accepts the Islamists assuming power and postpones dealing with the adverse consequences of this outcome until it is too late, especially for minorities in the firing line. Nurturing Salafism by default or by design is the Frankenstein in the US Middle East policy today. Did we not see this in Afghanistan in the 1980s, when the United States' support for the *mujahideen* in their fight against Soviet communism created Osama Bin Laden?

Given this potentially explosive picture, what can well-meaning people and concerned governments do to try and influence this possibly disastrous turn of events? I have four proposals:

1. Aim and work for a comprehensive deal over both Syria and Iran with Russia.

   This should be the US president's top priority after the November 2012 election. Russia has signaled it is ready for such a deal, while vehemently opposing any serious arming of the Syrian opposition or military interventions on behalf of it. The Russians have said that a settlement could involve Assad's departure—that is a good opening move toward a deal. Russia has important interests in Syria. They have the naval base at Tartus, and apart from their use of another smaller one in Algeria, that is it for them in the Mediterranean; the rest of the Mediterranean is an American lake. They also have legitimate fears about the rise of Sunni militancy. If you try to view the world from Moscow, you see that there are Chechens right there, supported by Saudi money. The United States refuses to call outrages perpetrated by Chechens "terrorism." The Russians also see the United States trying to cut a deal with the Taliban to quit Afghanistan, and they see the rise of Islamism in various Arab states. They will not easily let go of Iran and Syria. Russia may not be a match for the United States as a superpower, but it possesses vast disruptive capabilities; in a multilateral world, it makes eminent sense to sit and talk with the Russians.

Israel's fixation on Iran's nuclear program risks igniting the entire region, and dragging the United States into an unnecessary and calamitous conflagration. It also deflects attention from the real danger besetting the region—namely, a creeping advance to power of Wahhabi-inspired, radical Sunni Salafists, who in the long run will prove far more dangerous and destructive to Israel, the West, and the entire Middle East than anything Iran can muster. In my view, a deal over Iran could involve accepting that Tehran reaches the brink of nuclear breakout, short of actually manufacturing anything, with very intrusive monitoring by the International Atomic Energy Agency, in return for three things: renouncing all of this unnecessary and highly inflammatory anti-Israel rhetoric; curbing Hezbollah, Syria (if the regime survives), and other regional allies of Iran; and serving as a kind of counterbalance to Saudi Arabia and militant Wahhabism—in other words, acting like a responsible force for regional and Gulf stability. I still feel that we have not reached the eleventh hour regarding Iran. However, I do think it should be a top priority for the US president to talk with Mr. Putin.

2. The United States and the European Community must actively pressure Saudi Arabia and Qatar to temper Sunni agitation, and stop fanning the flames of Sunni fanaticism with money, arms, and propaganda.

   Blowing up the entire region is not the way to change a dictatorship, in Syria or elsewhere. The charade of arch-repressors like Saudi Arabia and Qatar leading a crusade against regional dictators with American and Western backing has to end. At the risk of sounding reductionist, I maintain that Saudi Arabia produces a great deal of the toxicity in the region and beyond; but the problem is that Saudi Arabia also happens to be the West's gas station. I conclude from this that the greatest challenge facing world statesmanship at present is how to decouple Wahhabism and the al-Saud dynasty, on the one hand, from the oil and vast amounts of petrol dollars it generates on the other—but that is for another day.

3. The United States and its Western allies must be induced by pressure from grassroots organizations to draw a thick red line to protect and preserve whatever meager freedoms already exist in parts of the Middle East, and build upon them.

   Freedom is a very rare and fragile commodity, especially in a place like the Middle East, so if you happen to stumble on it, it should be preserved. This means, among other things, active protection for minority rights and for pluralism as absolutely integral components of any meaningful move toward democratization. The specter of "one man one vote one time" posed by the Salafists must be fought, because it is a mortal threat to democracy. Raw majority rule in an Islamic environment can lead to what Alexis de Tocqueville termed "the tyranny of the majority." What needs to be emphasized are not just the formal aspects of democracy—campaigns, elections, and majority rule—but also the values that accompany the development of democracy: minority rights, respect for the rule of law, pluralism, and so on. These values are not emphasized enough when the discourse of democracy is addressed in an Islamic context. If freedom is what the West truly wishes for the people and societies of the Middle East, then wherever this rare and precious human commodity exists in the region, it should be nurtured and protected.

In Lebanon, freedom continues to exist despite the battering the country has endured since 1975. That freedom must be protected and defended at all costs. The Christian community there, despite its divisions and, I would say, lousy leadership, remains the freest in the region. And because of this, Lebanon itself is freer than all other Arab societies. Lebanon has no dictator. And its ex-presidents and prime ministers are alive, and usually thrive outside office until they die of natural causes.[5] The Taif Agreement, which ended the war in 1989–1990, does need to be revisited and modified, but not at the price of another war. If changing it involves another war, the Lebanese are not interested. We live with the Taif Agreement, with its many defects. Hezbollah's weapons can and should be regulated through internal agreement, not external pressures or attacks. If the region-wide Sunni–Shi'ite showdown is all but unavoidable, the West should exercise diligent damage control, in particular on collateral damage inflicted on exposed minorities such as the Christians, where freedoms tend to reside, and on behalf of whatever moderate Muslims may end up in the line of fire as well. Only the survival of such moderation and religious pluralism can offer the region some hope of a better tomorrow, once the dust of inter-sectarian confrontation between Shi'ites and Sunnis settles.

If indeed we are witnessing the region devolving into its primordial ethnoreligious aggregates after the artificial cobbling together of these various nations during the Sykes–Picot era, if we are now seeing a kind of renewed fragmentation, then the protection I am calling for may entail devising creative federal arrangements for beleaguered communities. Lebanon's unique share of the rare commodity of freedom means it must be insulated as much as possible from importation of the sectarian tensions plaguing Syria and the region.

4. An appeal to Europe.

I am issuing a cry for understanding and help, a cry on behalf of millions of native Middle Eastern Christians, and others like them, who feel exposed and endangered by the uncertainties of what is happening all around them. But this is also a cry of warning for people in Europe. If

Islamism is allowed to hijack the Arab uprisings while Europe is asleep, or looking the other way or, in some cases, working feverishly to make this happen, then Europeans will be adversely affected right here in their own homes. First of all, Muslim immigration to Europe will skyrocket as soon as people realize they cannot live by the shari'a the radical Islamists will surely want to impose. Secondly, if they are true to their ideology, militant Salafis will wish to carry their ideological confrontation with the West a step further toward active jihad; you will then have terrorism like nothing you have seen so far. Allowing an Islamist hijacking of the Arab uprisings will force Europe to contend with mass immigration and heightened Islamist terrorism in Europe. But doing all you can to spare the Middle East a slide into Islamism will, in the final analysis, protect Europe and the rest of the West.

NOTES

1. Francis Fukuyama, "The Failures of the Facebook Generation in the Arab Spring," *Newsweek*, May 21, 2012, http://www.thedailybeast.com/articles/2012/05/21/the-failures-of-the-facebook-generation-in-the-arab-spring.html.

2. See Elhanan Miller, "Syrian opposition names new leader, Iraq fails to depose old one," *The Times of Israel*, June 11, 2012, http://www.timesofisrael.com/syrian-opposition-names-new-leader-and-iraq-fails-to-depose-an-old-one/.

3. Kofi Annan made this statement on June 7, 2012, in front of the UN General Assembly in New York. See Patrick J. McDonnell, "Syria peace plan not working, U.N. envoy Kofi Annan says," *Los Angeles Times*, June 7, 2012, http://articles.latimes.com/2012/jun/07/world/la-fg-syria-violence-20120608.

4. For more details on this, see my book *Islamism and the Future of Christians in the Middle East* (Stanford: Hoover Institution Press, 2010).

5. Of course, there are exceptions to this rule, the most prominent of which are the assassinations of René Moawad in 1989 and of Rafiq Hariri in 2005. But many leaders in Lebanon died peacefully and of natural causes; this is not common in the Arab world. Thus, in focusing on the rule—and not the exception—one has to acknowledge that Lebanon is in a special position here.

WORKS CITED

Fukuyama, Francis. "The Failures of the Facebook Generation in the Arab Spring." *Newsweek*. May 21, 2012. http://www.thedailybeast.com/articles/2012/05/21/the-failures-of-the-facebook-generation-in-the-arab-spring.html.

Malik, Habib. *Islamism and the Future of Christians in the Middle East*. Stanford: Hoover Institution Press, 2010.

McDonnell, Patrick J. "Syria peace plan not working, U.N. envoy Kofi Annan says." *Los Angeles Times*. June 7, 2012. http://articles.latimes.com/2012/jun/07/world/la-fg-syria-violence-20120608.

Miller, Elhanan. "Syrian opposition names new leader, Iraq fails to depose old one." *The Times of Israel*. June 11, 2012. http://www.timesofisrael.com/syrian-opposition-names-new-leader-and-iraq-fails-to-depose-an-old-one/.

Chapter 4

Islamist Majoritarian Democracy in Egypt: What it means for Religious Minorities

(Zurich, November 28, 2012)

Mariz Tadros

Although recent events have brought Egypt back into the limelight, with President Morsi usurping power and taking executive, judicial, and legislative powers into his hands, the situation in Egypt has been worrying for quite a while, not only for religious minorities. What has happened since the revolution—a revolution that was celebrated in Egypt and worldwide for its inclusiveness, its non-violence, its demonstration of citizen and people power? What has happened to the dreams of the young people who sacrificed their lives so that Egyptians would enjoy three things: dignity, freedom, and justice? These were the three watchwords of the Egyptian Revolution; people wanted dignity, freedom, and justice. But in Egypt today, tear gas is being used against young people, in much the same spirit as when it was deployed by the Ministry of Interior of the former Mubarak regime. We see hundreds of people being imprisoned, hundreds of people disappearing, and we do not know where they are going. We see a great deal of violence, and we wonder: how did we get where we are today?

Today in Egypt there is talk of civil war. If the Muslim Brotherhood and the other Islamist factions—the Salafis, al-Gama'a al-Islamiyya, and others—mobilize their members and followers to go to the street, and if they run up against protesters who are there to express their unhappiness with the state of things in Egypt, at the very least we might experience an extraordinary amount of physical violence and bloody clashes, which would have the potential to develop into civil war. We are now in November 2012. The revolution happened in January 2011. How did we arrive at such a point in so short a time?

Skeptical commentators say perhaps the Egyptian Revolution—those 18 days of rebellion in Tahrir Square that we all saw on our screens—was not so wonderful after all. I was in Tahrir Square, not during those 18 days but afterwards, during the *millioniyas*, when more than a million citizens went to the streets. In those very first few months after the removal of Mubarak, there was a real inclusive space in Tahrir Square. I was sandwiched between hundreds of men and not subjected to a single moment of sexual harassment. The spirit of Tahrir Square brought together people of very different political orientations. It brought together rich and poor, Christians and Muslims, young and old—you saw grandmothers and pregnant women, sometimes sitting on those small chairs you take to concerts. The prevailing idea was, "We are all in this together"—one people against an authoritarian dictatorship that had clung to power for too long.

Of course, Egypt is not Tahrir Square, and the many inequalities that have long been entrenched in Egyptian society and politics did not disappear overnight simply because Tahrir Square was happening. Secondly, it is important to remember that the different political groups in Tahrir Square had agreed not to raise any political banners. The Muslim Brotherhood and the Salafis agreed not to raise their flags or make religious slogans. If religious slogans were displayed, the majority of the youth groups, which happened to have some Islamist factions but a lot of non-Islamist factions as well, would shout, "*Madaniyya!*" meaning, "This is civil, we are here fighting for a civil state." What was not reported was that this agreement was made so as not to disturb the West, which was very fearful of another Iran rooting itself in the Middle East. We tried to take attention away from the Islamist factions and focus on non-Islamist youth groups; and the Islamists agreed.

But something happened, I would say even before Mubarak was removed from power. I am not the only person who argues that a political agreement was reached between the Muslim Brotherhood and the Egyptian army. Days after the revolution began on January 20, the army went down into the streets and promised to protect the people. Yet something happened between that day—January 28—and the time when Mubarak was ousted. Many people believe the Muslim Brotherhood and the army agreed that the army would facilitate the Muslim Brotherhood's political ascendancy, in return for the army maintaining its budget and being guaranteed impunity and a safe exit for the generals who had been part of the Mubarak regime.

Recent events in Egypt appear to confirm this theory, because when President Morsi ordered retrials in November 2012, he specifically mentioned people involved in violations during Mubarak's regime. He made no mention of the violations perpetrated by the army once they took over from Mubarak, which were very bloody.

The settlement between the Muslim Brotherhood and the army meant that both the Muslim Brotherhood and other Islamist forces were able to register themselves as political parties. Conventionally, in the Egyptian constitution, political parties based on religion are not recognized. This does not mean that a force that has a long history, such as the Muslim Brotherhood, should not have the right to exist—I would argue that it does. But the constitution aimed to prevent what we have seen in Egypt recently; namely, the use of religion for political ends—that is, telling people that if you vote for us you will go to heaven, if you do not vote for us you will go to hell; that only the infidels, the unbelievers, will vote for our opponents; that good Muslims vote for those who are godly people, the guardians of Islam. You might think, "Did they really say that?" Yes, they did. There is evidence on YouTube and in newspapers. They instrumentalized religion and therefore nullified the prohibitions against making religious appeals in politics.

A year and a half ago, when I talked about my fears based on my study of the political thought of the Muslim Brotherhood and what I saw on the ground—when I said, "Be careful, this idea of an Islamic democracy sounds good, but there may be issues"—people were very skeptical and dismissive. They argued that the Muslim Brotherhood should be given a chance to rule, that the Brotherhood were the best political actors to lead Egypt in transition. They also argued that the Muslim Brotherhood have long condemned the use of violence as a way to reach power.

Their strongest argument, however, was that even if an agreement had been reached between the army and the Muslim Brotherhood, the Brotherhood nonetheless came to power through elections: people went to the polls and voted. They told the world which party they wanted to see in power. So, this argument goes, what is your problem? Why is it that when democracy does not bring the result you want, you start to object? I would argue that if the rules of elections had been respected—not using religion to mobilize people, and not bribing them with gifts to vote for you—the Muslim Brotherhood might still have gotten a majority of the seats in parliament, but not such a sweeping majority.

In the academic literature, a strong current argues that the Muslim Brotherhood are an organic political force which has existed since the 1920s; they have a constituency, they have resonance; when they speak on the streets of Egypt, people listen. So why import models from the West that the Egyptian people may not want? We know imported models fail. History tells us this. Contemporary events tell us this. But while the Muslim Brotherhood certainly represent a section of the Egyptian population, I think it would be problematic to say they represent all Egyptians, who are very diverse in their political and religious affiliations.

Yet another argument advanced in favor of the Muslim Brotherhood is that they have not had a chance to develop their political thinking along progressive or democratic lines, because they have suffered repression and torture for so long. Nobody can deny that the Mubarak regime severely repressed the Muslim Brotherhood, and that they were subject to the most horrendous forms of torture. However, we need to be aware of what is happening right now to those dissident voices within the Muslim Brotherhood that contest authority within the movement—those Muslim Brotherhood youths who participated in the revolution and discovered that the youths from other political forces were not infidel outcasts, that they all actually had something in common. These young people went back to the movement and tried to push the boundaries, but they were expelled. The numbers of Muslim Brotherhood youths who did not toe the line after the ousting of Mubarak and who therefore had to leave the movement are quite substantial.

Another of the arguments goes as follows: Well, look, Egypt is no longer ruled by the Mubarak regime. If people do not like the Muslim Brotherhood, they will vote them out in the next round of elections. It is just a matter of time; if they do not perform well, the people will elect others. The problem with this argument is that it ignores the instrumentalization of religion to mobilize people, the majority of whom have in any case relied for years on the Muslim Brotherhood's extensive welfare services, in existence for much longer than many other political forces. I am not saying it is impossible for the Muslim Brotherhood to be voted out; I am saying that when a party tells people that they represent God, it is difficult for other political forces to compete.

Another very important argument is that in any country that has abandoned authoritarian rule or is on the first steps toward a process of transition, the process is long. Give the Muslim Brotherhood time, it is said, they deserve to be given a chance to rule. The problem with this line of thought is that things seem to be getting far worse for the average Egyptian, not better. I go to Egypt every six weeks for field work, and I have been shocked to find people from every kind of background saying the same thing—villagers, hotel staff, and people working in transport and in civil society organizations. Nawara Fouad Negm, the prominent female activist who played a leading role in the revolution against Mubarak, said openly what other citizens have been saying on the streets: "We are experiencing days far worse than the worst days of Mubarak."

How did it happen that different sections of the population—Muslim and Christian, men and women, middle class and poor—have come to the conclusion that their daily realities are worse than in the days of Mubarak? Let me tell you, as a journalist who lived and worked under the Mubarak regime, that it was no fun at all. One of the jokes during the last days of Mubarak was that the secret police knew the color of your underwear—such was the extent of Egyptians' feeling that the secret police had infiltrated their lives. The fact that we have Egyptians today saying that the situation is far worse than the worst days of Mubarak means we have to listen to them. We cannot ignore voices just because we do not like them.

The context obviously has a bearing on the current situation—the presence of new strategic forces, the international economic crisis in food, fuel, and finance, and so on. But my argument has to do with the policies and forms of governance the Muslim Brotherhood has adopted in power. Before the parliamentary elections, the Muslim Brotherhood stated, "We are not going to be competing for the majority of seats, because we want to have an inclusive, representative parliament." Then they put up candidates in the majority of seats and ended up with the majority in parliament. Again, they said, "We will not put forward a president from the Muslim Brotherhood, because we want there to be an inclusive political order." And then again, they put forward a presidential candidate. They affirmed, "We are all going to write the constitution—different political forces, different religions, and different genders—it is going to be a representative constituent assembly." Islamists finally ended up with 67 percent of the constituent assembly. I am arguing that there is a pattern of exclusionary forms of governance, all justified on the following basis: we have come to power via the votes of the people. We represent the people and therefore we have the right to lead in a way that we see fit. It is a majoritarian understanding of democracy—the majority rules, whether you like it or not, because that is what democracy is about. Checks and balances and minority rights are missing.

Today, women who participated fully in the revolution have found themselves suddenly facing one of the worst backlashes in many decades. Today, non-Muslims who participated in the revolution believing the slogan "Muslim, Christian, one hand," and the youth coalitions who sacrificed most in the revolution, have been completely excluded from power, not part of any power-sharing deal, under a majoritarian system of governance that has started to act like an authoritarian ruler based on the idea, "We have the people's votes."

I think this is what the struggle in Egypt is now about. The people in Tahrir Square, and the people who are risking their lives across the different governorates in Egypt, are out there because they have had enough of being given promises of inclusion in the political system, only to find themselves time and again left out in the cold.

What has this meant for religious minorities? Of the 10 percent of Egypt's population that are Christian, about 99 percent belong to the Coptic Orthodox faith, and the remaining 1 percent are Catholics, Protestants and Church Orthodox. The Coptic Orthodox Church is one of the oldest Christian churches in the world. Historical accounts say that St. Mark the Evangelist visited Egypt between AD 48 and AD 60, and that is how an indigenous church was established in Egypt. This is not a faith brought to Egypt by missionaries in the nineteenth century; this faith has survived for centuries as part of the cultural and religious heritage of Egyptians.[1]

Following the ousting of Mubarak, there was a very strong belief that the decades of sectarian violence that Christians had experienced under his rule would now end. This was to be a new era, which would bring everyone together in the national project of building a new Egypt based on democratic values and social justice. The revolutionary movements of the youth were very much in favor of a non-Islamist state. Of course, there were young people from the Muslim Brotherhood in Tahrir Square who had a different vision, but overall the youth movements favored a non-Islamist political state. When I say non-Islamist, it does not mean anti-Islamist. It does not mean that they did not want to see Islamists share in power, nor that they did not want to see shari'a, Islamic law, represented in the constitution. It does mean that they did not want to see a system of governance based on instrumentalizing religion for political ends.

But what happened very shortly after the Egyptian Revolution? There was a move to change the governors of Egypt, since many of them had been generals and were associated with the Mubarak regime. This was a top-down measure. In only one governorate from among the 27, Qina, in Upper Egypt, a man was appointed who happened to be Christian. When this became public, protestors blocked the railway station and threatened to block the water supply to the rest of Egypt, and cut the electricity lines to factories in parts of Upper Egypt. The press argued that people were not against having a Christian as governor; they were against having another general. But generals had been appointed in other governorates too, and while there were protests against those generals, it was nothing like the situation in Qina. People came in from the towns and villages and congregated in front of the city council or its equivalent to say very clearly: "No, we do not want a Christian ruling over us. No, we do not want a quota Christian presiding over us"—implying that this governor had been appointed simply to prove that Christians were sharing power.

This put the Egyptian authorities in a very difficult situation. Would they ignore the popular clamor, thereby repeating the mistakes of Mubarak? Or would they remove the governor, thereby giving a clear political signal that if people do not want Christians, that is fine? (Perhaps if a woman governor had been appointed, there would have been similar protests; animosity toward women's leadership over a Muslim majority population is just as intense.) The Egyptian government eventually suspended the appointment of the governor, thus proving to the Islamist-led protesters that if they were able to flex their muscle, the government would comply.

In the space of a year and a half, we started seeing a very dangerous phenomenon in Egypt. Christians and Muslims have been living together in Egypt for hundreds of years, sometimes in conflict, but mostly in harmony. In poor villages you will find a Christian neighbor borrowing half a packet of sugar from her Muslim neighbor, or the Muslim neighbor bringing her children to her Christian neighbor to take care of while she goes out. Christians and Muslims do not live in all-Christian or all-Muslim communities. This does not mean we have not had sectarian violence; we have had horrendous cases, and the incidence was rising in the last 10 years of Mubarak's rule. But after the incident with the Qina governor—when the government's decision to suspend the appointment gave the signal that in the name of people power, people could get away with being exclusionary and tyrannical—a lot of mobilization started in the villages, in some cases led by the Muslim Brotherhood, in others by the Muslim Brotherhood in alliance with the Salafis. As a result, villagers started saying to their Christian neighbors, "We do not want you to live among us. We do not want you in our village any more. We believe God will not bless us if we have unbelievers in our community."[2]

In many instances where this has happened, people have simply packed up, left their homes and livelihoods, and tried to find relatives in other places where they could stay. Given the fact that many of these people were very poor to begin with, it has meant extreme hardship all around. After violence in Dahshur, one of the villages from which Christians were expelled, President Morsi intervened and said, "We are building a new Egypt, we do not want to see this kind of thing, we believe in citizenship." But the reality is that many Christians could not return to Dahshur, and those that did have miserable lives. They go down the street to buy cucumbers and carrots, and suddenly Muslims do not want to sell to them. Daily life has become very difficult.

We have seen a noticeable increase in the number of sectarian assaults on Christians since the revolution. I am still drawing up the data for 2012, but our analysis so far suggests the figure continues to rise. In 2010, there were 45 reported incidents; in 2011, there were already 70. These were the incidents reported in the Egyptian press, and my guess is many more were not reported. Nonetheless, the figures give a strong indication of the direction in which we are moving.

What is driving this sectarian violence? Some issues existed before the revolution. For example, you and I have a dispute in the market over the price of tomatoes. You, a Christian, insist they should only cost two pounds, because that is what you paid last time; I, a Muslim, insist that everything is getting more expensive and you have to pay three pounds. Because of the sectarian difference, the "infidel" Christian might be accused of not being respectful to the "superior" Muslim and things escalate into violence.

A second main driver has to do with the repair of churches. The ceiling in a church is collapsing; you get a permit, you start to repair it. Suddenly this is seen as a case of Christian enlargement of places of worship. It is taken as evidence of Christians wanting to build an empire and contest Islam, so the church is torched and the homes and property of Christians around the church are attacked.

Another driver of tension are cases where Christian women disappear, sometimes of their own free will—they have fallen in love with a Muslim man and they want to marry him (in Egypt interreligious marriages are not accepted), so they flee. Or women—especially young girls who are experiencing certain problems in their lives—are told, "If you convert to Islam, we will relieve you of all the hardship you are experiencing," and then those women disappear. There is no way to check whether the women chose to marry freely or were under pressure, because there is no legal mechanism that enables one to verify if this was a case of free will or not.

What is extremely worrying for me as an Egyptian is that since the revolution we are seeing cases where sectarian violence emerges out of the blue, because of a rumor, or because after Friday prayers people suddenly decide they have had enough of having Christians in their village. It is very alarming that communities are becoming so intolerant and refusing any longer to accept people who have been part of the fabric of their society for hundreds of years. What is even more alarming is that these incidents are happening more frequently because of majoritarian politics, which means that Islamists are able to use the power of numbers on the ground, and the fact that they are the majority in government, to get away with it.

What we are seeing is a growing trend of what is called in Arabic *natahir muqtamana*, that is to say, "cleansing our society" of Christians. As a political scientist doing political ethnography in villages and towns, I did not come across this expression before the revolution. Again, this is not to say that sectarian violence was not rampant in Mubarak's era—it was; but this explicit language was not used.

The second trend that is growing is to accuse people of being disrespectful to Islam. You and I may disagree during a discussion, and since you are a Christian, I might say, "Hey, guess what, everybody, she made fun of the prophet." This then becomes a rumor that spreads around and is enough to get innocent people sent to prison for two or three years.

The third trend is the increase in day-to-day harassment on the basis of religious affiliation. People who wear a cross are now being spat on and told, "Go and find a home outside this country, you infidels. This is not your country anymore." Christian women who are not veiled have had their hair cut by people belonging to the Islamist movement. Of course, the harassment of women is not just directed at Coptic women. I think they tend to be more fair game because they are not veiled, whereas the majority of Muslim women are veiled. Muslim women who are not veiled are subject to a great deal of harassment, but the fact of the matter is that even Muslim women who are veiled are subject to tremendous harassment.

The point is that the society is becoming more and more intolerant. This does not mean that we had a Scandinavia-like tolerant society before the revolution, where people enjoyed full freedom. It has never been a free society. But even the small space we enjoyed in society is being lost. We have been called a country in transition; and yes, we are in transition. The question is: transition to what? The evidence we have from President Morsi's most recent edicts is that we are moving to an Islamic dictatorship or an Islamic authoritarian regime.

Why do I say "Islamic"? An authoritarian regime is an authoritarian regime, and authoritarian measures are all alike: suppression of the media, harassment of protesters by the police force of the Ministry of Interior, etc. If authoritarianism is authoritarianism, is it biased against the Islamists to use the adjective "Islamic"? I argue that what we are seeing today is not just authoritarianism from above, but also authoritarianism from below. We are talking about people being mobilized to go out on the street to express support for authoritarian measures being taken by the president. The Muslim Brotherhood are mobilizing their own members and members of the Salafi movement to flex their muscle and tell the world, "We are in favor of this ruler; we do not care if he is acting in an authoritarian way." I think this is particularly dangerous. If you have a military-led authoritarian system, or even a foreign occupation, you can mobilize people against them. But if your message to people is that there is a life-or-death battle for the survival of Islam, and Islam depends on them going out and telling the world they want this particular leader, authoritarianism takes on an even more menacing character. People do cherish their relationship with God, but this relationship is being instrumentalized for political ends that are very problematic for non-Muslims and for society as a whole.

It is true that the Muslim Brotherhood promised an Islamic democracy—organic, with elements of the Islamic shari'a. Its democratic elements would be threefold: there would be elections, and elections would be accepted as the means of rotating power; secondly, there would be a constitution that would provide a normative framework for legislation and rulings; thirdly, this would be a "civil state," ruled neither by the clergy (as was the case in medieval Europe) nor by the military.

In my view, this "Islamic democracy" came with a number of qualifiers that in effect diminished the quality of citizenship and diminished rights. For example, we say we believe in equal citizenship for all—Christians and Muslims—as long as Christians espouse an Islamic identity and acknowledge Islamic civilization and the Islamic heritage as their foundation. But what if they do not? What if they prefer to say their identity is grounded in the pharaonic civilization (which they share with Muslims)? Egyptians say, "We are proud of having a civilization that is 5,000 years old." Yet saying so has become problematic, because you have to say you believe in an Islamic identity.

Secondly, the concept of equal citizenship for all stops short of a non-Muslim exercising leadership over a Muslim. This became very apparent when there was a discussion about the constitution and whether a Christian can become president. The Muslim Brothers' position was that neither Christians nor women can occupy such a position. They then changed their tune to say, "Well, if he comes to power via the people, we are fine with it," but in essence, the majority of Muslim Brotherhood thinkers argue that you cannot have a non-Muslim preside over a Muslim. How far will this idea reach? Will they argue against non-Muslim teachers because that is a form of leadership? Will they argue against Christian newspaper editors? In the Qina situation, people were saying, "We do not want a governor who is a Christian presiding over us." How far will this go?[3]

Some progressive political thinkers, students, journalists, and others have been careful not to criticize the Muslim Brotherhood, because they do not want to be seen as criticizing Islam. I think the time has come for us to differentiate between attacking Islam and critiquing a political movement in power. Just because the Muslim Brotherhood have "Muslim" in their name should not prevent us from analyzing and assessing their performance as a political actor—one which, moreover, has a monopoly on power in the presidency, the cabinet, the parliament, and the constituent assembly. Let us assess them for what they are—a political force in power—and not be silent because we do not want to appear to be associated with right-wing reactionary movements that are Islamophobic. Being intimidated into silence presents us with a very serious problem: firstly, it is unethical to decide that just because somebody is using religion in their name they deserve different treatment from other political forces; and secondly, we will become disconnected from what the citizens are thinking and feeling. If people on the ground are aware that religion is being instrumentalized by political forces, why should those of us who are abroad not recognize that?

I think now is the time for us to be sensitive to citizens' voices in all their diversity. Of course, there are people who support the Muslim Brotherhood in Egypt. But I think we need to come to grips with what it means to have a majoritarian regime in Egypt, free from checks and balances, using religion to strengthen its authoritarian hold while claiming to be a democracy, simply because it came to power through the ballot box.

NOTES

1. Egypt also has a Baha'i community, a small percentage of Shia followers, and, of course, atheists and free thinkers—in any context you have a number of people who do not want to be compartmentalized by religion.

2. There is a great deal more detail about this in my book *Copts at the Crossroads: the Challenges of Building Inclusive Democracy in Egypt* (Cairo: American University in Cairo Press, 2013).

3. This would be another example: believers are allowed places of worship commensurate with their numbers. But who determines the numbers? The Muslim Brotherhood argues that Christians and non-Muslim Egyptians amount to no more than 5 percent; others argue that the figure is between 10 and 14 percent. What are the implications of this for people's right to have places of worship?

WORK CITED

Tadros, Mariz. *Copts at the Crossroads: the Challenges of Building Inclusive Democracy in Egypt*. Cairo: American University in Cairo Press, 2013.

Chapter 5

The "Arab Spring" and Its Aftermath: Implications for Muslim–Christian Relations

(Zurich, May 30, 2013)

Michael Nazir-Ali

We live in very serious times—it is not an exaggeration to say world-changing times. So what I have to say is serious; sometimes it may be negative. But I hope that, nevertheless, we can draw positive lessons from it. Let us begin with recent events in London. On May 22, 2013, there was an attack on a soldier by two men who regarded themselves as converts to Islam. At first, the media—and also the government spokesman—said that this was an attack by "lone wolves," by people acting from their own ideas. Yet it gradually began to emerge that these people were not acting entirely on their own, but in concert with others. And so the question is: Who were these people connected with? How were they radicalized? Where were they radicalized? And who radicalized them?

Quite often, the tendency is to say that such actions in different parts of the world are the actions of a small minority of people who are extremists, who have been radicalized; I have just used the expression myself. And yet, the more I look at the situation in the Middle East and beyond, the more I see that the "lone wolves," and even small extremist groups, are acting against a background that is by no means monochrome, but is broadly that of what we might call, for the time being, an "Islamic resurgence"—that is a neutral-sounding expression. There are, of course, many progressive and positive aspects to this resurgence. I have for a long time been friends with Anwar Ibrahim, the Malaysian politician, and Chandra Muzaffar, who is engaged in the modernization of Malaysian society; their work is admirable. I also have connections with Nahdlatul Ulama in Indonesia, a large body of Sunni Muslim professionals who work to uphold the principle of *pancasila*, by which the Indonesian state recognizes various religions and no one of them is privileged more than another. In India, the work of Asghar Ali Engineer is notable, as is the work some scholars have been doing at al-Azhar in Cairo, the central place of Sunni learning—particularly the former Grand Mufti of Egypt, Sheikh Ali Gomaa, who issued certain progressive *fatwas* which are, of course, now in jeopardy. Also, both in Iran and Iraq, there is a stream of Shi'a religious thought that makes it possible to have dialogue on certain issues.

Unfortunately, however, this is not the picture generally. Islamic resurgence in many places is marked by being backward looking, not forward looking. In general, I have found this looking back (that is what the word *salafi* means somebody always looking back to the foundations of something) is always accompanied by a specific and comprehensive political, economic, and social program, and is characterized by a suspicion of plural societies where people of different faiths can live together. In my own experience, in many such societies—the Holy Land, Pakistan, Iran, Iraq, where people were to some extent at ease with one another—the situation has recently changed out of all recognition.

Obviously, there is hostility to the West and Israel. But there are particular tensions with Christians. I believe the tensions with Christianity sometimes occur because both are missionary religions, and are now to be found in many parts of the world where, perhaps even a hundred years ago, they would not have been present. We are to a very great extent competitors in these places.

What characterizes this backward-looking aspect of the resurgence? I think there is a difference between Sunni and Shi'a versions. As far as Sunni Islamist extremist agendas are concerned, there are certain constant factors. The first is the belief in the unity of the Islamic *umma*, or community; this is why young British Muslims are volunteering to go and fight far away in Syria, for instance.

Secondly, in Sunni thinking about Islamic polity, the *umma* needs a leader. Throughout the course of Islamic history, up to the 1920s, there was indeed such a leader, known as the caliph. At first, the caliph had to be an Arab from the Quraysh tribe, that is, the same tribe prophet Muhammad belonged to. But later on, the Ottomans claimed to be the rightful caliphs because they were the only leaders then continuing *jihad*. The caliphate was abolished in the 1920s, after Turkey's defeat in the First World War. Since then, both moderate and extreme Muslims have looked toward the restoration of the caliphate.

The third constant factor is implementation of the shari'a as it is understood by people involved in the resurgence. The way in which shari'a has been enforced in, for example, Pakistan and the countries of the Arabian Gulf, and campaigns to enforce it in other parts of the world, demonstrate a particular understanding of shari'a; namely, an attachment to a strict form of shari'a. This leads us to the idea of the *dhimmi*, the particular way in which the Islamic world accommodated Christians and Jews at first, later on Zoroastrians, Buddhists, and Hindus. These minorities were tolerated under certain conditions: paying extra taxes, not being able to propagate their faith, hold public office, and so on. If you are attached to implementing shari'a in the way that many of these movements are, then, of course, non-Muslims will have to be treated differently from how they have been treated in the past hundred years, during which Western secular notions of equal citizenship gained ground.

The final constant factor is the idea of recovering lands lost to Islam. Which are they? The whole of the Iberian peninsula, India as a country, and, of course, Israel. In the view of people who have an Islamist agenda, here is land that had been conquered by Islam, and is now no longer governed by Islam. This state of affairs is regarded as contrary to God's will, and thus unacceptable. These are the five constant factors that characterize Sunni Islamism.

Shi'a Islamism is somewhat different. There is the same desire to enforce the shari'a in a particular form. I remember a senior ayatollah saying to me at the time of the Iranian Revolution that the real question in Shi'a Islam was the relationship between revelation and reason, and there are still Shi'a thinkers in Iran and in Iraq, who are pursuing this question. But, on the whole, this intellectual challenge has not characterized the Revolution.

Since the Iranian Revolution, there is a new understanding of theocracy in Iran which is not really paralleled in any Sunni country. This is the idea of what they call *velayat-e faqih,* the rule of the religious scholar. Formally, Iran is ruled by Shi'a religious scholars. Sometimes people claim that this idea of *velayat-e faqih* was invented by Ayatollah Khomeini. But my research has shown that as early as the constitution of 1906, room was being made to give the Shi'a *ulama,* that is, the Shi'a body of scholars, a supreme place in law-making.

What is characteristic of Shi'a Islamism in Iran, for example, but also elsewhere, is the positive value that Shi'a Islam places on suffering and martyrdom. During the Iran–Iraq war, I was in the area, and saw those plastic keys painted silver, the keys to Paradise, that were given to young boys—sometimes hardly teenagers—as they were pushed out to be cannon-fodder for the Iraqi guns. The idea that martyrdom is something to be desired characterizes Shi'a Islam in quite a unique way. Of course, the idea of martyrdom is there in Sunni Islam as well. But in Shi'a Islam it is directed to a particular end—namely, the coming of the absent leader (*imam*). If you fight for justice as they understand it, if you fight for the supremacy of Islam as they see it, that will hasten the coming of the *imam.*

There are some Islamist organizations—both Sunni and Shi'a—that claim to be non-violent. The Muslim Brotherhood in Egypt and elsewhere claim that they have renounced violence. The Sunni movement Tablighi Jama'at in Pakistan is a very large missionary organization with its headquarters in Raiwind, where I used to be bishop. How many Muslim missionaries did the

Tablighi get at their annual convention while I was there? Around 800,000, from all over the world. The present bishop tells me it is now nearly a million! Of course, they claim that as a missionary organization, they are completely non-violent—and I believe them. But sometimes people who come to a fundamentalist view of Islam through these organizations move on to something else. Having been radicalized in this way, they can then be further radicalized. There is some evidence, particularly in the Western world, that this happens.

Part of the title of this talk has to do with the "Arab Spring," or rather: the so-called Arab Spring. The Western media, and some politicians, had a love affair with what was happening, and either did not want to see, or perhaps could not see more deeply into what was happening. A number of questions about democracy have resulted from the "Arab Spring." The first is whether people who have come to power through the ballot box are also willing to give up power through the ballot box. The test of democracy is not winning an election; the test of democracy is losing an election. And there, the jury is out.

Many Islamist organizations believe in what is called *Fath Mubīn*, the "manifest victory of Islam"—once you have a "manifest victory," what happens if you lose the election? What happens to the "manifest victory"?

Secondly, and this is more serious, neither in the Middle East nor anywhere else is democracy enough. The West tends to speak as if democratic elections are all that is needed. However, such elections are not enough. They can simply result in the tyranny of the majority. The Morsi government in Egypt, for example, won an election; it supposedly won a referendum. Yet if you look at the absolute figures, they are not majority figures, they are actually absolute minorities. Suppose they were majority figures: would that be enough? My own view is that Egypt desperately needs a Bill of Rights, either as an independent document, or incorporated into the preamble to the constitution. What would such a Bill of Rights contain? It would be clear that there was one law for all Egyptians. Under shari'a, the *dhimmis* can, to some extent, have their own law. But then what happens to freedom of expression, to freedom of belief, to freedom to change your beliefs, to the freedom not to believe? These freedoms are not protected under shari'a.

I am a great admirer of former Coptic Pope Shenouda; I met him about a year before he died. One of the things he said after the recent Revolution, which caused me some concern, was, "Well, if they want to have their shari'a, then let them have shari'a, as long as we have our own law." That is precisely what should not happen in Egypt, because that immediately reduces the Christian population to *dhimmi* status, rendering equal citizenship invalid. Abdullahi An-Na'im, the Sudanese reformist Muslim scholar, says that in the presuppositions of shari'a law there are three inequalities: between men and women, between Muslim and non-Muslim, and between slave and free.

The third question about democracy that the "Arab Spring" has provoked relates to the idea of a common citizenship. When the Ottoman Empire abolished the *dhimma* and the *millet* systems in the nineteenth century, gradually the Christians and other minorities (at that time, there were significant Jewish populations in these countries), found themselves equal citizens, for the first time since the rise of Islam. This is what led to the awakening (*nahda*), the rise of Arab nationalism, to which Christians contributed out of all proportion to their numbers: Constantin Zureiq, Antoine Farah, Michel Aflaq, Boutros Ghali (the grandfather of the present Boutros Boutros-Ghali), and so forth. They were only able to do this because they were, at last, recognized as fellow-citizens. What we do not want, in Egypt and elsewhere, is a retreat to the status of *dhimmi* from this common citizenship that has been achieved with so much struggle.

Western politicians sometimes claim that the phenomenon of Islamism, even in its extreme forms, is due to economic circumstances, and if the economic circumstances change, the phenomenon will disappear. It is true that in the great cities of the Arab world, for example Algiers or Cairo, there is now a large cohort of young men—and I use all those words advisedly—who have had enough education to know they are not getting what they should be getting. They are easy recruits to one kind of Islamism or another; that is true.

In the rural areas on the Afghanistan–Pakistan border, on the other hand, there are large numbers of rural families who cannot afford to educate their children, partly because of the failure of the educational policies of the government of Pakistan; I say this openly. They have to send their children to the *madrassas*, that is, Qur'anic schools, where they are radicalized. So it is true that economic circumstances aid recruitment to Islamism; but the resurgence of Islamism, be it Sunni or Shi'ite, cannot be equated with these economic circumstances.

The former Archbishop of Canterbury, Lord Williams, said in an article in *The Times* that a true Islamic state would ensure the freedom of Christians and other religious minorities. I have seen attempts at a true Islamic state in Afghanistan, in Pakistan, in Iran, and also in Northern Nigeria; and I cannot say, hand on heart, that a true Islamic state would mean an easy, or easier, life for Christians and others. This is a completely mistaken view, and it leads to a false optimism that we should not entertain. We have to be realistic.

The murder of the soldier in Woolwich, London, was an attack by Islamist extremists. Some media reports, however, dropped the term "Islamist." I think it is a mistake not to identify the kind of extremism we have to deal with. If we do not, how are we ever going to find a solution? Such Islamist extremists understand their mission to be rooted in Islam, and many moderate Muslims feel that they are completely mistaken about this. They may be; it is not for me to say, for I am not a Muslim. What I can say, however, is that when my Muslim friends have said that this is a mistaken interpretation of Islam, in nearly every case that I can think of, it is the extremist interpretation that has prevailed, and not the moderate one. Now I regret this very much; but the fact has to be recorded.

The West spent a great deal of money, time, and some heroic work by the armed forces in enforcing no-fly zones in Saddam Hussein's Iraq. I was once asked by a pilot to sit in the cockpit in which he flew the no-fly zones as part of his duties. It is a tiny space, and I asked, "How long do you sit in this cockpit?" He said, "Seven hours." These no-fly zones meant the survival of the Kurdish people in the north and the Marsh Arabs in the south. Whatever one might say about what happened next, the no-fly zones were laudable.

I was in Iraq fairly recently. In many parts, the Shi'a and Sunni communities are protected physically by walls. People criticize the wall that the Israelis have built. But Baghdad is full of walls—green walls, red walls, yellow walls, all sorts of walls—behind which people are protected. They have their own militias that are supposedly there to protect them. Christians in Iraq, however, have no such protection; they are particularly exposed, and have been savagely attacked: their clergy, their bishops, laypeople, their shops, their homes, and their churches. Of course it is right for the West to be concerned about the safety of the Kurdish people and the Marsh Arabs; but what about Christians in Iraq? Who is concerned about their safety? And how can their safety be ensured?

Some Iraqi Christians think there might be some territorial provision for them, as there has been for the Kurdish people, and may soon have to be also for the Shi'a community in the south; and maybe also for the Sunnis. In the end, I think the future of Iraq—if there is a future—is as a very loose confederal arrangement, not in a unitary state. If not, how is the international community to safeguard this ancient community, which predates the coming of Islam to Iraq by many centuries—and not just Christians, but also other communities like the Yezidis, the Mandaeans, and others?

Let me address the situation in Syria. Whatever we may say about the Assad regime, it is true that what is happening now in Syria is pay-back time for what happened under the rule of President Assad's father in the 1980s, when he tried, and succeeded to a large extent, in violently suppressing the Muslim Brotherhood. No one can in any way approve of what he did at that time.

Syria is a very delicately balanced society. Not only are there Christians, there are Druzes, and many different kinds of Muslims, that is, the Alawites, the mainstream Shi'a, the Sunni, Sufi-oriented people, and so forth. How will this delicate balance—which I think the Assad regime has succeeded in maintaining—survive if an Islamist regime comes to power, as desired by the Western powers, Saudi Arabia, and Qatar? And also, what will be the international situation with an Islamist regime right on the doorstep of Israel? The Assads found a Cold War–type of *modus vivendi* with Israel. We cannot assume that will carry on.

In Afghanistan, Western intervention has meant—no question about it— greater freedom for the people of Afghanistan than they have ever known, under any regime whatsoever. Especially for women: the possibility simply of going to school, of having a job, of going out into the streets for the shops, all of which had been curtailed by the Taliban. I hope, for the sake of our common humanity, that the Taliban never return to power in Afghanistan because of the incredible human rights abuses of which they were guilty, particularly against women and girls, and their cultural vandalism.

Afghanistan is now a better place, no doubt—but not for Christians. Mr. Abdul Rahman became a Roman Catholic in Afghanistan and was arrested for apostasy, then tried and convicted to death for apostasy. (This was one of the agenda items for the Anglican dialogue with al-Azhar that year). I asked a friend of mine, an Afghan lawyer who is one of the prominent shari'a lawyers responsible for the new Afghan constitution, "What are you doing? The West is spending billions of dollars in Afghanistan. You have drafted, along with others, a new constitution; and yet, Mr. Abdul Rahman can still be sentenced to death for apostasy?" He said, "Look, Michael, we have done the best we could. We have even incorporated the UN Declaration of Human Rights into the preamble to the Afghan constitution. But no one in Afghanistan can trump the shari'a." So, what does that mean? What is the value of this constitution?

Pakistan is a paradox. On the one hand you have a multiparty political system that holds elections, from time to time, a reasonably independent higher judiciary, a reasonably free press, and civil institutions. Civil society can appear to be quite strong. Yet terrorists have untrammeled freedom to do whatever they like, kill whomever they like, occupy whatever they like, change the character of society in any way that they want, threaten women and girls who are receiving education. A Roman Catholic school in the Swat Valley that had been educating girls for 75 years—mainly Muslim girls—was blown up when the Taliban occupied the valley.

The big question in Pakistan, from a legal point of view, is the Blasphemy law, which prescribes the death penalty for insulting the Prophet of Islam. Of course, Christian belief in itself can be taken as a form of an insult, since if Christians believe that prophecy came to fulfilment in Jesus, it may be difficult for them to recognize any other prophet after that. The very beliefs of a non-Muslim—or even sometimes a Muslim, if you include the Ahmadiyya—can be taken as blasphemy. Every attempt to modify the law, or even to make administrative provisions to ease the force of the law, have been resisted by the ulama—and there have been the killings of the governor

of Punjab, progressive Muslim Salmaan Taseer, and the Christian Minister
for Minority Affairs, Shahbaz Bhatti.

The central importance of Shi'a–Sunni relationships in this part of the
world cannot be overestimated. Sometime in the past few years I went to see
my senior surviving uncle, who is a Shi'a religious leader still in Bahawalpur
in Pakistan. He said, "Well, we sympathize with what is happening to your
community. But just listen to what I have to say about three of your own
cousins in the last few weeks." I asked, "What happened?" He replied, "They
were in the Shi'a mosque. A *Lashkar*, one of the Sunni Islamist extremist
groups, came to kill the imam. The imam had already gone home, so they
killed these three boys."

That is a microcosm of what is going to happen throughout the region: a
Shi'a–Sunni conflict on a huge scale. It is already happening in Iraq, it is happening in Syria, it will be exported to Lebanon, and it may well be exported
to Turkey, because there is a large number of Shi'ites in Turkey. It is already
happening in Pakistan on a large scale. What will be the reaction to this in
Iran, for example? What happens to Christian groups will happen in the context of this larger Shi'a–Sunni conflict in the region.

Naturally, we also have to ask, "What about Muslim minorities in non-
Muslim societies?" India, as a non-Muslim country, has a Muslim minority
that is larger than the population of Pakistan; Sri Lanka is another example.
We now also have significant Muslim populations in Britain, France, Switzerland, Belgium, Holland, and Germany. It is up to both the Muslim and host
communities to decide what the future will look like.

The policy of multiculturalism in Britain has largely been a failure. Instead
of welcoming the new situation on the basis of Christian hospitality, Christian
engagement, or Christian service, multiculturalism was created on the basis
of mere tolerance, which in Britain at least means leaving people alone. When
you leave people alone, what happens? They become isolated; people become
segregated, one from another. There is no idea of a common citizenship, and
most of all in this situation, there is the opportunity for extremists to radical-
ize the young. That is what has happened.

What are the issues that have been raised by the situation I describe? The
first has to do with the role of religion in public life. The West, particularly,
has gotten used to what could be called the Westphalian situation: since the
1648 Treaty of Westphalia, religion has been separated from public life.
But Islamism, in the West and elsewhere, means this is no longer an option.
There can no longer be a Westphalian consensus. The question now is not
whether religion should have a role in public life; it is instead what sort of
role this should be. We have to say clearly that the role cannot be theocratic.
The relationship of religion to public life cannot be that of coercion; it has
to be one of persuasion. Religious people must contribute to public life,

but on the basis of the strength of our arguments, rather than merely on the basis of privilege or because we lay claim to some kind of legal or religious tradition.

Will our partners in dialogue be willing to accept such a role for Islam? Some Muslims will be, and others will not. Democracy in the form we have it now has arisen from the Christian view of the person. People go back to Athenian democracy and Greek democracy. However, Greek democracy only applied to free men, not to women and not to slaves. Aristotle called slaves "living tools," and if you went to ancient Greek cities, you would find plenty of public facilities for men, none for women. The origin of the democratic idea was under the influence of the Christian teaching that men and women are in God's image. Of course, that democratic idea has extended itself in a number of ways.

Can people from a non-Judaeo-Christian background develop democracies on their own terms? That is the question. Some Muslims claim that there is material that can be used to foster democracy—for instance, the idea of the *shura*, that is, consultative council, in the Qur'an; and, in certain cultural contexts, the idea of *bay'ah*, that is, of offering allegiance to a leader, thus legitimizing his or her rule; or the idea of the *jirga* system, which was reformed and used recently during the constitutional process in Afghanistan. That may be. But we have to see whether people are willing to lose power democratically, and secondly, whether provision can be made for fundamental human rights in addition to democratic voting procedures. Thirdly, the question of the relationship of religion to law: in the Western context, law has largely arisen from Christianized Roman law and from the Canon law of the church. At the same time, Public Law has achieved an autonomy that is independent of any particular religious tradition, and that is how it should be.

The question in the West is: what should be the relationship of shari'a to public law? Some years ago, the former Archbishop of Canterbury and the Lord Chief Justice, the highest judicial officer in England, both publicly argued that shari'a should be recognized in terms of public law.[2] When they were criticized, they said, "Oh, we do not mean the cutting-off of hands and public executions. What we mean are the softer aspects of shari'a, for example, family law." If shari'a family law was recognized in public law in Britain, what would happen? In Britain, bigamy is a crime. If shari'a law is recognized, would it be a crime only for some people, and not for others? What happens to the principle of equality of all before the law? Under shari'a, a man can divorce a woman much more easily than a woman can divorce a man. Where is the equality there? Custody of children: at the very time that the Lord Chief Justice was saying shari'a law should be recognized in terms of public law in Britain, the Law Lords—the highest judicial court in the country—were ruling on the appeal of a Lebanese Muslim woman against deportation. As the bishop on duty that day, I sat with them. The Law Lords ruled that the woman could not be deported to Lebanon, because if she was, under shari'a law her son would be taken from her and given to her husband, and this would be a violation of her fundamental human rights. At the same time, the Chief Law Officer was saying, "Recognize shari'a family law in terms of public law in the country!" What about inheritance also? Under shari'a, a non-Muslim cannot inherit from a Muslim, and there is inequality between women and men.

The question of *jihad*: it is possible, in Islamic terms, to think of *jihad* in ways that have to do with social reform or with a deepening of spirituality. Some Muslims are now talking about *jihad* in terms of self-defense. But historically, *jihad* has meant opening the way for Islam in lands that are not Muslim. When the Ottoman caliph claimed to be the caliph, what he was saying was that he was opening up land. Which land was he opening up? Southern and Eastern Europe. As you know, the Ottomans reached right up to the gates of Vienna before they could be stopped. In a debate on television in Egypt between a secularist and an Islamist, the secularist said, "Why did the Muslims come to Egypt?" The Islamist replied, "To open the way for Islam." The secularist then said, "Now that you have opened the way, you can go back." There is, of course, no going back.

Finally, reciprocity: in many countries of Western Europe, there are mosques, and I believe it is right for these mosques to exist because of the principle of freedom of religion. However, in many Muslim countries, it is impossible to have churches. In Egypt, much of the violence against Christians occurs because they are accused of building a church, or repairing a church, or building a church-hall. When I was Bishop of Raiwind in Pakistan, I was given a plot of land in a nice middle-class area, with very educated Muslim people living round about. They came to me and said, "Bishop, please do not build a church here. Build a school, and we will send our children to your school. Please do not build a church." In another place we did build a church, but the present bishop tells me that 25 years later, the Muslim community in the neighborhood has still not allowed this church to be used. I was talking to a long-serving Saudi diplomat about this, and I said, "You have mosques here in London, Regent's Park Mosque, hundreds of mosques. What about some churches in Saudi Arabia?" He replied, "But there are no mosques in the Vatican." This is an unsatisfactory answer.

My approach in dialogue, however, is to seek a common commitment to human freedom by the partners, as a proper expression of reciprocity. I have found, since I began this work, that dialogue is more and more a commitment to fundamental human freedoms. And if we do not have that, in the end, there will be no dialogue at all—not in the Middle East, and not in the West.

NOTES

1. In fact, the word *taliban* means "students." Students where? Students of the *madrassas*, used as the "shock troops" of the Taliban. It follows that the solution to the question of the Taliban does not lie in Afghanistan, but in Pakistan.

2. See "Sharia law in UK is 'unavoidable,'" *BBC News*, February 7, 2008, http://news.bbc.co.uk/2/hi/7232661.stm (accessed April 6, 2017). See Patrick Wintour and Riazat Butt, "Sharia law could have UK role, says lord chief justice," *The Guardian*, July 4, 2008, https://www.theguardian.com/uk/2008/jul/04/law.islam (accessed April 6, 2017).

WORKS CITED

BBC News. "Sharia law in UK is 'unavoidable.'" *BBC News*. February 7, 2008. http://news.bbc.co.uk/2/hi/7232661.stm.

Wintour, Patrick, and Riazat Butt. "Sharia law could have UK role, says lord chief justice." *The Guardian*. July 4, 2008. https://www.theguardian.com/uk/2008/jul/04/law.islam.

Chapter 6

Preventing Genocide in the Middle East: The Continuing Relevance of the Turkish Experience and the Problem of Bias within the United Nations

(Zurich, May 2, 2013)

Hannibal Travis

There has been a tendency of late to look to Turkey—a state ruled by a Muslim Brotherhood-related so-called Islamist party—as a political model, or even a political miracle. Western policy-makers increasingly claim that Turkey can inspire democratic change in places that have been dictatorships for many years, such as Egypt, Iraq, and Syria. Both President Bush and President Obama have upheld Turkey as such a model for the Islamic world, citing its dynamic economic growth, its "moderate" Islamist government, and its "secular" constitution. These American presidents have gone so far as to promote Turkey's membership in the European Union on the questionable grounds of its strong democratic credentials. It has become commonplace for American statesmen to cast Turkey as a source of peace and stability in the two regions it geographically straddles—that is, the Middle East and Europe. I, however, profoundly disagree. To uphold Turkey as a model for the development of the Middle East is not only wrong, it is dangerous and will prove counterproductive.

The trends in the Middle East since the eruption of the "Arab Spring" uprisings of 2011 are alarming. Instead of the "transition to democracy" that President Obama has forecast, we see the development of conditions for genocide. What are the warning signs for genocide? Scholars have identified a number of warning signs, with civil war being the number one warning sign—we saw that in Rwanda, in Bosnia, in Cambodia, and in many other places. Secondly, there is the formation of clandestine death squads. Thirdly, there is the demonization of certain groups, blaming them for the country's problems. Fourthly, institutionalized inequality between different groups is an important factor. Upcoming elections are an excuse or trigger for genocide in many cases. Competition for land and resources, undue concentration of political power in an undemocratic system, censorship of the mass media—so that reports of atrocities do not get out—celebration of past genocides and crimes against humanity, and misuse of humanitarian aid are all warning signs of genocide and politicide.

American policy based on promotion of the Turkish model for the Islamic Middle East has contributed to the creation of such conditions. The first part of my talk will challenge policy based on the Turkish model. In the second part, I will draw attention to reforms that need to be undertaken in the United Nations system to more effectively prevent the genocidal eradication of religious minorities in the Middle East.

The "Arab Spring" uprisings were initially projected by the Western media as a peaceful "Facebook Revolution," led and driven by young, liberal, idealistic users of social media. But we have seen a shift from peaceful protest calling for reform to rebellion in Tunisia, Egypt, Libya, Yemen, and Syria. These rebellions have triggered international interventions of one kind or another. President Obama demanded that Egypt's President Hosni Mubarak and Yemen's President Ali Abdullah Saleh to resign; NATO intervened militarily in Libya to overthrow Colonel Gaddafi, while the United States and its Western and Sunni regional allies employed military means and economic sanctions to try to remove Syria's secular Alawite President Bashar al-Assad from power.

A pattern of reprisals has also developed—reprisals not only against members of a deposed regime, but also against ethnic and religious minorities. The seeds of genocide are being sown in the "Arab Spring" countries that are subjected to American regime change policies. What has happened in Iraq since the United States invaded it and overthrew Saddam Hussein should serve as a warning. Some still persist in claiming that Iraq has successfully managed a transition from dictatorship to democracy. But I question this. Up to 1 million excess deaths have occurred in Iraq compared to the prewar mortality rates. The ethnic and sectarian violence is such that you can see it from space, with the lighting of different neighborhoods changing as people flee. There are 4.5 million refugees and internally displaced people, and perhaps 3 million widows according to the relevant government ministry, with child malnutrition reaching almost a third. Nearly half of the population was living on a dollar a day at one point.

The targeting of religious minorities has also been widespread in Iraq. Half of the Assyrian Christian population has fled the country; 2,000 Christian families fled Mosul in October 2008 in the midst of an anti-Christian campaign of death threats and targeted assassinations. In 2009, six churches were bombed in Baghdad in a single month, while in Mosul three churches and a convent were bombed. In 2009, Senator Carl Levin of Michigan introduced a draft resolution on minorities in Iraq, which stated that there were "grave threats to religious freedom in Iraq, particularly for the smallest, most vulnerable religious minorities in Iraq, including Chaldeans, Syriacs, Assyrians, and other Christians, Sabean Mandaeans, and Yezidis." The resolution also said there had been "alarming numbers of religiously-motivated killings, abductions . . . rapes . . . and displacement from homes."[1]

The Mandaeans—followers of John the Baptist—have been hit particularly hard by the widespread violations of human rights and religious freedom in Iraq. According to the Mandaean Human Rights Group's 2005 report, a recent surge in religious extremism had made Mandaean lives even worse, in the context of targeted violence against religious minorities, which was fueled by some Muslim religious leaders preaching that it was religiously acceptable to take money, property, and women from "infidels." Another non-Muslim minority community, the Yezidis, complain of a similar pattern of incitement of violence against them. While Yezidis were flocking for pilgrimage to their holy shrine at Lalish in August 2007, up to 500 lost their lives in a single terrorist bombing. This atrocity was preceded by the execution in Mosul of 27 Yazidi workers who were hauled off a bus and shot near Mosul. According to the traditional Yazidi leader, Prince Tahseen, "The Islamic terrorists had made it very clear that they wanted to see rivers of Yazidi blood. I'm sure it will happen again unless we take steps to protect ourselves."[2] None of the Iraqi authorities, nor the US army, he noted, have shown concern about this growth in anti-Yazidi violence.[3] Such proceedings raise large questions about the fate of religious minorities in countries where the United States tries to impose regime change.

Turkey's genocidal past does not augur well for its role as a model for the Islamic Middle East. Nearly one hundred years ago, millions of Christian subjects of the Ottoman Turks—then about 20 percent of the population of Anatolia—were ruthlessly driven en masse from their homes. Many were massacred in flight. This grim reality was confirmed by of the founder of modern Turkey, Mustafa Kemal Ataturk.[4] The United States ambassador to the Ottoman Empire at the time, Henry Morgenthau, spoke of "a devilish scheme to annihilate the Armenian, Greek, and Syrian Christians of Turkey."[5] Documentation of this anti-Christian religious cleansing abounds, although its genocidal character is still denied by the Turkish state.

Religious cleansing and other forms of anti-Christian persecution survived the collapse of the Ottoman Empire and became features of the current Turkish national state. The "cleansing" of Greek Christians from Turkey continued under the leadership of Ataturk, and even after the end of World War II. The policy of eradicating Christian minorities in Turkey achieved the desired results. If we consider the percentage of the population that is Christian as an index of the religious diversity of Turkey, the Armenian, Greek, and Assyrian populations constitute a lower percentage than that of the Jewish population in Germany. While Jews were a quarter of a percent (0.23 percent) of the German population in 2006, Armenians were less than a tenth of a percent (0.09 percent) of the Turkish population, Greeks less than a hundredth of a percent (0.004 percent), and Assyrians also less than a tenth of a percent (0.02 percent). To this day, the pressure on Turkey's few remaining Christians continues.

Turkey's attitudes toward issues of non-domestic genocide are also problematic. They appear to be determined more by sectarian dogmatism than by the Genocide Convention. The Turkish government has habitually condemned massacres of Muslim populations as genocide, while refraining from recognizing the religious cleansing of non-Muslims as genocide. In Cyprus, even before it invaded, Turkey claimed a genocide of the Turkish population of Cyprus at the hands of Greek Christians. In Bosnia, it claimed genocide in 1991 and 1992, just as a rebellion was getting started. A massacre of 44 people in Kosovo was called genocide. Turkey has described the killing of Muslims in East Turkestan and China as genocide, and has described Israel's military actions in Palestine as genocide. But in the case of Darfur, where a jihadist government conducts acts of genocide against Black African Muslims, Turkey sides with the perpetrators. Speaking in defense of Sudan's government, Turkish President Recep Tayyip Erdoğan went so far as to claim that "it is not possible for those who belong to the Muslim faith to carry out genocide."[6] He furthermore claimed that Israel's "war crimes" in Gaza were worse than anything that had taken place in Sudan, and even worse than anything Hitler had done.

As the "Arab Spring" uprisings unfolded, Turkey has consistently supported extremist forces that strive to impose discriminatory norms on society, including non-Muslim minorities. In Egypt, we see that Turkey has been outspoken in its support for the country's new Muslim Brotherhood President Mohammed Morsi, despite a pattern of impunity for those who attack the Coptic minority and Coptic churches. There is also a linkage between Turkey and violent extremist groups in Libya and Syria. In both cases, the territory of Turkey has urged a blockade (of Tripoli and Damascus) and has played a key role in the provision of massive aid to jihadist rebel forces. By October 2011, press reports were appearing highlighting that the Libyan rebel forces were systematically killing and torturing Black Africans. In Syria, al-Qaeda linked groups have come to the fore. Fighters and weapons are flowing to the Syrian rebels. A full-blown civil war is now underway as jihadist rebels arrive from Iraq and Libya, often via Turkey, and wage war with AK-47s, hand grenades, heavy machine guns and mortars, and anti-armor missiles. Some observers speak of an Afghanistanization of Syria—not an uplifting prospect as over two million Afghans have died as a result of war since 1979, with life expectancy at 44 years at one point.

If the United States is committed to genocide prevention and the preservation of religious minorities in the Middle East, it will drop the notion of Turkey as a model for the Middle East. But more is needed. Washington needs to be proactively strengthening the anti-genocide institutions of the United Nations.

What is the UN response and how can we reform the UN to prevent these warning signs of genocide from evolving into actual genocide? There are various stages of UN involvement: there can be concern, condemnation, or censure; there can be an offer of peacekeepers, with the sides agreeing that they will not attack the peacekeepers; there can be a referral to the International Criminal Court; and there can be an authorization of the use of military force. Outside of that list, many of the interventions that are being practiced are arguably illegal. In the case of Syria, there is already a deadly combination of non-UN sanctions against the government and arms to the rebels, a combination that violates norms of international law and creates conditions for genocide. There is also an argument that in the case of Libya, the Security Council authorization for the use of force was exceeded. Russia argues that the Libya resolution authorized the protection of the people of Benghazi, and was exceeded to support the coming to power of a particular group or a set of groups. There are double standards, of course, in various situations. There have been referrals of some cases to the International Criminal Court, but not others. There have been authorizations for the use of force in some cases, but not others. And there is a problematic pattern of a lack of objectivity and universality in UN resolutions.

For example, while Israel has drawn the most condemnations by the United Nations for more than 100 deaths in Palestine in 2012 and about 800 in Gaza in 2008, there were more than 7,000 deaths in Sri Lanka in 2009. These killings were not censured, not condemned, and not referred to the International Criminal Court. In 1991, during the suppression of the Kurdish and Shi'a uprisings in Iraq, more than 50,000 people were killed. There was no referral to any court, and only a limited intervention, which did not save the principal victims. Political violence in Algeria killed more than 200,000 people, with no referral and no clear condemnation. Nor have the victims of Darfur received an answer from the International Criminal Court to their appeals for a trial.

In the case of the International Criminal Court, the Sudanese president, who has been indicted for having committed war crimes in Darfur, travels to other countries without being clearly sanctioned. The cases of Libya, Côte d'Ivoire, Kenya, the Democratic Republic of the Congo, and the Central African Republic, which involve dozens or hundreds of victims, are moving forward in the International Criminal Court. The Darfur case involves hundreds of thousands of victims. It is not being pursued. Human Rights

Watch is calling for Syria, Sri Lanka, and Gaza to be addressed by the International Criminal Court, but this has not been done. There is no action in the International Criminal Court regarding Iraq, Afghanistan, Pakistan, Somalia, or Colombia. There is a pattern of inaction, double standards, and incongruity in the referrals to the International Criminal Court and the UN Security Council's responses.

What is the legal solution to this problem, this pattern of double standards? We could reform the International Criminal Court. We could decouple it from UN Security Council referrals and we could speed up its process so that Darfur would receive action as timely as the action that happened in Libya. And we could also achieve universality and non-discrimination in the International Criminal Court, so that both sides of a conflict, if they commit crimes, may be referred and not simply the losing side or the side that is less popular in some kind of voting bloc.

Some scholars advocate UN reform with more representation from the developing world, establishing greater transparency, and publicizing draft resolutions so that the public can make its voice known; others propose enforcing human rights more effectively in the middle zone between condemnation and a Libya-style intervention, so that overthrowing a government, which often engenders even more crimes, is not necessary to remedy human rights violations.

Another series of legal solutions that is absolutely essential is access to and control over cultural property. International law talks about a right to preserve one's cultural heritage against forced assimilation, violence, deportation, and other kinds of pressure. There should be an effective remedy for obtaining access to and repatriation of one's ceremonial objects and church buildings, as the Convention on Biological Diversity and the Declaration of the Rights of Indigenous Peoples talk about. Some of the buildings that have been destroyed in Turkey, Iraq, or Egypt can someday be reclaimed by the relevant community.

Self-determination in cultural affairs is essential. A UN report has talked about a right to one's homeland not being violated. The UN Declaration on the Rights of Indigenous Peoples talks about a right of self-determination in social and cultural development, and the right to maintain and strengthen a people's distinct political, legal, and cultural institutions, as Native Americans are beginning to have in the United States. The Native American Graves Protection and Repatriation Act speaks of returning cultural patrimony to Native Americans from federal government holdings and museums; that is a model for enforcement of the Declaration of the Rights of Indigenous Peoples.

Compensation for the destruction of cultural heritage is important. According to the International Court of Justice, a state has an obligation to make reparation for damage caused to all persons concerned. And there should be compensation for the destruction of cultural property under the Fourth Geneva Convention, which talks about it as a war crime and which can be the basis of civil reparations. Corporations that aid and abet violations of international law are increasingly being sued for damages. There are cases like Almog v. Arab Bank, a case in New York where Jewish victims of Palestinian suicide bombers hope to receive compensation, claiming an extermination campaign against the Jewish race in Israel by means of suicide bombing.

There are potential objections to these legal reforms. Some scholars talk about "cultural imperialism," saying that for the majority to respect the minority is a Western model of liberalism. There are often complex ownership issues around land and cultural objects, including complex changes of title. Museums often make this argument, claiming there could be an inhibition of scholarship and access if governments do not clearly control cultural relics, and a Pandora's Box of claim and counter-claim for reparations. But there has not been a huge backlash in the United States to modest efforts to achieve reparations for Native Americans. In Germany, there were substantial reparations to Jews without much backlash. In Guatemala, there are increasing reparations to the Mayan population for genocide in the 1980s without a terrible backlash. In South Africa, there have been reparations to the black population without a violent backlash or a large-scale violent backlash. And there are also internal movements within most of the countries I have spoken of, movements toward autonomy and equality for minority populations. Many of these countries have signed up to the international covenants and treaties that require them to do these things; thus, it is not entirely an external imposition.

Also, there are negative effects of continued cultural violence that should not be ignored. Destroying pluralism tends to facilitate extremism, and existing inequities within countries are probably worse than having to make reparations; in other words, the cure is not worse than the disease. These are the legal solutions we should be looking to for preventing and remedying cultural and religious violence in the Middle East.

NOTES

1. US Senate Resolution 322, "Expressing the Sense of the Senate on Religious Minorities in Iraq," October 26, 2009.

2. Quoted after Michael Howard, "'They won't stop until we're all wiped out': Among the Yezidi people, a people in mourning," *The Guardian*, August 18, 2007, https://www.theguardian.com /world/2007/aug/18/iraq.topstories3.

3. See ibid.

4. For further information, see my book *Genocide in the Middle East: The Ottoman Empire, Iraq, and Sudan* (Durham: Carolina Academic Press, 2010).

5. *The New York Times*, "Morgenthau Calls for Check on Turks; Says Their Devilish Scheme for Annihilation of Other Races Must Not Go On," *The New York Times*, September 5, 1922.

6. Quoted after Seth Freedman, "Erdogan's blind faith in Muslims," *The Guardian*, November 11, 2009, https://www.theguardian.com/commentisfree/2009/nov/11/erdogan-muslims-turkish-sudan-gaza.

WORKS CITED

Abdelmassih, Mary. "Coptic Pope, Morsi in War of Words Over Attacks on Coptic Churches." *United Copts.* April 11, 2013. http://www.unitedcopts.org/index.php?option=com_content&view=article&id=8523&catid=15&Itemid=124.

Agence France-Presse. "Syria at risk of 'genocide.'" *The Telegraph.* June 6, 2012. http://www.telegraph.co.uk/news/worldnews/middleeast/syria/9314359/Syria-at-risk-of-genocide.html.

Clinton, Hillary. "Clinton highlights Turkey's growing economic leadership." *States News Service.* October 31, 2011. https://advance.lexis.com.

Davies, John et al. "Dynamic Data for Early Conflict Warning." In *Preventive Measures: Building Risk Assessment and Early Crisis Warning Systems*, edited by John Davies et al., 79–88. Lanham: Rowman & Littlefield, 1996.

Diehl, Jackson. "Turkey's government is the new normal in the Middle East." *The Washington Post.* January 19, 2012. http://www.washingtonpost.com/opinions/tukeys-government-is-the-new-normal-in-the-middle-east/2012/01/19/gIQA-5GRaJQ_story.html?wpisrc=nl_headlines.

Fein, Helen. "The Three P's of Genocide Prevention: With Application to a Genocide Foretold—Rwanda." In *Protection Against Genocide: Mission Impossible?* edited by Neal Riemer, 41–66. Westport: Praeger, 2000.

Freedman, Seth. "Erdogan's blind faith in Muslims." *The Guardian.* November 11, 2009. https://www.theguardian.com/commentisfree/2009/nov/11/erdogan-muslims-turkish-sudan-gaza.

Freedman, Rosa. "Improvement on the Commission? The UN Human Rights Council's inaction on Darfur." *University of California at Davis Journal of International Law and Policy* 16 no. 1 (2010): 81–129.

Freedman, Rosa. "The United States and the UN Human Rights Council: An early assessment." *St. Thomas Law Review* (2010): 91–136.

Gordon, Philip. "Remarks at Transatlantic policy network: A new era for Transatlantic cooperation." *States News Service.* September 30, 2009. https://www.lexisadvance.com.

Gruenberg, Justin. "An Analysis of United Nations Security Council Resolutions: Are All Countries Treated Equally?" *Case Western Reserve Journal of International Law* 41 (2009): 469–511.

Hauslohner, Abigail. "Lost in Libya's turmoil: Workers from the Third World." *Time Magazine.* February 27, 2011. http://www.time.com/time/world/article/0,8599,55709,00.html.

Howard, Michael. "'They won't stop until we're all wiped out': Among the Yezidi people, a people in mourning." *The Guardian.* August 18, 2007. https://www.theguardian.com/world/2007/aug/18/iraq.topstories3.

Ignatius, David. "Endgame in Syria." *The Washington Post.* January 31, 2012. https://www.washingtonpost.com/blogs/post-partisan/post/endgame-in-yria/2012/01/31/gIQA9aHzfQ_blog.html?utm_term=.5f1bbdcd0112.

Kennedy, Elizabeth. "In complicating move, al-Qaida backs Syrian revolt." *Associated Press/U.S. News & World Report.* February 12, 2012. https://www.usnews.com/news/world/articles/2012/02/12/al-qaida-chief-urges-outside-help-for-syria-rebels.

Laub, Karin. "Score-settling after Libya's war casts shadow." *The Associated Press/Yahoo! News.* October 29, 2011. https://www.yahoo.com/news/score-settling-libyas-war-casts-shadow-185528901.html.

Miles, Tom. "Russia says 15,000 foreign 'terrorists' in Syria." *Reuters.* March 8, 2012. http://www.chicagotribune.com/news/sns-rt-us-syria-russiabre82714e-20120308,0,556393.story.

The New York Times. "Morgenthau Calls for Check on Turks; Says Their Devilish Scheme for Annihilation of Other Races Must Not Go On." *The New York Times.* September 5, 1922.

Obama, Barack. "Remarks by President Obama in Address to the United Nations." *The White House.* September 21, 2011. https://obamawhitehouse.archives.gov/the-press-office/2011/09/21/remarks-president-obama-address-united-nations-general-assembly.

Özkan, Mehmet and Birol Akgün. "Turkey's Darfur Policy: Convergences and Differentiations from the Muslim World." *Insight Turkey* 12 (2010): 147–162.

Philip, Catherine. "Video: The hidden massacre: Sri Lanka's final offensive against Tamil Tigers." *The Times.* May 29, 2009. http://www.timesonline.co.uk/tol/news/world/asia/article6383449.ece.

Pollard, Ruth. "Fighters, weapons flow into Syrian war zone." *Sydney Morning Herald.* February 17, 2012. http://www.smh.com.au/world/fighers-weapons-flow-into-syrian-war-zone-20120217-1tefb.html.

Prosecutor of the International Criminal Court. "Twentieth Report of the Prosecutor of the International Criminal Court to the UN Security Council pursuant to UNSCR 1593 (2005)." *International Criminal Court.* December 12, 2014. https://www.icc-cpi.int/iccdocs/otp/20th-UNSC-Darfur-report-ENG.PDF.

Quist-Arcton, Ofeibea. "In Libya, African Migrants Say They Face Hostility." *National Public Radio.* February 25, 2011. http://www.npr.org/2011/02/25/134065767/-African-Migrants-Say-They-Face-Hostility-From-Libyans.

Reuters. "Satellite Images Show Ethnic Cleanout in Iraq." *Reuters.* September 19, 2008. www.reuters.com/article/2008-09-19/us-iraq-lights-idUSN1953066020080919.

Rohan, Brian. "Displaced black Libyans tell of beatings, expulsion at gunpoint." *Reuters.* October 17, 2011. http://www.reuters.com/article/2011/10/17/us-libya-displaced-idUSTRE79G2CY20111017.

Rosenthal, John. "Al-Qaeda in rebel Syria." The *National Review.* March 8, 2012. http://www .nationalreview.com/articles/292904/al-qaeda-rebel-syria-john-rosenthal?pg=2 &.

Travis, Hannibal. *Genocide in the Middle East: The Ottoman Empire, Iraq, and Sudan.* Durham: Carolina Academic Press, 2010.

———. "Wargaming the 'Arab Spring': Predicting likely outcomes and planning UN responses." *Cornell International Law Journal* 46 (2013): 75–142.

UN Fact-Finding Mission on the Gaza Conflict. *Report.* UN Doc. No. A/HRC/12/48. September 25, 2009. http://documents.un.org.

UN Human Rights Council. *Report of the International Commission of Inquiry on Libya.* UN Doc. No. A/HRC/19/68, paras. 59, 63. Geneva: United Nations, 2012.

UN Human Rights Council. *Report on the implementation of Human Rights Council resolutions S-9/1 and S-12/1.* UN Doc. No. A/HRC/22/35/Add.1, para 6. Geneva: United Nations, 2013.

UN Human Rights Council. Special Sessions (2-12). http://www.ohchr.org/EN/HRBodies /HRC/Pages /Sessions.aspx.

UN Secretary-General. *Report of the Secretary-General on the implementation of the Five Point Action Plan and the activities of the Special Adviser on the Prevention of Genocide, Annex.* UN Doc. No. E/CN.4/2006/84. March 9, 2006. http://documents .un.org.

US Department of State. *2006 report on International Religious Freedom.* https://2001-2009.state.gov/g/drl/rls/72131.htm.

US Senate Resolution 322. *Expressing the Sense of the Senate on Religious Minorities in Iraq.* October 26, 2009.

Weaver, Matthew, and Gethin Chamberlain. "Sri Lanka declares end to war with Tamil Tigers." *The Guardian.* May 19, 2009. https://www.theguardian.com/world/2009/may/18/tamil-tigers-killed-sri-lanka.

Weizman, Eyal. *The Least of All Possible Evils: Humanitarian Violence from Arendt to Gaza.* London: Verso, 2012.

Chapter 7

Remarks on the "Arab Spring" and Religious Minorities in a Shari'a-State

(Zurich, November 19, 2013)

Bassam Tibi

The uprisings in the Middle East and North Africa of 2011 have been dubbed the "Arab Spring." Many people initially hoped that these uprisings were a sign that the Middle East was now riding a global wave of democratization. But democratization failed to materialize. Instead, the "Arab Spring" has turned into a bloody, lethal winter, a catastrophe for religious minorities. Why? Today, I offer some remarks on a subject with which I have long engaged as a Muslim from the Levant, and as a scholar working mainly in the West. Greater depth and a broader context will be found in my latest book, *The Sharia State: Arab Spring and Democratization* (Abingdon: Routledge, 2013).

The issue under discussion is a personal one for me. I am a native Syrian, born in Damascus, and I lived there until the age of 18. Now, in the aftermath of the "Arab Spring," the Syrian national air force, which was supposed to protect the country from evil—any evil, as the propaganda of the state had it—is bombing the residential areas of Damascus, including the places where I grew up. In Damascus, 20 percent of the population was Christian. In my youth, I had Christian friends, and Christians had no serious problem in the country because they were Christians. There was, and still is, a Christian part of Damascus, called Bab Touma. In addition to the Christians who had very deep roots in Syria, there were also Armenian Christians. Most of them found refuge in Syria during the Armenian Genocide in Turkey during the First World War. I had Armenian friends in Damascus. There is also a Kurdish area in Damascus; Damascus is a tolerant place. Or rather, it was—things are changing, and not for the better. The Middle East is no longer a good, secure place for Christians. They are leaving in large numbers, especially for Europe, the United States, Canada, and Australia. A kind of de-Christianization of the Middle East is taking place.

65

WESTERN POLICY

I have lived in the West since the early 1960s, mainly in Germany. But I have also lived for extended periods in the United States. Something unhealthy is also going on in the West. After the 9/11 terrorist attacks in the United States in 2001, I became aware that the American government was actually at war against Islam, in the guise of a "war against terror." At the time, I was a professor at Cornell University. Every time I entered the United States with my German passport, I had to go through a second inspection full of humiliation and intimidation, and I said to myself, "Why am I coming to this country?"

Back in 2002, I was with the American ambassador in Jakarta, Indonesia. We both had a common interest in combating anti-Americanism in the Islamic world. I told him, "If you want to fight terror, you have to use an Islamic–American approach; otherwise, the policy will be derailed." And it was derailed. Washington's "war on terror" was waged against Muslims like me. On the one hand, I would be invited to consult with the United States government officials on jihadism at the RAND Corporation. But on the other, I would be taken aside at the airport as a terrorism suspect while on my way to the consultation. I asked the immigration offers who detained me, "If I am a terrorism suspect, how could I be invited to advise your government?" They told me, "The best thing you can do is shut up." These immigration officers had the discretionary power to arrest me. The "war against terrorism" seemed to be more directed against Muslims like myself who believe in democracy and human rights than against Islamists who work to subvert both those ideals. America had been my dream country, but after 9/11, it lost its charm. The Islamophobic atmosphere was intense. In Germany, I could never be arrested for being a Muslim. Germany is a *Rechtsstaat*, that is to say, a country where the rule of law prevails. Is this the case in America? I am not so sure.

I was happy when Obama was elected president, and expected positive developments. Early in his presidency, Obama made two important speeches regarding the Islamic world, one in Ankara[1] and the other in Cairo.[2] The gist of his message was: "I will end the war between the United States and Islam." At the time, I thought this was wonderful. What I did not know at the time of the Cairo speech was that the American Embassy had invited 15 leaders of the Muslim Brotherhood to attend. President Mubarak's security agents got advance wind of this and protested to the Americans. But even in Egypt, America is stronger than the Egyptian head of state, and the protests were to no avail. By this action the United States upgraded the Muslim Brotherhood. It seems that the Obama administration's termination of the war against Islam suddenly became support for Islamist movements.

Washington's policy of supporting Islamists was on full display after the outbreak of the "Arab Spring" uprisings, when the US Secretary of State

Hillary Clinton rushed from Washington to Cairo in July 2012 to endorse the newly elected Islamist President of Egypt, Mohammed Morsi. She was then received by demonstrators from the Christian Coptic minority, which comprises about 10–12 percent of the population. They were protesting because they did not share Secretary Clinton's conviction that Morsi and his Muslim Brotherhood backers were introducing genuine democracy. The Coptic community had suffered under the Muslim Brotherhood. They understood realities about Islamism that Secretary Clinton apparently failed to grasp. So the demonstrators carried banners saying, "Clinton, go home—you are not welcome in Egypt." These demonstrations were not anti-American. Copts are not hostile to the United States. The Christian demonstrators were only protesting against American support of the Islamist movement. This was the case in 2011–2012, and, I maintain, it remains the case today.

In the United States, there is much talk about human rights and democracy; whether Democrat or Republican, it makes no difference. Members of both parties talk about these issues, and in much the same way. But at the Harvard *Human Rights Journal*, in which I published, there was a consensus among my colleagues that American foreign policy is *not* unequivocally promoting human rights and democracy in the Middle East; it promotes instead American interests. Of course, every state pursues its own interests. But when American politicians pursue national interests, they do not say, "We are pursuing the national interests of the United States." They say instead, "We are pursuing the promotion of human rights and democracy," even if fundamental principles of human rights and democracy are trampled on. We have to keep this in mind when considering American support for Islamists in the Middle East and elsewhere. That support is customarily cloaked in language of democracy and human rights. The Obama administration regards the Muslim Brotherhood as a peaceful, non-violent Islamist network, and as such as the best possible partner in its war against transnational jihadist Islamists. That is why the United States came to accept and empower the Muslim Brotherhood as an ally. Washington projects its support for the Muslim Brotherhood as the promotion of democracy in the Middle East. There is nothing wrong with fighting transnational jihadist Islamists, but it is not the same thing as promoting democracy.

Support for Islamism is also a European phenomenon. A few astute European observers were quick to notice when the Muslim Brotherhood began to infiltrate the uprising and to express concern about the prospect of demands for shari'a norms overtaking demands for democracy. But European statesmen tended to throw caution to the wind. One such was Catherine Ashton, the European Union's High Representative for Foreign Affairs and Security Policy. I have to say that she is really quite ignorant about the Middle East and has no idea how to fashion a foreign policy to meet the challenges of the region. Ms. Ashton advocated in *The New York Times* a policy of trust in, dialogue with, and support for the emerging Islamist political forces, noting that "we will show humility in front of this huge task."[3] Such thinking is misguided and dangerous for the EU, the rest of the West, and for the Middle East.

I am not opposed to any cooperation with Islamist powers. But to do so effectively requires the ability to make a distinction between the religious faith of Islam and Islamism. Islam is a religion, not a political ideology. Islamism is not a religion, but is a political ideology. Some people in the West say Islam is by definition a political religion, but I do not agree. Islam has been politicized to create an ideology called Islamism. Islamism is not Islam, as I argue in my book, *Islamism and Islam* (Yale: Yale University Press, 2012).

THE "ARAB SPRING": DEMOCRACY AND ISLAMISM

The "Arab Spring" started in December 2010, when a young man in a village in Tunisia protested against his humiliation by his government by burning himself. There were huge non-violent demonstrations, and within a few weeks the president, Ben Ali, fled the country. Next came Egypt. Millions of Egyptians demonstrated in and around Tahrir Square, the center of the protest. The demonstrators could not compel Mubarak to leave office; it was the army that did it. The overthrow of Mubarak by the army was erroneously called a revolution by the Western media. But when the same army toppled Morsi, also against the background of mass demonstrations, the Western media spoke of it as a "putsch," a coup d'état.

At the beginning of 2011, everyone talked about democratization. But we have to be honest with ourselves: the people who took to the streets did not go primarily for democracy and freedom. The majority wanted an improvement in the standard of living. The Middle East and North Africa region is distinguished by a growth of population. In 1900, Cairo had one million people; today, Cairo has 20 million people. The Egyptians of today number between 85 and 90 million. There has been huge demographic growth, but economic development has failed to meet basic needs. A term was coined for this generation of Egyptian youth: the "no-future generation."

Such people took to the streets. They wanted to have bread, they wanted to have decent housing. Many people in Cairo live in the streets. Their top priority was to have respectable standard of living. Political freedom was a secondary issue. The early demonstrators were not Islamists. The "Arab Spring" was not of Islamist making. I have very strong evidence, based on my work in Cairo, that in the first two and a half weeks, Islamist participation in the demonstrations was negligible. The highly disciplined Muslim Brotherhood, the strongest Islamist movement in Egypt, determined that this would be the case. It is often not understood that the Muslim Brotherhood is much more disciplined than Western democratic political parties. If you are European or American and want to join a political party, you sign up, perhaps pay the membership fee and the next day you are a full member of the party. If you want to join the Muslim Brotherhood, you need to wait eight full years. You join as a sympathizer, as the first step, and then there is a system of strict surveillance. You are observed and if, after a long period of observation, they have confidence in you, you can become a full member. But even when you are a member, you never get anything like an overview of the movement. You belong to a cell of three, maximum five, people, and you do not know any others. The leadership of the movement controls all this. About five percent of the Egyptian population is organized in the Muslim Brotherhood; it is a very strong movement, and the Brotherhood instructed their people *not* to join the demonstration at Tahrir Square. Only after the breakdown of the security apparatus did they join in, following negotiations between Islamists and non-Islamists about the terms of cooperation.

Islamists were not part of the initial uprising in Tunisia, nor in Libya, nor in Syria. The younger generation of progressive activists did the organizing. At the beginning, the Islamist movement stood aloof from the rebellion, fearful of the security apparatus. The uprising in fact took the Islamist movement by surprise. But in the end, they succeeded in hijacking the "Arab Spring." How were they able to do this?

First, they are well-organized. The Muslim Brotherhood was monitored by the secret police, because they were regarded as a security threat. But they were the only political force able to withstand surveillance. Why? Because they work underground as religious groups with high secrecy, and the secret police were not able to penetrate them. Their cell structure meant the police could break perhaps one or two cells and arrest a handful of people, but they could not reach the whole movement. Another reason is that the Muslim Brotherhood established a very efficient network in Western Europe. Lorenzo Vidino of the Center for Security Studies in Zurich produced a very informative book, *The Muslim Brotherhood in Western Europe* (New York: Columbia University Press, 2010). It demonstrates the Brotherhood's strength, which, as we have seen, managed to secure the support of Washington and Brussels for the Islamist cause.

Secondly, the Muslim Brotherhood has a clear agenda. The people who were demonstrating in Cairo were against Mubarak; this was the only thing that united them. There was no consensus among the demonstrators about what should come after Mubarak. Islamists have a clear agenda, so they were able to seize the "Arab Spring" and run with it.

THE ISLAMIST POLITICAL ORDER

There are two tendencies in Islamism: one is peaceful, and one is violent. I call the peaceful Islamists "institutional Islamists," because they participate in the game of politics and work through institutions. They are not moderate, but they are institutional, and they forego violence. The Muslim Brotherhood is an example; they are not a violent jihadist movement. Al-Qaeda is an example of violent jihadist Islamism. (Jihadism, by the way, is not jihad. Jihad in Islam is not terror; it can encompass violence, but it is not terror. The United States is rightly fighting al-Qaeda and its terrorism. But the Obama government thinks it is possible to cooperate with peaceful Islamists against jihadist Islamists, and that the best partner for this is the Muslim Brotherhood. That is why the Muslim Brotherhood came to be seen as an ally by the United States, which says it is promoting democratization by helping the Muslim Brotherhood to be empowered. There is nothing wrong with fighting terrorism, but this is not the same thing as promoting democracy.

What is democracy? Is democracy only based on elections? When I was interviewed on Swiss radio recently, the journalist said, "Well, there were elections in Egypt"—as if free elections equal democracy. Of course, without elections there can be no democracy. But elections are not enough. Hitler was elected in free elections. Hitler came to power peacefully, not through violence. Democracy requires much more than elections. My intellectual mentor in the field of democracy is Karl Popper. I am a believing Muslim, and the Qur'an is my holy book; but when it comes to democratic politics, my holy book is Karl Popper's *The Open Society and Its Enemies* (1945).[4] At the very beginning, Karl Popper makes it clear that democracy is not about the rule of the majority; democracy is about the prevention of despotism. If this is not guaranteed, there will be no democracy. The Muslim Brotherhood argues, "We are a democratic movement. The majority of the people in Egypt and elsewhere are Muslims. When we rule on their behalf, we are an expression of democracy."

Here we have to return to the distinction between Islamism and Islam: Islam is a faith; Islamism is about a political order. Of course, Islam has to do with politics, but only in ethical terms. There can be an Islamic ethos of democracy. But if you read the Qur'an, if you study Islamic tradition, you will not find any system of government. I know the Qur'an by heart. The term *daula* (state) does not occur in the Qur'an: this is modern Arabic. The term *shari'a* occurs only once in the Qur'an: *Thumma ja'alnaka 'ala shari'atin mina alamri faittabi'ha* ("We have given you the shari'a, so live according to it," 45:18). This is ethics, not a system of government.

In my book *Islamism and Islam*, I define six features of Islamism, one of which is political order. The founder of the Muslim Brotherhood said Islam is *din wa daula*, religion and the state. So for them, faith is not only spiritual; faith is also expressed in the political order, the shari'a-state. But there is no shari'a-state or shari'a-order in the Qur'an. When you talk to Islamists in Cairo, they have always said "al-Shari'a," *the* Shari'a, with the definite article. But if you study Islamic history and jurisprudence, you find that there is no one understanding of shari'a. There are three basic forms: ethical shari'a, classical shari'a, and Islamist shari'a. The Qur'anic meaning is ethics—a Muslim has to be an ethical person. The shari'a of the Muslims, in the language of the Qur'an, is *al-amr bi 'l-ma'ruf wa 'n-nahy 'an al-munkar,* to enjoin the good and forbid the evil.

In the course of Islamic history from the eighth to the twentieth centuries, Muslim scholars developed a system of *legal rules* covering three areas: worship, *ibadat;* civil law, *muamalat;* and penal law, *hudud.* That is all. This has nothing to do with politics. If you read any detailed history of Damascus, my home city, you will find references to the Banu al-Tibi. This is my family. The muftis and the qadis of Damascus were from Banu al-Tibi, my family, for 300 years, from the thirteenth to the sixteenth century. My family had nothing to do with politics. They were legal scholars. The mufti is the highest-ranking authority in Islam, the one who issues a *fatwa,* or legal judgment. This form of shari'a has nothing to do with politics. *Classical* shari'a is about civil law and worship. The *Islamist* shari'a was established with the birth of the Muslim Brotherhood, and is about the order of the state. The core feature of Islamism is preoccupation with the order of the state.

In 2002, I was in a group of five advisers to the US armed forces. The American invasion of Iraq was then being planned. All of us were against the war. We told one general, "Do not go to war. There is no need for war. This is an unnecessary war." But the general said the decision had already been taken in Washington—and this was in 2002. One general asked me, "Can you tell me, in one sentence, how I can distinguish between a Muslim and an Islamist?" He stressed the "one sentence," explaining that "I am a general; I have no time to read books." I said, "Yes. You simply ask a person if Islam is a religious faith or the order of the state, and if he says (it is always a he and not a she, for Islamism is a male-chauvinist movement) that Islam is a political order, then he is an Islamist."

In traditional shari'a, there are four types of people: first, the true Muslims, who comply with the rules of Islam and subject themselves to the ruler. Then there are the *munafiqun*, the hypocrites, who say, "I am a Muslim," but do not comply with the rules. If you are critical of the way things are, you run the risk of being viewed as a hypocrite, a *munafiq*. The third category is the *kafirun* or *kuffar*, the infidels, the unbelievers—in other words, all the people who are not Muslims. Christians and Jews constitute the fourth category in classical shari'a: the *dhimmi. Dhimmis* are *kafirun* or *kuffar*, but as subjugated

Christians and Jews—the People of the Book—they are allowed to practice their religion, to have synagogues and churches and to live by Christian or Jewish culture, but as second-class citizens. A Christian or a Jew, under Islamic rule, does not have the same rights as a full Muslim.

Perhaps in medieval times, the situation of Christians and Jews in the Muslim Middle East was better than that of Muslims in Europe. My Jewish friend and teacher at Princeton University, Bernard Lewis, wrote a book about Jews in Islam and rightly observed, "It is really better to be a second-class citizen than to be killed."[5] *Dhimmitude* is often upheld as Islamic tolerance, but in the twenty-first century, we need more than this precarious, second-class citizenship: Jews and Christians cannot be minorities under the protection of *dhimmitude*; they need to be full citizens. If the Islamists apply shari'a in Egypt—a process that got underway during President Morsi's one-year tenure in office—they will be treated as second-class citizens. This is not acceptable.

THE PERTINENCE OF ISLAMIST RULE
TO CHRISTIAN MINORITIES

We must again distinguish between Islam and Islamism. Islam protects the life and property of Jewish and Christian minorities, if they accept to live as submissive subjugated minorities, as second-class citizens. We can see there is a distinction between Islam and Islamism with regard to minorities. It is better to be a minority under Islam than under Islamism. But the shari'a-state is a state under Islamist rule. The founder of Islamism, Hassan al-Banna, who lived in Ismailia near Cairo and established the Muslim Brotherhood in 1928, speaks of *the* shari'a. I myself accept shari'a as ethics, and in my life I try to practice shari'a as ethics. Shari'a as *law* is not acceptable to me, because law is constructed by human beings; it is not in the Qur'an. And shari'a as a legal constitutional framework is not acceptable to people who want real, modern democracy.

The Freedom Foundation in Madrid has published a paper by an Egyptian legal scholar under the title "Tyranny of the Majority?" (Moataz El Fegiery, FRIDE, 2010). He studied the program of Islamists in Egypt and in Tunisia and came to the conclusion that they want to institutionalize, as the law of the state, their own interpretation of shari'a. This is wrong. But there is a larger wrong. A Swiss person might criticize the Swiss constitution, or I, as a German citizen, might criticize the German constitution (*Verfassung* or *Grundgesetz*), intellectually or legally. A constitution is made by human beings. But if you say shari'a comes from God and is based on Revelation, then if you criticize shari'a, you are criticizing what God has revealed, and if you do so, you cannot be a Muslim. You make yourself vulnerable to *takfir*, which is excommunication or banishment from the Islamic *umma*, from the whole community of Islam. When this happens you become an apostate, which is a capital offense according to the shari'a as law. Therefore, shari'a as a political order is not acceptable to Muslims who really want democracy. This is even more true for non-Muslim religious minorities, because they have very limited rights under shari'a, even when *moderate* Islamists rule. When *radical* Islamists rule, non-Muslim minorities have no rights at all.

In Egypt, even before the Muslim Brotherhood gained power, no Christian could become president, and Christians were not allowed to enter some professions. There was no attempt to destroy the Christian community. Now radical Islamists have been burning down churches; 80 were burned down on August 14, 2013. This is a catastrophe in a country like Egypt, which was once famous for its tolerance.

CONCLUSION: SOLUTIONS

Many things are happening in what we call the Arab world, although there is, in reality, no *one* Arab world: Egypt is a highly developed society compared with Libya; Tunisia is a highly civil society compared with Algeria; and so on. There are great differences within the Arab world, culturally, religiously, and also with regard to politics and society. But just about every Arab country is caught up in a crisis.

There are many possible responses. One response is democratization. Another is better economic development. Population control would help, so that poor people do not have to have ten children without choosing to have them. I do not support the Chinese solution of one child per family. But people can be convinced without coercion. When I talk to poor people in Egypt, I ask, "Do you believe in Allah?" They say, "Yes." Then I ask, "But does not Allah ask you to treat what he gives you in a proper way?" And they say, "Yes, children are a gift from God." I reply, "But if you do not give those children food, education, and shelter, you are treating the gift of God badly, and insulting God."

The Islamists see the solution in Islam. But Islam is a religion. If people stop drinking wine and going to bars, will the crisis end? If the police monitor people's observance of shari'a, will this be a solution? No. However, there are also many Islamist movements. The most important one is the Muslim Brotherhood of Egypt, but it has produced many offshoots. There is Ennahda in Tunisia; Hamas in the Gaza Strip. You cannot ignore these movements. So far there have been two attempts at solutions to Islamism, in Algeria and in Turkey. The Algerian solution is *exclusion*: get rid of the Islamists,

exterminate them, oppress them, do whatever you want with them, but get
them out of the way. This is how the Algerians have dealt with the Islamists
since the 1990s, and it is why the "Arab Spring" did not reach Algeria. But
the Algerian approach is absolutely not acceptable in a democracy.

The Turkish solution is *inclusion:* allow the Islamists to engage in politics
and participate in the political game. We need to remember the distinction
between *engagement* and *empowerment.* I think the danger of the Turkish solution is that it empowers the Islamists, which I believe needs to be
prevented. If they come to power and establish a shari'a-state, that will be
the end of democracy in Turkey. I have had difficulties explaining this to
interviewers in Zurich these past few days. They say, "You want to engage
with them, but you do not want to allow them to have power? How are you
going to manage this?" I say that if you do not engage with them, you have
to suppress them, and this is against democracy. But if you allow them to be
empowered (as, for example, the United States has been doing), this does not
promote democracy either. So this is a dilemma.

While keeping the distinction between Islam as a faith and Islamism as a
political religion, I have unfolded a critique of Islamist human rights violations in the Middle East and North Africa, in particular against Christians.
The trend in the Middle East is one of de-Christianization. The Christians, at
least those who have the means, are migrating to Europe, the United States,
and South America.

Saddam Hussein was a dictator, but his regime in Iraq was positive for
Christians; they made up five percent of the population. Today, perhaps one
percent of the population is Christian; the rest have left the country. The same
thing is taking place in Egypt. In Lebanon, Christians used to represent the
majority of the population, and the constitution still reflects that. But a lot of
Christians have left Lebanon, and now live in the United States. The largest
segment of the population in Lebanon now is Shi'a Muslims, which is why
Hezbollah is so strong there. If you want to maintain the rights of minorities in the Middle East, you have to stop the process of de-Christianization.
Christians have their place in the Middle East, and they should be helped to
keep it, not only to protect their own rights, but also to protect interests of
human rights in general.

One of the obstacles to finding solutions is the widespread acceptance of
Edward Said's theory of Orientalism. Classic orientalism, as Said defined it,
says, "People of the Orient are *bad* people." But if you say, as Said's writings
might suggest, "All oriental people are *good*," this is orientalism in reverse.
Orientalism has become an instrument of censorship. Middle Eastern studies in the United States is deteriorating, in part because of the prevalence of
Said's Orientalism in academia. Ten years ago, the United States was still
the leading place for Middle Eastern studies in the world, but today this is

no longer the case. The reason is that Islamic studies have been tainted with accusations of Orientalism. I myself, coming from an aristocratic traditional Islamic family in Damascus, have been told, "You are being Orientalist— come on, stop it!" I reply, "I am a Muslim. You are a Christian. You are blonde. I am a Middle Easterner. And you accuse me of Orientalism?" They say, "OK, you are not an Orientalist, but you are Orientalizing yourself." Self-Orientalization? This is nonsense.

Even worse than Orientalism is the accusation of Islamophobia. If you criticize Islamism—not the religion of Islam, but the political doctrines of Islamism—you are accused of Islamophobia. For that reason, in the last chapter of my book, *The Sharia State* (Abingdon: Routledge, 2013), I ask: Is it acceptable today in scholarship and in the media to speak critically of what is going on in the Middle East and North Africa in particular and in the world of Islam in general? The only parts of the world where you have freedom of speech are the United States and Western Europe. But this is dwindling. Freedom of speech is increasingly being sacrificed in the name of fighting Islamophobia. I am fighting for freedom of speech. We must be allowed to speak critically about what is going on in the world of Islam.

The fate of religious minorities in the Middle East is not promising, to say the least. We must, in the name of democracy and human rights, talk about these problems. Freedom of speech and a vigilant observation of human rights violations are imperative. Individual Christians may seek refuge in the West, but this is not a solution for entire communities. We have to face the existing problems head-on. Most of them have nothing to do with the religion of Islam: they are economic, social, and political problems, but they have been "religionized." In the past 10 years, I have introduced this term to the English language, and also to German. In Egypt, for example, there are social problems—unemployment, health, education, and so on. If you say the West is responsible for this—that the Christian West is oppressing Muslims, and thus turn these social, economic, and political problems into a Christian–Islamic problem, you "religionize" what are essentially non-religious problems. We should be aware of this religionization of the problems, but we should also take urgent steps to confront these social, economic, and political problems head-on.

I think only a common approach by the West, and in particular by Europe, can have any effect. I think Europe is more important to the Middle East, and the Middle East to Europe, than the United States that is far away. When something happens in the Middle East, the problems spill over into Europe; refugees come, for example, from the Middle East to Europe. That is why Europe must be engaged in protecting human rights and democracy and helping Middle Easterners to solve their problems. We must have the freedom to identify the problems and talk about them, including the fate of non-Muslim minorities. If we are forbidden from doing that, for fear of being accused of Islamophobia, then forget it!

In the UN Human Rights Council, there are two states, Saudi Arabia and Pakistan, that are actively trying to prevent free and open discussion about the plight of Christians and other non-Muslims in the Middle East by calling it "Islamophobia." To stifle this, they want to establish an international legal prohibition against blasphemy—that means anything that they regard as offensive to their understanding of Islam. If they succeed, there would be an international law against freedom of speech. We cannot allow this. In Saudi Arabia and Pakistan, there is no freedom of speech, and there is no respect for religious minorities. These countries have been allowed to instrumentalize the United Nations as a forum for promoting their own repressive policies. We should not listen to such self-proclaimed representatives of Islam; we should not buy anything they say.

NOTES

1. See Barack Obama, "Speech in Ankara. Full Text," *Hürriyet*, April 8, 2009, http://www .hurriyet.com.tr/full-text-of-the-us-presidents-speech-at-turkish-parliament-11376661.

2. See Barack Obama, "Speech in Cairo. Full Text," *The New York Times*, June 4, 2009, http://www.nytimes.com/2009/06/04/us/politics/04obama.text.html.

3. Catherine Ashton, "Supporting the Arab Awakening," *The New York Times*, February 2, 2012, http://www.nytimes.com/2012/02/03/opinion/supporting-the-arab-awakening.html.

4. The volumes were written in 1945. In 2011, Routledge published an edition that contains both volumes, see Karl Popper, *The Open Society and Its Enemies* (Abingdon: Routledge, 2011).

5. See Bernard Lewis, *The Jews of Islam* (Princeton: Princeton University Press, 1984).

WORKS CITED

Ashton, Catherine. "Supporting the Arab Awakening." *The New York Times.* February 2, 2012. http://www.nytimes.com/2012/02/03/opinion/supporting-the-arab-awakening.html.

El Fegiery, Moataz. "A Tyranny of the Majority? Islamists' Ambivalence about Human Rights." *FRIDE Working Paper* 113 (October 2012).

Lewis, Bernard. *The Jews of Islam.* Princeton: Princeton University Press, 1984.

Obama, Barack. "Speech in Ankara. Full Text." *Hürriyet.* April 8, 2009. http://www.hurriyet.com.tr/full-text-of-the-us-presidents-speech-at-turkish-parliament-11376661.

————. "Speech in Cairo. Full Text." *The New York Times*. June 4, 2009. http://www.nytimes.com/2009/06/04/us/politics/04obama.text.html.

Popper, Karl. *The Open Society and Its Enemies*. Abingdon: Routledge, 2011.

Said, Edward. *Orientalism*. London: Vintage, 1979.

Tibi, Bassam. *Islamism and Islam*. Yale: Yale University Press, 2012.

————. *The Sharia State: Arab Spring and Democratization*. Abingdon: Routledge, 2013.

Vidino, Lorenzo. *The Muslim Brotherhood in the West*. New York: Columbia University Press, 2010.

Chapter 8

The Impact of the Arab Uprisings on *Dhimmitude*: Non-Muslims in the Middle East Today

(Geneva, March 20, 2014)

Bat Ye'or

The impact of the recent Arab uprisings on the Middle East's non-Muslims is an issue that has far-reaching human, moral, and political implications for Europe and for the Christian world. I will start by giving a quick overview of the history of Christians in the Middle East, the largest of the religious minority communities threatened by *dhimmitude*. This term, which is rooted in the Arabic word for conditioned protection, is one that we shall return to.

The Christians still living in this region of the world are the remnant of various peoples who converted to Christianity during the six centuries that preceded the seventh-century Islamic invasion of their countries. At the time of the Islamic imperial conquests, Christians constituted the overwhelming majority of the populations of the Levant, Mesopotamia, and Northern Africa. Their pre-Christian roots were Jewish or pagan. Their churches—whose ethnic identities are deeply rooted in the history of the Middle East—include the Greek Orthodox that bore the culture and civilization of the Byzantine Empire, and the Coptic Church as heir to the ancient Egyptian civilization. We should also mention the Syriac Orthodox Church of Syria and Iraq, the Armenian Church, the Maronite Church, and the "Nestorian" Church of the East, all of which also reflect ancient pre-Islamic civilizations. This geographical and historical overview provides an indication of the various Christian populations that existed in Egypt, the Levant, and Mesopotamia at the time of the Islamic invasions.

The ethnic character and ancient language of these Christian populations is preserved in their liturgy, historical annals, and personal accounts. These peoples and civilizations—so highly advanced in terms of art, literature, and the scientific knowledge of the time—were conquered and subjugated by a power that was numerically, economically, educationally, and technologically

79

weaker. The Muslim conquests were followed by a continuous wave of emigration of tribes from Arabia and their resettlement in conquered Christian countries and Mesopotamia. These invasions were the start of a period of chaos and clan wars between rival Arab tribes, whose aim was to appropriate and control land and villages belonging to Christians. Documents of the time speak of massacres, enslavement, and the exodus or deportation of indigenous peoples as the conquerors consolidated their power. What we witness today in Syria and Iraq is reminiscent of these tragedies.

The Islamic conquerors developed the system of *dhimmitude*. It spread across all Islamized Persian and Christian territories. It was this coercive institution that was the main factor in producing the Islamization of the Middle East, an institution that turned a majority into a tiny minority. *Dhimmitude*, the condition of the conquered Christians, Jews, and Zoroastrians, encompasses the Islamic shari'a laws governing non-Muslim peoples subjugated by jihad and its consequences. Now a few words about the term *dhimmitude* and the way in which I use it so that you might understand what is meant.

I coined the term *dhimmitude* to designate a particular system of Islamic theology, politics, and law that determines the condition of non-Muslims.[1] When I speak of *dhimmitude*, I do so on the basis of the study of a set of historical texts and laws. This painstakingly collected data allow us to identify what I call the civilization of *dhimmitude*, in which subjugated Christians and Jews are to be protected by their Muslim conquerors on condition of accepting discriminatory social, political, and economic conditions, upon pain of death. If we know what elements make up this civilization, we can make a fairly good assessment of their stability, their geographical reach, and above all their durability. Does *dhimmitude* still exist? Will it spread? What is its future and what future do Christians living in Muslim countries face?

Some nineteenth-century observers believed that the institution of *dhimmitude* was in terminal decline, and they had good grounds for thinking so. The great Islamic Ottoman Empire, ruled by a caliph on the basis of the shari'a, had weakened to the point where the possibility of its collapse weighed heavily on the minds of European statesmen. Western powers, especially England, advocated political and social reforms, including the concept of equal citizenship, in the hope of preserving the empire—but on a modern, non-Islamic basis. The weakness of the Ottoman Empire allowed European powers to exercise their own protection of the vulnerable Christian churches. Under these conditions, the institution of *dhimmitude* did weaken but it did not disappear.

During this era of Western-inspired reform, there were sometimes large-scale massacres of Christians and Jews. These religious minorities were accused of seeking to free themselves from servility of *dhimmitude* and claim equality with Muslims. Traditionalist Muslims never accepted the idea of the abolition of *dhimmitude*. This reformist notion was widely perceived as being an affront to Allah and his laws, as reflected in the shari'a. The Islamic resurgence of the second half of the twentieth century has given rise to political Islamism that seeks to restore and strengthen once embattled shari'a norms, including discriminatory *dhimmitude.*

I have chosen to detail all these aspects because it is often claimed that the system of governing non-Muslims based on shari'a norms—what I call *dhimmitude*—does not exist. It is sometimes said that its discriminatory character toward Christians and Jews is not consistent with the shari'a, or that this discrimination is random or incidental, or often caused by the bad behavior of Christians and Jews themselves. Such interpretations see humans as existing in a chaotic, incomprehensible world over which they have no control. I hold the opposite view. The Islamic laws prescribing *dhimmitude* for non-Muslims are listed in many Muslim legal compendiums accompanied by comments and justifications. They can be recognized as such, as they have endured for centuries in all Muslim countries with some degree of variation. Thus, they can be observed in North Africa, the Levant, Mesopotamia, and beyond—most dramatically in areas controlled by Wahhabi Saudi Arabia, the Islamic State, al-Qaeda, and other jihadist groups.

If we accept the reality of *dhimmitude*, we will be able to recognize it, anticipate its spread, and oppose it and thereby protect ourselves from it. We can respond by helping victims of *dhimmitude*. If we want to control our own destiny and help victims, it is very important that we know and understand this shari'a-prescribed condition.

What are the signs of *dhimmitude* today? *Dhimmitude* is an outworking of jihad. The jihadist movements seek to both impose their law, shari'a, and an Islamic government on conquered and Islamized countries. Non-Muslim populations must necessarily comply with the laws of *dhimmitude*, incorporated in shari'a law, or convert to Islam. Today we see jihadist groups operating on various fronts, in Asia, Africa, Europe, and America. Jihad is now a global phenomenon. In the Middle East today, there are several types of war that are linked to jihad:

1. Wars between Arab tribes or clans that use the seventh-century vocabulary of the great conquests. These tribes fight among themselves for control of a particular territory, accusing their Muslim rivals of not being religious enough, betraying shari'a, and being apostates. These charges incur the harshest punishments.
2. Wars between Shi'ites and Sunnis in Iraq, Lebanon, and Syria that date back to the beginnings of Islam. They stem from the power rivalries between Muawiyah and Caliph Ali in the seventh century.
3. Wars to destroy national entities inherited from the period of European colonization, with the aim of recreating the Caliphate to govern all the Islamic countries.

The restoration of the Caliphate is the ultimate goal of the Islamic State of Iraq and Syria (ISIS) jihadist group, now called the Islamic State (IS). The IS uses extreme violence to achieve this end. But it is also the goal of the Organization of Islamic Cooperation (OIC), which comprises 56 Muslim countries and seeks—mainly through political means—to install the seat of the Caliphate in Jerusalem, as stated in the organization's statutes.

These different religious wars between Muslims aim to re-establish strict Islamic government, shari'a, and *dhimmitude* for non-Muslims—practices which were abolished during European colonization or which have gradually lapsed in Muslim countries during successive stages of modernization in the twentieth century. However, it is important to note that *dhimmitude* has not completely disappeared from Muslim countries. In Egypt, during the presidencies of Sadat and Mubarak, the Copts were victims of discrimination. Coptic girls were kidnapped, forcibly converted, frequently raped, and forced to marry Muslims. Copts were also forbidden to build new churches, or to restore or paint old ones. Discriminated against in professional life and under the law, Copts suffered many injustices, humiliations, and accusations incurring heavy penalties.

Even in Turkey, a country considered secular and modern, discriminatory laws continue to penalize non-Muslims, including through the confiscation of land belonging to Assyrian monasteries erected long before the Islamic era, such as Mardin (fourth century). The difficulties created for the Greek Orthodox Patriarchate underline the continuing inferior status of Christians in what is nevertheless considered to be one of the most progressive Muslim countries.

The various wars and conflicts we have been witnessing for several years now in the Middle East are conducted according to the rules of jihad laid down in the shari'a. In other words, the warfare is not governed by modern international law. Civilians, women, old people, and children who are perceived as belonging to the enemy camp are taken hostage or are victims of terrorist attacks. Often women and children are raped, held captive, and treated as slaves. Modern humanitarian laws that protect civilians in armed conflict do not apply in jihad. Islamists do not recognize legal instances and instruments that are not shari'a-compliant.

The "Arab Spring" uprisings have not all produced the same results. The worst excesses have been seen in countries where the system of clans and tribes has remained since the seventh century. Even today, Arabs identify with ancestral affiliation.

When ISIS seized Raqqa, a metropolis in the north of Syria frequently mentioned in Christian chronicles of the Middle Ages, they rushed to impose the laws of *dhimmitude* required by shari'a on the Christians living there. These include payment of the *jizya*, an obligatory tax prescribed by the Qur'an and imposed on non-Muslims in exchange for their protection. *Jizya* is often compared with a capitation tax. However, since a capitation tax is not necessarily religious but is rather economic in nature, it may be questioned or abolished. On the other hand, the *jizya* is mentioned in the Qur'an. The Qur'an, being the uncreated word of Allah, cannot be subject to review or change. An Islamic regime therefore cannot abolish the *jizya*, but must keep the tax and ensure it is paid.

Through this humiliating practice, non-Muslims redeem themselves and purchase the right to live under Muslim authority. In other words, the right to life is not a natural inalienable right attached to the person but a favor that the non-Muslim purchases from the ruler, who in return imposes a tax and a set of discriminatory measures. This underlines the sense of vulnerability of peoples subject to the rules of *dhimmitude*. They have often lost their immunity under some pretext. This situation still continues to this day for Christians in Pakistan who are accused of blasphemy and, not being able to contradict the testimony of a Muslim in court, are sentenced to death. Muslims and even Pakistani government ministers—such as Salman Taseer[2] and Shahbaz Bhatti[3]—who opposed this law have been murdered.

Today, this *jizya* is required of Christians in Raqqa by the IS, which has re-established the collection methods prescribed by Muslim jurists in the eighth century; namely, the payment twice per year according to a scale: four dinars for a rich person, two dinars for a moderately wealthy person, and one dinar for a poor person. In addition it has re-established other fundamental elements of *dhimmitude*: the ban—never lifted—on building or renovating churches and monasteries, the ban on displaying the cross or wearing different Christian symbols in public, the prohibition on church bell ringing, the requirement that Christians pray quietly so as not to disturb Muslims in the vicinity, and the ban on public displays of Christian worship, such as the organization of funerals and religious ceremonies. Lastly, there is a prohibition on insulting Muslims verbally and criticizing them. Therefore, we are forced to conclude that such jihadi rebel movements are again imposing laws of *dhimmitude* on non-Muslims, and that these are not the result of chance and inexplicable events but rather form part of a coherent legal and religious system maintained for more than thirteen centuries.

These jihadi wars have several sponsors and receive significant financial support, notably from certain OIC countries whose charter proclaims adherence to shari'a. What is more surprising, however, is the support of Western countries—including the United States—for jihadist wars, and this in the name of "transition to democracy."[4] These countries are in such chaos that we cannot predict the outcome of the fighting. However, it is clear that a victory for jihadist groups would see the return of extreme forms of *dhimmitude*—as I outlined earlier—and an exodus of Christian populations from their historic birthplace.

What would the disappearance of the Christian populations from the Middle East mean for Europe? It would certainly be deplorable were Europe to lose more of its historical memory and identity. Jihad will repeat itself here, in Europe, if we do not heed the warning, if we do not pay attention to what is happening in the Middle East.[5] Powerless and failing to grasp what is happening, an uncomprehending and indifferent Europe will experience the suppression of a large part of European history, and witness a major historical and human tragedy on its own soil.

I believe that one of the reasons for this powerlessness is the denial of *dhimmitude*. When we deliberately deny a blinding reality, we no longer see it and no longer understand it. It is not possible to understand something whose existence we deny. The only way to combat *dhimmitude*—which I believe already exists in nascent forms in Europe and the United States—is to recognize it in order to be able to expose it. That would encourage many Muslims who are fighting for a modern, egalitarian, and open society.

The recent "Arab Spring" uprisings have not been entirely negative. They have led to the release of new forces: forces of progress and change that have highlighted the courageous struggle of the Muslim peoples to establish freedom and democracy in their countries. Several encouraging signs can be seen. First is the fact that the fundamentalist Muslim Brotherhood movement was rejected by Tunisia as it strives to modernize. Another point that deserves to be highlighted is that Egypt has ousted the Muslim Brotherhood government of Mohammed Morsi and moved to recognize the equality of men and women and to open up Egyptian Muslim society.

We too, if we are courageous enough, can support this process. It is now again the case that many of the Christians of the Middle East cannot speak about *dhimmitude* for risk of being killed. They are at the mercy of the governments and terrorist groups that strive to sustain discriminatory shari'a norms. It is therefore up to us to confront the realities of which so many are unaware. In so doing we can fight together to ensure the equality of all human beings and respect for the sanctity of life.

NOTES

1. I elaborate on the *dhimmitude* term in the following books: *The Dhimmi: Jews and Christians under Islam*, trans. David Maisel et al. (Madison: Farleigh Dickinson University Press, 1985), *The Decline of Eastern Christianity Under Islam: From Jihad to Dhimmitude, Seventh–Twentieth Century*, trans. Miriam Kochan and David Littman (Madison: Farleigh Dickinson University Press, 1996), and *Islam and Dhimmitude: Where Civilizations Collide*, trans. Miriam Kochan and David Littman (Madison: Farleigh Dickinson University Press, 2002).

2. Salman Taseer, the governor of Punjab Province, was shot dead on January 4, 2011. See Salman Masood and Carlotta Gall, "Killing of Governor Deepens Crisis in Pakistan," *The New York Times*, January 4, 2011, http://www.nytimes.com/2011/01/05/world/asia/05pakistan .html.

3. Shabhaz Bhatti was a Christian and Pakistan's minority minister. He was shot dead on March 2, 2011. See Dean Nelson and Javed Siddiq, "Pakistan's only Christian minister shot dead over blasphemy law opposition," *The Telegraph*, March 2, 2011, http://www.telegraph .co.uk/news/worldnews/asia/pakistan/8356777/Pakistans-only-Christian-minister-shot-dead-over-blasphemy-law-opposition.html.

4. Barack Obama, "Remarks by the President on the Middle East and North Africa," *The White House*, May 19, 2011, https://obamawhitehouse.archives.gov/the-press-office/2011/05/19 /remarks-president-middle-east-and-north-africa.

5. Also see my book *Europe, Globalization, and the Coming of the Universal Caliphate* (Lanham: Rowman & Littlefield, 2011).

WORKS CITED

Bat Ye'or. *The Dhimmi: Jews and Christians under Islam*. Translated by David Maisel et al. Madison: Farleigh Dickinson University Press, 1985.

———. *The Decline of Eastern Christianity Under Islam: From Jihad to Dhimmitude, Seventh–Twentieth Century*. Translated by Miriam Kochan and David Littman. Madison: Farleigh Dickinson University Press, 1996.

———. *Islam and Dhimmitude: Where Civilizations Collide*. Translated by Miriam Kochan and David Littman. Madison: Farleigh Dickinson University Press, 2002.

———. *Europe, Globalization, and the Coming of the Universal Caliphate*. Lanham: Rowman & Littlefield, 2011.

Masood, Salman and Carlotta Gall. "Killing of Governor Deepens Crisis in Pakistan." *The New York Times*. January 4, 2011. http://www.nytimes.com/2011/01/05/world/asia/05pakistan.html.

Nelson, Dean and Javed Siddiq. "Pakistan's only Christian minister shot dead over blasphemylaw opposition." *The Telegraph*. March 2, 2011. http://www.telegraph .co.uk/news/worldnews/asia/pakistan/8356777/Pakistans-only-Christian-minister-shot-dead-over-blasphemy-law-opposition.html.

Obama, Barack. "Remarks by the President on the Middle East and North Africa." *The White House*. May 19, 2011. https://obamawhitehouse.archives.gov/the-press-office/2011/05/19/remarks-president-middle-east-and-north-africa.

Chapter 9

The IS Caliphate and the West's Wars in Syria and Iraq: A Challenge to Religious Pluralism in the Middle East

(Zurich, October 8, 2014)

Patrick Cockburn

This is a particularly appropriate moment to be talking about the wars in Syria and Iraq and religious pluralism in the region. It is appropriate because this is the year that the Islamic State, ISIS, came forth as a new, powerful political factor in the Middle East. ISIS is, as of now, besieging the Kurdish-held city of Kobane in northern Syria, right on the border with Turkey. And this particular week is also a very important moment in the history of the Middle East, of Iraq, Syria, and the neighboring countries, because in the last couple of days ISIS entered the suburbs of Kobane. 160,000 people have fled. Turkey has said that it will not help stop the carnage. The United States has been bombing hard to try to stop ISIS, but they may not succeed.

This is a critical point in President Obama's plan to "degrade and destroy ISIS."[1] The United States started bombing on August 8, in Iraq and extended that to Syria on September 23. At the time, there was much rhetoric about how ISIS was going to be eliminated; there were many exciting pictures on television of plumes of smoke rising, and videos of vehicles being targeted and then being destroyed. But ISIS has not only *not* been degraded and destroyed; it is still expanding—at Kobane, in other parts of Syria around Aleppo, and also in Iraq.

One of the reasons that we all know about Kobane is that it is on the Turkish border, and journalists can see it from across the border. But there are battles and violence occurring throughout Iraq and Syria that *nobody* sees, because journalists like myself cannot go there—they will chop our heads off. Even for local journalists, it is extraordinarily dangerous. ISIS has produced an 11-point guide for local journalists, which basically says, "If you do anything, we will kill you." So there is a paucity of information coming out.

The Islamic State, so-called, which was announced on June 29, now extends from the borders of Iran northeast of Baghdad right across northern Iraq up the Euphrates in eastern Syria to the outskirts of Aleppo. This is an area about the same size as France; it really is very big, and it is not getting any smaller. In Iraq, a country I have been going to since the 1970s, the Islamic State has been moving into Baghdad. They have overrun Iraqi garrisons and taken lots of equipment; and this despite American air strikes. At this point, nearly four months after they took Mosul in northern Iraq, the Islamic State is growing and getting more powerful. And the attempt to hold them back through air strikes alone is not working.

Why is this happening? One reason has to do with the type of enemy ISIS faces. In Iraq, the army remains extremely weak, and the state is extremely corrupt. I was talking to an Iraqi politician recently and I asked him, "Why is the Iraqi army not fighting back?" He told me that the Inspector General of the Iraqi army had been to see their only armored division, which is meant to have 120 Abram tanks and 10,000 soldiers. He found that in fact there were only 68 tanks and 2,000 soldiers, although 10,000 were being paid for. Why has this happened? Because quite a lot of soldiers in this army are ghosts. They never existed as soldiers. But somebody is taking their salary. If you join the Iraqi army, you get paid, but you return half your salary to the officers and never go near the barracks. So the Islamic State is not facing very powerful opponents at the present time.

What is happening in Kobane is also very important, because it is splitting the Turks and the Kurds. For the Kurds, this is their Battle of Thermopylae; this is the moment when they are trying to hold their own against superior forces. They think that the Turkish army has stabbed them in the back, that supplies are not being allowed through, that, basically, the Turkish government has decided that it is in its interests to let the Kurds be destroyed. Consequently, there have been riots and demonstrations all over Turkey by Kurds wherever there is a large Kurdish community, and in cities like Istanbul and Ankara. 18 people have so far been killed, and a well-known human rights lawyer was shot in the head in Istanbul. The Kurdish crowds were very angry; at one point, they took the head of the Turkish leader Ataturk from a statue and started kicking it around the streets, which is very dangerous in Turkey because of the strength of Turkish nationalism.

Not all of this is reported outside Turkey, because the Turkish media is heavily censored, or restrained, by government pressure. CNN's Turkish affiliate became famous during the 2013 protest riots over Gezi Park; while riots were going on all over Istanbul, they ran a documentary on penguins, which created some hilarity. This time round, while riots were going on throughout Turkey, with fires and smoke rising in every street, they ran a documentary on honeybees.

So Kobane is, I think, a crucial moment in the history of this part of the Middle East. There is a very peculiar aspect to the opposition to the Islamic State. Obama created an alliance of countries, 44 in all, who are pledged to oppose the Islamic State. Yet not many of them are actually *doing* it. And some, like Turkey, have made it clear they consider the Kurdish guerilla organization, the Kurdistan Workers Party (PKK), just as bad as the Islamic State. Judging by their actions, it appears they would prefer the Islamic State to their own Kurdish separatists. Saudi Arabia, the United Arab Emirates, Qatar, and Bahrain have been participating in attacks against ISIS. But these are the very states that spent a great deal of money and supplied a great many weapons to set up the jihadi movement in Syria at the outset; in Iraq too. So they are not really committed to acting *against* ISIS.

What is also strange about this American-led alliance is that its members are not those actually fighting ISIS on the ground. The people who are doing this are the Syrian Kurds, the Syrian army, Hezbollah in Lebanon, and the Iraqi Shi'ite militias. I am not saying that these are great guys, but they are the ones who have been doing the fighting. Yet they are being held at arm's length and are not being assisted to hold ISIS back. It seems to me this is a recipe for failure. And ISIS has been very acute in exploiting the divisions of its enemies.

What is the bottom line? ISIS is not going to go away. In the last few months, in America and in every country in Europe, the TV screens were filled with people saying they were going to eliminate ISIS. It simply has not happened. In fact, ISIS is getting bigger and stronger.

WHERE DID ISIS COME FROM?

So where did this organization come from? How many other organizations have declared their own *state* in recent years? And not only declared it, but done something to achieve it? ISIS comes out of war—out of the war in Iraq in 2003. And ISIS is very much the child of war: it combines religious fanaticism and military expertise. Its leadership and its core members have all fought in wars against the Americans and against the Iraqi government since the fall of Saddam Hussein in 2003, and then again in Syria since 2011. Some officers from Saddam's old army have provided military knowledge. But my own suspicion as to why they are so effective is that they have simply been fighting for a long time. If you have been fighting pretty efficient armies, like that of the Americans, and you have survived after 10 years, you are probably pretty good at your job.

Where does the fanaticism come from? I think this issue is not discussed enough. The ideology of the Islamic State is not that much different from the variant of Islam, Wahhabism, which is prevalent in Saudi Arabia. Wahhabism is very sectarian. It regards Shi'ite Muslims as non-Muslims. It regards Christians and Jews as completely beyond the pale. It regards women as somewhere between second-class citizens and chattels. Its punishments and its implementation of shari'a law are violent. The only other place that beheads people continually outside the Islamic State is Saudi Arabia. It is the only country in the world where women are not allowed to drive. No public manifestations of religion other than Islam are permitted. Non-Muslims cannot be Saudi citizens. In many respects, the Islamic State is only Saudi Wahhabism carried to its logical and most violent conclusion. Wahhabism, I think, is one of the trends of the last 40 years, which has been perhaps not noticed enough in Europe and elsewhere. This is unfortunate, because Saudi Wahhabism has taken over the mainstream of Sunni Islam—and this is a critical factor in why all these movements, not just ISIS, are so sectarian. There are 1.6 billion Muslims in the world. Over 80 percent of them are Sunni, and Wahhabism has come to be the dominant ideology. And this is where religious minorities are all threatened: Christians, Shi'a, Sufis, Yezidis, Jews, you name it.

When I first went to Baghdad in 1977, one of the reasons I liked it was the diversity of people there. You had lots of different types of Christians, who had been there for the last 1,600 years. You had strange groups like the Yezidis, who had elements of Zoroastrianism, the old Persian religion, in their beliefs. Likewise, when you go to Damascus, you find churches that have been there almost since the beginning of the Christian era. And now, all this is ending. I mean that it is ending as we speak. The Christians are fleeing, the Yezidis have fled, and some of the other minorities have gone. It is difficult to see how this will be reversed.

Why has this happened? We can talk about the Islamic State. But it is Saudi Wahhabism, I think, that really changed things dramatically in the region, without it being countered by Western or outside powers. A friend of mine in London told me the other day that he thought very few Sunni or Shi'a in London had the address of a member of the other variant of Islam in their address book. They simply do not talk to each other anymore. Certainly, the Sunni are very ignorant of the Shi'a. There used to be a time when Shi'a were regarded simply as a different type of Muslim. Now, they are not regarded as Muslims *at all*. And there is increasing sectarianism in countries where there are small Shi'ite minorities—Malaysia, Indonesia. I did not think there were many Shi'a in Egypt. But a year or so ago, in one village, four of them were dragged out from their houses and lynched in the streets. It was all shown on YouTube. These are horrific events. This has spread to Tunisia, and to all those other places where there are small minorities, including the Christians. There was quite a big Christian minority in Mosul in northern Iraq, the second biggest city in Iraq. There were Christian monasteries around Mosul for a thousand years. There is an ancient Christian quarter in one part of the city, where the buildings are so old they look as though they went back to Roman times (though they cannot be much older than early medieval). All this is being extinguished and the churches are destroyed. So there is a reign of terror among all the minorities in the Middle East—it is at its worst in Iraq and Syria, but it is spreading everywhere else as well.

Why is there not more opposition to it? I think, partly, it is because of the wealth of Saudi Arabia. If somebody in Bangladesh wants to build their own mosque, they need $20,000. Saudi Arabia is about the only place they can get it from. Even in Syria before 2011, the Syrian government had, rather unwisely, accepted an offer from the Saudis to pay for many imams in local mosques. The Saudis deployed their wealth to change the nature of Islam in Syria, toward a more sectarian variant. There really was not much opposition in America or Europe, because the Saudis had a lot of money. The last time I looked, America had $86.1 billion worth of arms contracts with Saudi Arabia. The British have big contracts too, though less in value. In Britain, my home country, politicians are always willing to denounce some local imam for being sectarian or pro-jihadi, but you never see them summon the Saudi Ambassador to the Foreign Office to ask why Saudi Arabian billionaires are funding satellite television channels that are used by sectarian preachers of hate to call for the death of Shi'a, the death of Christians, for everybody to go on jihad. If you look on YouTube, you will find that millions of people have already watched these channels—extraordinary numbers.

I think there is a very open alliance between Saudi Arabia and America, dating back to World War II. The Americans supplied security; the Saudis supplied oil. Then the Saudis played a big role in Afghanistan, supporting the *mujahideen* against the Soviets. And I think that having let the Saudis into the house, America could not get them out again. Look at 9/11 and the destruction of the Twin Towers: 15 out of the 19 hijackers were Saudi. American official reports say they were financed by Saudi private donors. Bin Laden himself comes from the Saudi elite. Yet after 9/11, who was pursued? Saddam Hussein in Iraq. He may have been a bad man, but one thing he had not done was being involved in 9/11, as official inquiries showed. That is one of the reasons why we have the Islamic State now. The people who were most important in creating the conditions for 9/11 and for backing ISIS—I do not mean the Saudi government, but important Saudi citizens—all got off scot-free.

If you look at American documentation, you will find information about the funding of terrorist organizations like al-Qaeda in Pakistan. Invariably, there is a connection with Saudi Arabia. For example, WikiLeaks published a cable, dated 2009, from Hillary Clinton, the then-Secretary of State, saying that Saudi Arabia is the biggest funder of organizations that included al-Qaeda.[2] But that never produced political consequences. A price is being paid now for this tacit acceptance of Saudi behavior.

SOCIAL MEDIA

One of the peculiar things about the last three years is that it is the most bigoted and sectarian people who have become most adept at using social media. In 2011, it was said that social media—YouTube, Facebook, Twitter, etc.—were progressive and positive because they avoided official censorship and would reduce the power of police states to control information. What has happened has been rather different. The people who have become really astute at using social media are the Islamic State. They put out propaganda that is primeval in its nature, but often very skillfully made. Those awful movies in which the Islamic State is shown executing people are actually well-made movies. And it is very effective. One of the reasons the Iraqi army ran away is that they had all seen these productions in which Iraqi soldiers on their way to their bases are dragged out of cars and shot in the head. First they show the man with his military ID, and then they show the body.

You can imagine the effect on the families of Iraqi soldiers in Baghdad when they see this, and they all do. The same is true for the Syrian army. These are very visual cultures. A friend of mine in southeastern Turkey found some children in a refugee camp looking at a video on the internet of two men having their heads chopped off with chainsaws. He recognized that it was not from the Middle East at all. The film originally came from Mexico—a Mexican drug lord had murdered some of his rivals in this way, and put it on YouTube. But the video shown to those children said, "These are Alawites, the ruling Shi'ite caste in Syria, murdering Sunnis." You can imagine the impact that had.

EFFECTS OF CORRUPTION

Is this becoming irreversible? I wish I could say it was not. But the situation does not look good. The Iraqi army and the state are extremely weak. The Americans spent around $26 billion training the Iraqi army, but it immediately ran away from ISIS. Why did this happen? Under Saddam, almost all the officers were Sunni, about 95 percent of them. There were not many Shi'ite officers. But the present government is Shi'ite, and they want Shi'ite officers. Most are not very well-trained. Another reason is simply corruption. After the fall of Mosul, I was talking to a four-star Iraqi general who had recently retired. When I asked him why the Iraqi army had run away, he said, "Corruption! Corruption! Corruption!" He said it began when the Americans outsourced supplies to the Iraqi army, in keeping with their economic philosophy. But it turned out to be a very bad idea in the circumstances of Iraq. The officer of a battalion of 600 would get paid to feed his men. Fortunately for him, however, there would only be 200 men in his battalion. And he would pocket the difference, or share the money among the other officers.

The Iraqi army has checkpoints all over Iraq. If you are a foreigner, you sail through. If you are an Iraqi truck driver coming through, you have to pay. These checkpoints all act really like customs posts, and they are a big source of revenue. As a consequence, being an officer in the Iraqi army became very profitable, and people paid for it: if you wanted to be a colonel, it would cost you about $200,000; if you wanted to be a divisional commander, about two million. But they ended up with an army that could not fight effectively. Last year in Baghdad, a politician said to me, "The Iraqi army will not fight *anybody*." I said, "But surely, some of them will fight." And he said, "No, no! You do not understand. These guys have bought their jobs: they are not soldiers, they are investors. They are not a colonel in order to perform any activity militarily, but in order to make money." I was sitting in Baghdad, and people were telling me, "You know, Baghdad cannot fall, because it is a city of seven million, it has a majority of the Shi'ite militias, the Iraqi army." We were all telling each other the same thing, but I am not so sure it is true.

The Americans fostered a very peculiar sort of state in Iraq. People debate whether foreign intervention does good or bad. It seems to me that on certain occasions you can justify foreign intervention, for example, in a place like Kobane, where the Islamic State is advancing and trying to murder people. It is good when American planes bomb them and try to stop them. But the problem in Iraq was that when you have an outside power occupying another country, whatever its motives, that power basically looks after its own interests. At the moment American interests might coincide with those of Iraq, but, in the long term, they will not.

Iraq had an extraordinarily incompetent prime minister called Nouri al-Maliki, who has recently been dismissed. Why was he the prime minister of Iraq? Basically, the American ambassador had appointed him, and the Iranians had said they would go along with it. The Iraqi government was in any case a creation of foreign powers, which robbed it of legitimacy, and of competent people: those who disagreed with the Americans did not get promoted.

WHAT TO DO?

What can be done now? As I said earlier: ISIS is the creation of war; it comes out of war. In some ways, I think there might be a parallel with European fascism in Italy and Germany in the 1920s and 1930s, which came out of the First World War, from paranoid people who were used to dealing with the world around them with extreme violence. ISIS is somewhat similar, very paranoid, very sectarian. A Shi'ite friend of mine said, "I think I must feel like Jews in Germany felt in 1934—with a sense of continual threat." There *is* a parallel between what happened in Europe then and what is happening in Iraq now.

How do we deal with it? It seems to me that one thing that should have been done, has not been done, but might still be done, is to end the war in Syria. It is what detonated Iraq again. Why did Iraq erupt all over again, after the war that started in 2003 reached its height in 2007, then ebbed? By 2010, things were not satisfactory, but violence was reduced. The Sunni were not happy, but they did not think there was much they could do about it. The explosion of violence is often blamed on al-Maliki, on the persecution of the Sunni, and so forth. I think that is wrong. I think what really happened was very simple: the Syrian war started. Syria is 60 percent Sunni Arab, and Iraq is 20 percent Sunni. For ISIS and the jihadis, there was a much bigger opportunity in Syria. And that destabilized Iraq. The Saudis gathered funding for Sunni organizations. I remember at the time the Iraqi Foreign Minister saying to me, "If this war goes on in Syria, it will restart our civil war." It was not that the Iraqis did not see it coming; there was simply not much they could do about it.

Outside powers made a great miscalculation about Syria in 2011–2012. They thought that Assad would go down the same way as Gaddafi had. I thought it was never going to happen—because of the 14 provincial capitals in Syria, Assad controlled 13 of them, with the backing of Russia, Iran, and Hezbollah. Gaddafi was isolated. But the outside powers were convinced Assad would go down, so the only negotiating platform the United States and the West would agree to was one of transition, in which Assad would go. Since Assad controlled most of the country, he was not going to go. The peace negotiations known as Geneva II in fact provided a recipe for continuing the war by insisting that Assad had to go. This is important, because this is the ground on which ISIS, the Islamic State, flourishes. They know how to deal with war; they do not know much of anything else. They are sort of like an Islamic Khmer Rouge: I do not know how many people recall what happened in Cambodia in the 1970s, but there you had an ideological group, a fanatical group that was good at war, that dealt in extreme violence, murdered a million of their own people, institutionalized torture, and so on. In some ways, they resemble the Islamic State.

How do you defeat this group? I think the first thing you do is to try and reduce the level of fighting. In Syria, people ask, "What is the solution?" I do not think there is a short-term solution. People hate each other too much. But what you *could* do, if you had the support of Iran and Saudi Arabia, America and Russia, is to institute ceasefires, broker truces. I said this to somebody in Lebanon, who replied that Lebanese truces never lasted—apparently there were 600 truces during the 15 years of civil war in Lebanon. This is true, but a lot of people are alive, who would otherwise be dead, because of those truces. You have to bring down the pace of violence before you can even begin to negotiate between people. Otherwise, you have what in Northern Ireland we used to call "the politics of the last atrocity." Everybody is dominated by the last atrocity; they cannot talk to anybody. I think bringing down the level of violence is just feasible if the great powers adopt a more responsible attitude. Otherwise, I think they will just have to fight it out. But when it comes to the Islamic State, the Americans and other outside powers are dealing with a group for which martyrdom is at the center of their ideology. You get killed fighting: this is an expression of your faith, and you will go straight to Paradise.

Of course, the problem with the outside powers is that once they have gone down the road of mistaken policies, it is very difficult to do a U-turn. No politician or leader likes to say, "Let us do a U-turn, we have got it wrong." In fact, they *do not* say that. A former Syrian government official who now lives in Lebanon told me, "The problem with all the political leaders, all the Western powers is that they all climbed up the tree so high and shouted, 'We are going to get rid of Assad!' But they cannot now say, 'This is not possible, we have got it wrong,' and adopt a more realistic policy." Vast numbers of Syrians have died or have become refugees as a consequence of their inability to do a U-turn. I do not put this forth as an argument for being pro-Assad, just for recognizing the realities on the ground. Any successful truce, any successful negotiation, is basically a recognition of a certain balance of power on the ground. If you do not recognize what the balance is between the opposition and Assad and the others, then you do not have peace.

There was this hope that the local Sunni population would eventually turn on the Islamic State because of their repression. I think this is a naive hope—how *do* you turn on people who are incredibly violent, very well-organized, and constantly anticipating a stab in the back? They are bound to kill you first. So I do not think revolt is going to happen. Most of the minorities in the Middle East, in Baghdad and Syria, just want to get out now. They do not see that they have a future in the region. The only way anyone can help those that remain is by ending the war in Syria, which is eating away at, and destroying, the whole region.

NOTES

1. See Barack Obama, "Statement by the President on ISIL," *The White House*, September 10, 2014, https://obamawhitehouse.archives.gov/the-press-office/2014/09/10/statement-president-isil-1.

2. See Hillary Clinton, "Terrorist finance: action request for senior level engagement on terrorism finance," *WikiLeaks*, December 30, 2009, https://wikileaks.org/plusd/cables/09STATE131801_a.html.

WORKS CITED

Clinton, Hillary. "Terrorist finance: action request for senior level engagement on terrorism finance." *WikiLeaks*. December 30, 2009. https://wikileaks.org/plusd/cables/09STATE131801_a.html.

Obama, Barack. "Statement by the President on ISIL." *The White House*. September 10, 2014. https://obamawhitehouse.archives.gov/the-press-office/2014/09/10/statement-president-isil-1.

Chapter 10

Religious Pluralism in the Middle East: A Challenge to the International Community

(Boston, March 25, 2015)

Amine Gemayel

I would like to take a few moments to define terms and provide context. Firstly, I will speak about religious pluralism rather than about religious freedom. Freedom implies the right of individuals to decide on matters of faith for themselves, and even to change, or give up, their religion. In the present Middle East climate, both religious pluralism and religious freedom are important issues—and *both* face mounting obstacles. Nevertheless, I believe that, under present conditions, in which pluralism is under daily assault, we must start by doing everything possible to safeguard religious pluralism. Because this region is the birthplace of the three great faiths, upholding religious pluralism is a sacred task.

Secondly, when I speak of the Middle East, I mean primarily the Arab countries of this region, or what is often called the Arab world. This world is really a remarkable mosaic of religions, ethnicities, and cultures. Also, I employ the phrase "international community" in a broad sense, to cover states as well as non-state actors, most especially religious institutions and civil society organizations. Finally: I speak tonight as a former head of state from a country, Lebanon, where Christians have always played a leading political and cultural role. I am myself Christian, and we have convened at Boston College, a Christian-run institution, under the auspices of Christian Solidarity International.

For those reasons, I make no apologies for focusing my remarks on the extreme plight of Arab Christians. At the same time, when discussing the crisis of pluralism in the Middle East, this fact must be understood above all: if Christians are among the first victims of persecution, they are by no means the *sole* victims of persecution. Within a Middle East environment that features a steadily contracting space for pluralism, religious extremists oppress, and even *kill* anyone who does not submit blindly to their authority. They murder Shi'a, Sunni, Druze, Alawites, and more. In short, they kill the *other*, who are many—virtually everyone.

THE CRISIS OF CHRISTIANITY IN THE ARAB WORLD

I condemn all forms of persecution, no matter who is targeted. But the Christian dimension of the crisis of pluralism is worthy of particular attention, because it carries special and tragic implications for civilization. There is absolutely *no* danger that the Middle East will lose its Muslim character. In contrast, if the present negative trends intensify, we must start thinking the unthinkable, namely, the extinction of Christianity in the region. We should all care about the possible disappearance of Christianity from the Middle East, not only because of the human toll this process is imposing, but also because it will destabilize the region for generations, perhaps permanently. A former Human Rights Watch researcher recently stated that the presence of Christianity in the Middle East has often served as a "bulwark against fanaticism."[1] If Christianity were extinguished in the Middle East, then we would also need to alter the very lexicon we use to describe the region.

In 2011, the Lebanese scholar Kamal Salibi wrote that "it is the Christian Arabs who keep the Arab world Arab, rather than Muslim."[2] Salibi indicated the dire consequences of the collapse of religious pluralism in the Middle East. The *essence* of this crisis is revealed in the words used to describe the latest atrocities in Iraq and Syria: massacre, execution, beheading, crucifixion, murder, rape, sexual slavery, and so on. Witnessing these events, even seriously circumspect observers have correctly raised the specter of genocide. For example, the Vatican's representative in Geneva has issued an extraordinary call for the creation of a UN-approved multilateral force to stop genocide. This is the word he used: *genocide*. Against Christians and other groups. A human rights investigator of the United Nations has accused ISIS of committing acts of genocide against the Yezidis in Northern Iraq. Years ago, Christian Solidarity International had the foresight to circulate a genocide warning, alerting the world to the impending fate of religious minorities in the Middle East.

I am an indigenous and life-long resident of a small country that, for better or for worse, has absorbed every imaginable Arab, Middle Eastern, and global trend. I have been a close student of, and participant in, Middle Eastern politics on the national and regional levels where, for over half a century, I have served in government as a peacetime parliamentarian and wartime president. I have directed an international think-tank and one of the Arab world's oldest political parties. In all of these capacities, I have travelled extensively and visited almost every country in the Middle East over many decades. I am deeply saddened to report that I have *never* in my political life witnessed Arab Christians in such extreme danger. For my community, 2014 truly was an *annus horribilis*, a year of existential crisis.

The designation of 2014 as a disastrous year for the Middle Eastern Christians is doubly disturbing, given that their numbers were steadily dwindling even before the rise of ISIS. At the beginning of the twentieth century, Christians constituted approximately 20 percent of the total population of the Middle East. Today, that figure has been reduced to less than 5 percent. The persecution of Christians is often blamed on the conditions created by the occupation of Iraq in 2003 by the United States. Although the reverberations of the Iraq War have certainly hit Arab Christians particularly hard, it should be remembered that, in the last two decades of the twentieth century—that is, during the period ending just before the 2003 Iraq War—it is estimated that about two million Christians left the Middle East to settle in Europe, the Americas, and other regions. Projecting current population trends forward, the Middle East's remaining 12 million Christians may be reduced by 50 percent in less than a decade.

Given the long-term and immediate catastrophes that have befallen Arab Christians, it is inexplicable how little attention they have received from the media and national policy-makers. A respected journalist, Jeffrey Goldberg, has called the persecution of Arab Christians "one of the most undercovered stories in international news."[3] We do not know why, but there is a kind of blackout concerning these events. And, despite the most recent bloodshed, not much has changed. *Foreign Policy* has referred to "Washington's passivity in the face of an ongoing wave of atrocities [in the countries] of Iraq and Syria."[4]

I would like to place these atrocities in a human context by focusing on the fate of the Christian town of Ma'aloula in Syria, which is occupied by an al-Qaeda splinter group. The town's ancient church was completely demolished and its Christian residents, including a community of nuns, were forced to flee for their lives. In the wake of this, and all such attacks, the response from the United States has been a resounding *non-response.* We have seen, for instance, the failure by the White House to name an incumbent to the newly created position of Special Envoy for Christians and other groups under assault by ISIS, failure by the US military to deploy war planes to protect internally displaced Christians in Iraq, and failure by executive branch officials and members of Congress even to speak up on behalf of targeted Christians.

Every reasonable critic, myself included, must recognize that the United States is constantly buffeted by demands that it do more to intervene in crises around the world. And so, even as we criticize the United States, we must also recognize its numerous and significant contributions as a force for good.

The United States, for instance, has been a prime supporter of the beleaguered Lebanese Armed Forces, which represent the last best hope for a democratic Lebanon. Yet, as we witness Christianity disappearing from the Middle East mosaic, appealing to the United States is logical because it has the military means to do more. The United States is also politically positioned to act if it has the will, thanks to its strong relationships with regional governments and its leading position within the United Nations. What must be done?

MILITARY AND DIPLOMATIC MEASURES

Options for aiding Arab Christians and other minorities include policies that could be pursued by states unilaterally, bilaterally, and multilaterally. What I think the international community must consider, first and foremost, is creating a region-wide strategy for dealing with the Middle East crisis of pluralism—and by the international community, what I really mean are the leading democracies of Europe and North America. As early as 2011, Dr. John Eibner of Christian Solidary International offered a wise proposal that is even more necessary today. He urged President Obama to "establish a high-level inter-agency task-force [within the US government] to prepare a strategy aimed at securing religious freedom and diversity in the Middle East."[5] Without a well-conceived plan to secure religious pluralism over the long term, this critical goal will almost certainly be lost, amid the confused and confusing welter of problems and crises that the Middle East has become.

Previously, I mentioned the call by the Vatican's representative in Geneva for the creation of a UN-endorsed military force to combat ISIS. It is surely the case that the Islamic State will only be contained, and then destroyed, if it is subjected to sustained military attack. We must remember how well-equipped ISIS is, thanks to its capture of equipment and heavy weapons from Iraqi and Syrian government arsenals, its control of oilfields, its funding by wealthy and naive Muslim supporters, and its rampant criminality, including bank robberies, kidnappings, and extortions. ISIS constitutes a real force, military and financial.

Beyond military operations, the United States and other leading powers should activate diplomatic channels to assist Arab Christian communities. Such diplomatic measures could include the creation of a contact group at UN Headquarters which, if properly constituted, could collect information and anchor policy responses not only by the United Nations agencies and individual UN members, but also by other multilateral organizations such as the Arab League, the Gulf Cooperation Council, and the various Arab and international development funds.

Hopefully, the seed for a new integrated diplomatic approach will be planted in March 2015, when the French Foreign Minister is scheduled to chair a UN Security Council Session devoted to the plight of Christians in the Middle East. A search for diplomacy on behalf of Arab Christians and other endangered groups could be guided by a document circulated by the Vatican, Russia, and Lebanon, entitled "Supporting the Human Rights of Christians and Other Communities." This is the first official paper on this topic to be submitted to the UN Human Rights Council in Geneva. Adroit diplomacy would mean working in tandem with diplomats and religious and diplomatic leaders from majority Muslim countries, for example, the UN High Commissioner for Human Rights, Zeid Ra'ad al-Hussein, himself a Muslim and a member of the Jordanian royal family. He has strongly condemned ISIS, invoking widely accepted Muslim teachings to do so. Similar declarations against religious extremism and the persecution of non-Muslims have been voiced by leading Muslims, such as HRH King Salman of Saudi Arabia, President Abdel Fattah al-Sisi of Egypt, Grand Imam Ahmed al-Tayyeb of Egypt's al-Azhar University, former Prime Minister of Lebanon Saad Hariri, and the Grand Mufti of Lebanon, Abdel-Latif Derian.

Among the most important declarations by Muslim authorities in support of non-Muslims, the following two statements particularly gratified me. In late 2013, HRH King Abdullah II of Jordan said, "The protection of the rights of Christians is a *duty* rather than a favor. Christians have always played a key role in building our societies and defending our nations."[6] And, in September 2014, following the lightning rise of ISIS and the start of its reign of terror, the rector of the largest mosque in Paris, Dalil Boubakeur, declared, "We are all, no matter our religion, Christians of the Middle East."[7] These strong voices that have spoken out in favor of religious pluralism are the true Muslims, the genuine defenders of Islam.

Now is the time to bring together these sentiments and instill them into a comprehensive plan of action. People should act, not only speak. The forum for such an effort already exists in Vienna, in the International Centre for Interreligious and Intercultural Dialogue (ICIID), founded by the late King Abdullah of Saudi Arabia in 2011. To better engage institutions such as ICIID, the United States and its European allies should perhaps consider training their diplomats so they can address with greater skill these issues of religious faith.

REGIONAL SAFE HAVENS?

A proposal which has received some attention is the creation of safe havens within targeted countries, which would allow citizens to remain in their home countries. The Archbishop of Canterbury, the Most Revd Justin Welby, is among those who have advocated such an approach.[8] Safe havens, as an alternative to refugee centers abroad, could offer certain advantages. After conditions stabilize, safe havens would enable Christians to return to their home communities far more rapidly than if they were abroad.

However, the placement and conditions of proposed safe havens need to be considered with extreme care. There must be a sufficiently strong local force to provide on-the-ground security. And this force will need logistical and air support provided by international partners who enjoy the legal authority and political will to act swiftly and decisively. In considering the establishment of protected zones, we must recall the tragic fate of the UN safe area in Srebrenica, Bosnia, created in April 1993, but overrun little more than two years later, resulting in the massacre of more than 8,000 Muslims at the hands of Serb paramilitaries.

After establishing the necessary background conditions, including international military guarantees, it might be possible to create an officially declared safe haven for Christian and other groups in the Nineveh plains region of northern Iraq. Historically, this region has been a bedrock of Christianity, and its Christian residents have for centuries lived in harmony with their Muslim neighbors. A proposed safe zone for Christians in the Nineveh area would only be secure if created in cooperation with the Muslim communities in the region. The approval of Muslim communities for support at the local level is symbolic of the region-wide necessity for cooperation among different faith communities. An officially declared safe zone must function as an integral and cooperative component of the surrounding communities. Over time, such an approach will help to rebuild trust among Iraq's various religious and ethnic groups.

WHAT MUST BE DONE CONCERNING LEBANON?

Lebanon is central to religious pluralism, because it is *both* a symbolic and an applied center of interfaith dialogue. For this reason, the international community has a fundamental interest in protecting Lebanon's international security, which acts as a shield for its positive internal dynamics. Lebanon is, in fact, the only Arab country with an intricate array of confessional communities that has not experienced widespread internal conflict in recent decades. Therefore, it can, and *should*, serve as a springboard for a regional effort to protect and extend religious pluralism. For Lebanon, and the Arab world generally, the two most pressing religious pluralism issues are: firstly, securing the status of Christians, and secondly, placing Sunni-Shi'a relations on a long-term peaceful footing.

I have already mentioned the important aid that the United States has provided to the Lebanese army. Other countries, such as Saudi Arabia and France, have been forthcoming with military assistance as well. But to secure Lebanon against attacks and infiltration by ISIS and other terrorists, more needs to be provided in terms of money, equipment, advisory personnel, and training.

The consequences for Lebanon of the ongoing Syrian crisis have been tremendous. In Germany, an official of the United Nations High Commissioner for Refugees (UNHCR), told America's National Public Radio, "The international community has got to provide more support for Lebanon."[9] We estimate the number of refugees currently in Lebanon as between 1.2 and 1.5 million. Even if low estimates are accepted as valid, the fact is that one in every four people now residing in Lebanon is a refugee. Translated into American terms, this is the equivalent of hosting 80 million desperate people in need of every possible necessity of life—from food to housing, education, employment, and medical care.

If the international community does more to support Lebanon, then the Lebanese must demonstrate that they are worthy partners. I refer here to the embarrassing, counterproductive, self-defeating, and partially self-inflicted fact that the Lebanese Presidency is vacant. We have been unable to elect a president for 300 days (as of March 25, 2015). Simply put, the Lebanese system of shared powers among the various communities cannot work if it is disrupted at the summit, where the Christian President, the Sunni Prime Minister, and the Shi'ite Parliamentary Speaker are expected to provide individual and collective leadership. Lebanon needs a strong, capable, and experienced president who can engage in three critical issues: first, reconciling internal Lebanese differences and contradictions through sustained dialogue; second, coordinating governmental reforms and economic development; and third, serving as the voice of Lebanon in the international community by defending sovereignty and core national interests.

WHAT MUST BE DONE AT THE INTERNATIONAL LEVEL?

There is an urgent need to promote the concepts of democracy and human rights in the Arab world. These goals, of course, are related to—but broader than—the struggle to preserve religious pluralism. In the present maelstrom, Arabs are confronted by three competing realities of government: the old failed states, the so-called Islamic State (ISIS), and what can be called citizen states. For some years, I have been discussing a concept that could help move the Arab world toward citizen states: a concept called the Arab Marshall Plan. This is not a detailed blueprint that specifies funding levels, matrices, and timetables; rather, it is meant to encourage Arabs, especially young Arabs, to embrace democratic ideals as a prelude to democratic systems. Other priorities of the Arab Marshall Plan are physical reconstruction, economic development, and a new system of governance both domestically and at the level of regional cooperation.

One may well ask how, with a rampant force like ISIS on the loose, alternatives like the Arab Marshall Plan can succeed. In response, we must remember the advice given by the wily French statesman Talleyrand to that great believer in military force, Napoleon: "The only thing you cannot do with the bayonet is to *sit* on it." He meant that power does not in itself create legitimacy. The only basis for stable and long-term good governance is diplomacy. I say to those who support the best aspects of Arab civilization, including religious pluralism: The ideological and actual bayonets of ISIS will fail—because the mental and physical bayonets of an evil army will not frighten us. ISIS will not intimidate us or deflect us from our goal of building up freedom and dignity for Lebanon and across the Arab world.

NOTES

1. Daniel Williams, "Christianity in Iraq is finished," *The Washington Post*, September 19, 2014, https://www.washingtonpost.com/opinions/christianity-in-iraq-is-finished /2014/09/19/21feaa7c-3f2f-11e4-b0ea-8141703bbf6f_story.html?utm_term=.e0af86640784.

2. Quoted after William Dalrymple, "Lost flock," *The Guardian*, October 30, 2001, https://www.theguardian.com/world/2001/oct/30/pakistan.israelandthepalestinians.

3. Quoted after Kirsten Powers, "Middle East Christians need our protection: Column," *USA Today*, April 2, 2013, https://www.usatoday.com/story/opinion/2013/04/02 /middle-east-christians-need-our-protection-column/2047473/.

4. Bethany Allen-Ebrahimian and Yochi Dreazen, "The Real War on Christianity," *Foreign Policy*, March 12, 2005, http://foreignpolicy.com/2015/03/12/the-real-war-on-christianity-iraq-syria-islamic-state/.

5. PRNewswire, "CSI Urges Obama to Promote Religious Freedom and Diversity in Islamic World," *PRNewswire*, January 2, 2011, http://www.prnewswire.com/news-releases/csi-urges-obama-to-promote-religious-freedom-and-diversity-in-islamic-world-112779134.html.

6. Quoted after Christa Case Bryant, "What the Middle East would be like without Christians," *The Christian Science Monitor*, December 22, 2013, http://www.csmonitor.com/World/Middle-East/2013/1222/What-the-Middle-East-would-be-like-without-Christians.

7. Quoted after Lori Hinnant, "French imams to use pulpit against Islamic State," *Associated Press*, September 9, 2014, http://wtop.com/news/2014/09/french-imams-to-use-pulpit-against-islamic-state/.

8. See John Bingham, "Welby warns offering asylum to Christians could 'drain' Middle East of 2,000-year-old communities," *The Telegraph*, November 18, 2014, http://www.telegraph .co.uk/news/religion/11237755/Welby-warns-offering-asylum-to-Christians-could-drain-Middle-East-of-2000-year-old-communities.html.

9. Ron Redmond, quoted after National Public Radio, "Lebanon Imposes Restrictions On Syrian Refugees," *National Public Radio*, January 6, 2015, http://www.npr.org/2015 /01/06/375308947/lebanon-imposes-restrictions-on-syrian-refugees.

WORKS CITED

Allen-Ebrahimian, Bethany and Yochi Dreazen. "The Real War on Christianity." *Foreign Policy*. March 12, 2005. http://foreignpolicy.com/2015/03/12/the-real-war-on-christianity-iraq-syria-islamic-state/.

Bingham, John. "Welby warns offering asylum to Christians could 'drain' Middle East of 2,000-year-old communities." *The Telegraph*. November 18, 2014. http://www.telegraph.co.uk/news/religion/11237755/Welby-warns-offering-asylum-to-Christians-could-drain-Middle-East-of-2000-year-old-communities.html.

Case Bryant, Christa. "What the Middle East would be like without Christians." *The Christian Science Monitor*. December 22, 2013. http://www.csmonitor.com/World/Middle-East/2013/1222/What-the-Middle-East-would-be-like-without-Christians.

Dalrymple, William. "Lost flock." *The Guardian*. October 30, 2001. https://www.theguardian.com/world/2001/oct/30/pakistan.israelandthepalestinians.

Hinnant, Lori. "French imams to use pulpit against Islamic State." *Associated Press*. September 9, 2014, http://wtop.com/news/2014/09/french-imams-to-use-pulpit-against-islamic-state/.

National Public Radio. "Lebanon Imposes Restrictions On Syrian Refugees." *National Public Radio*. January 6, 2015. http://www.npr.org/2015 /01/06/375308947/lebanon-imposes-restrictions-on-syrian-refugees.

Powers, Kirsten. "Middle East Christians need our protection: Column." *USA Today*. April 2, 2013. https://www.usatoday.com/story/opinion/2013/04/02 /middle-east-christians-need-our-protection-column/2047473/.

PRNewswire. "CSI Urges Obama to Promote Religious Freedom and Diversity in Islamic World." *PRNewswire*. January 2, 2011. http://www.prnewswire.com/news-releases/csi-urges-obama-to-promote-religious-freedom-and-diversity-in-islamic-world-112779134.html.

Williams, Daniel. "Christianity in Iraq is finished." *The Washington Post*. September 19, 2014. https://www.washingtonpost.com/opinions/christianity-in-iraq-is-finished.

Chapter 11

Revisiting Turkey's Policy toward Religious Minorities on the Centenary of the Armenian Genocide

(Zurich, April 1, 2015)

Cengiz Aktar

What is Turkey's policy toward religious minorities? Is there *one* Turkey with one attitude? I do not think so. There is less and less *one* Turkey. There is one *official* Turkey on the one hand, and on the other there is the *social* Turkey, the *other* Turkey, the Turkey that reflects on what happened in these lands a hundred years ago. Let me give you some snapshots of what is happening nowadays after a century of official genocide denial in the Kemalist Turkish Republic.

- The Armenian Catholic Church in Turkey represents a minority compared to the main Armenian Apostolic Church. But the Turkish state has recently granted legal status to the Armenian Catholic Church. This is an interesting development.
- 2015 is the year of the Venice Biennale. The artist chosen to represent Turkey in the official Turkish pavilion is Sarkis Zabunyan, a very famous Turkish Armenian artist who lives in Paris. Sarkis is unlikely to restrain himself when speaking about genocide and other grim realities in Turkey.
- Syriacs have been allowed to open a primary school in Istanbul, on land given by the Catholics—a first since 1928, when their schools were completely shut down by the Kemalist republic. Furthermore, of the religious foundations belonging to non-Muslim minorities and confiscated by the state, 10 percent have been returned. These are official actions by the state.
- On April 23, 2014—the day before Armenian Genocide Remembrance Day—the then-Prime Minister, Recep Tayyip Erdogan, made a statement, for the first time in the history of the Turkish Republic, saying he shared the pain of the descendants of those who died in the massacres. He of course did not use the word *genocide*. But it was an acknowledgement that many innocent people were murdered; that a terrible crime had been committed.

- On March 26, 2015, the Great Synagogue of Edirne near the Bulgarian border was re-opened after restoration. It dates back to 1909, and it is a jewel—a replica of a synagogue in Vienna that was destroyed by the Nazis. The Edirne synagogue was abandoned after the forcible departure of the Jews from the town in the 1930s. The building was restored with public funds and reopened. Moreover, it will not just be a museum; Jewish religious services will take place there. The same thing happened in 2007 to another religious monument, namely, the Armenian Cathedral of the Holy Cross on Akdamar Island in Lake Van. It was also restored with public money. But in this case it re-opened as a museum, not a functioning place of worship.

How is it that this hitherto denialist Kemalist state now carries out acts that are reminders of the tragedy that befell the Armenians, the Syriacs, and all the other non-Muslim minorities? Such deeds were unthinkable only a few years ago. The state that does so is governed by the Muslim Brotherhood-related Islamist AK Party of Recep Tayyip Erdogan. Why is it doing these things?

EMERGENCE OF COMMUNITIES AS POLITICAL ACTORS

In the mid-1980s, Islamist Muslims and Kurds started to become significant political actors in Turkey. They were, of course, rejected right away by the ruling class adhering to the secular, Turkish national ideology of Kemalism. But they did not give up. Some Kurds took up arms, but the Islamist Muslims began to take control of the municipalities through the ballot box. By these means, they became more powerful political actors. The Islamist Muslims had so much success that they attained power in the national elections of 2002.

The empowerment of Muslims qua Muslims and Kurds challenged the myth of a beautiful homogeneous nation, one in which there were no ethnic or religious differences. This myth was invented at the end of the Ottoman era and became the basis of the Turkish Republic. As soon as Kurds and Muslims became political actors as Kurds and as Muslims, they opened up a Pandora's Box of other identities, which had been either erased, or hidden, or simply ignored in the official narrative. Moreover, these two big political groups are not too shy to talk about non-Muslims, because they did not bear primary responsibility for the decision to annihilate them. That responsibility rested fully on the shoulders of secular nationalist statesmen. Of course, Kurds and Muslims were involved in the operations of annihilation; it was mainly Kurds who massacred the Armenians. Some Muslim clerics—not all—incited their followers to kill as many Christians as possible in order to go to heaven.

Nowadays, the political descendants of these henchmen of genocide say that their people were manipulated by the state. I think that even if they find an excuse and say *mea culpa, mea maxima culpa*, "We were involved, but we were manipulated," this is extremely important, because it constitutes an act of remembrance of what happened. This is part of how we are slowly getting to what I call *memory works* at the level of society in Turkey.

The Turkish state, however, is still schizophrenic and paradoxical on this issue. I mentioned several examples of positive actions that challenge the old Kemalist narrative of complete denial. But on the other hand, there are still negatives. For example, the Greek Orthodox seminary on Halki remains closed, and Turkey put heavy pressure on the Geneva authorities to cancel the planned Armenian art project, *Les Réverbères de la Mémoire*.[1] I mentioned the religious foundations getting back their confiscated property. But the court of cassation in Turkey still operates by a landmark decision in 1934, which proclaimed all non-Muslims foreigners. This year on Armenian Genocide Remembrance Day, the Turkish government will divert attention by staging a huge national celebration to commemorate the sensational Turkish victory over the Australian and New Zealand Army Corps, ANZAC, in the World War I Battle of Gallipoli. As for the reconstruction of the synagogue in Edirne, I will cite the reality as reported by a Turkish Jew: "Buildings might be protected, but the people who visit them are subjected to regular hate speech and threats."[2]

Despite all these contradictions and paradoxes, the hegemonic political forces in Turkey, both Islamists and Kurds, are not impeding the *memory works*. The *memory works* continue to penetrate deeper and deeper into Turkish society. These political forces are not applying the brakes, as the Kemalist old guard used to do. The use of the word *genocide* is still forbidden by Article 305 of the Turkish Penal Code, but no one is punished for using it. The word is everywhere; people not only talk openly about genocide, but are starting genocide studies. Something really new is happening in Turkey. This is why it is difficult today to talk about *one* Turkey, or Turkey's policy in relation to the genocide. There is one *official* Turkey, for which genocide is still a taboo. Yet for the society and its active elements and forces, things have changed dramatically.

FORCES FOR CHANGE

The first cluster of active elements is people involved in academia and publishing. When I was a student in Istanbul, it was impossible to find a single book about the genocide or the other massacres of religious minorities that happened in Anatolia. Now academia is extremely active and publishing houses are blossoming. There are books translated and everything is available, including the magnum opus of Raymond Kévorkian, *The Armenian Genocide: A Complete History* (London: I.B. Tauris, 2011), which details village by village, city by city, what happened to the Armenians in 1915 and 1916.

Pioneering work was done by my friend Ragip Zarakolu, who opened the Belge Publishing House in 1977. Every single book that he has published or had translated was pursued by the authorities, but he never gave up—a very courageous man. Aras, an Armenian publishing house, continued the good work, and today almost all publishing houses in Turkey publish books about what happened a hundred years ago in Anatolia, not only about the genocide, but about many other things that happened. The Kurds have their own publications, in Kurdish, which nobody else reads, but in these works they discuss what happened to their Armenian neighbors in eastern Anatolia. Taner Akçam has been a pioneering scholar, but what is interesting about the present is that he is now not the only one. Young researchers are more and more interested in examining the reality.

In September 2005, a landmark conference took place in Turkey. The state was very unhappy about it, but it happened anyway. The conference was entitled "Ottoman Armenians during the Decline of the Empire."[3] It opened the floodgates. Now there are so many conferences touching this theme that we cannot keep track of them. The public interest is not only in the Armenians. The fate of Syriacs, Jews, Kurds, and Greeks is also addressed. Just 10 years ago, such conferences took place only abroad. Now they are taking place not only in Istanbul, but in more remote Anatolian towns like predominantly Kurdish Diyarbakır, and Mardin, once populated by many Syriac, Nestorian, and Chaldean Christians. All these are new and very encouraging developments.

MEMORY RESEARCH BY INDIVIDUALS

The second cluster of active forces comes under the heading of individual memory research. In Turkey, before these new developments, to call someone an Armenian, or to talk about Armenian or Greek or Syriac ancestors, was impossible, practically a sin. People themselves were afraid of talking about this sort of thing. Now, more and more, people are searching for their ancestors and proudly mentioning their Armenian grandmothers. Boys were extensively slaughtered in the genocide, but Armenian girls were kept, so they became mothers and grandmothers, mainly in Kurdish families. There is a saying among the Kurds: "There is no Kurdish family without an Armenian grandmother." People are now talking about these things, and searching for their roots, and this is something precious. My friend Fethiye Cetin (who happens to be the lawyer of Armenian editor Hrant Dink who was assassinated in 2007) published a book called *My Grandmother—An Armenian-Turkish Memoir* (trans. Maureen Freely, New York: Verso, 2012). There are now 13 or 14 books of the same nature; before, it was impossible even to mention these grandmothers.

Another interesting subject is that of forcibly Islamized Armenians. In 1915, the Ottoman government issued a decree allowing Armenians to convert to Islam. In some places, so many people converted that the government annulled the decree, and issued another one forbidding conversion. Conversion of course saved the lives of many Armenians. Some were slaughtered despite having converted, but that is another matter; the majority of those who converted were saved. These people always existed. The state knew about it. Their neighbors knew about it; they still know about it. They talk about a village that is 100 percent Muslim but is still described as "the Armenian village." The people in such villages are now talking openly about their Armenian roots. Some estimates put the figure of descendants of converted Armenians in the millions, which I do not think is an exaggeration. Armenian sources say there were some 300,000 or so whose lives were spared thanks to conversion; their descendants could easily number in the millions.

Now some of these people are re-converting. The Church is not always happy, because the converts include some who do not know much about Christianity. But the fact is they want to be baptized, they are being baptized, and slowly they learn the religion. In the process they also often learn the language of their Christian ancestors.

PUBLIC AWARENESS

The third cluster in what I call *memory works* is public awareness, and the increasing visibility of non-Muslim minorities, who are almost literally being discovered by Turkish society. There are only 2,000 Greeks remaining in Turkey, and they live mainly in Istanbul. Some say that they can still encounter their fellow Turkish citizens on the street and be asked: "Oh, you are a tourist; how do you like Istanbul?" Ignorance still abounds. Nevertheless, public awareness is developing by the day.

There used to be only one Armenian friendship association, but now there are eight such associations. All are in Istanbul, because no Armenian communities are left in Anatolia. They are all active; they all have, as we say in French, *pignon sur rue*—they are public, they do not hide any more. Armenian newspapers of course always existed—they were not forbidden—but in the past, they did not reach a readership beyond the Armenian community. *Agos,* the paper of the late Hrant Dink, had the genius idea of publishing in both Turkish and Armenian. In 2016, *Agos* will have been publishing for 20 years, thus increasing public awareness and the visibility of the Armenians among the general population.

The first public commemoration of the anti-Greek pogroms of September 6 and 7, 1955, took place in 2005. While Greeks were the main targets, some Armenians and other non-Muslims were also attacked and their property was destroyed. The public did not have a collective memory of these events until the commemorative exhibitions were held, an effort I was involved in. It has now happened every year since 2005. Similarly, the 1964 expulsion of most of the remaining Greeks in Istanbul was commemorated for the first time in 2014. Now it is on the radar of the Turkish public.

Diaspora organizations are coming back to Turkey. This is a fascinating development. The Civilitas Foundation, based in Yerevan, Armenia, has opened an office in Istanbul. The National Congress of Western Armenians is intending to open an office. Yerkir, which means "the country," is also opening offices.

Another group of people associated with the genocide is emerging into the daylight: the upright people, those who saved Armenians. Of course, when it was impossible to talk about what happened to the Armenians per se, it was not possible to talk about those who saved them. But now we can, and it is extremely important because they were many. Some were public figures—officials, mayors, governors, sub-governors, and so on, who refused to obey the orders from Istanbul. There were anonymous people who simply decided to save the lives of their fellow citizens. Now people are saying things like, "I remember my mother telling me that our grandfather saved so many Armenians." Naturally, some of the rescuers had ulterior motives, such as wanting to keep Armenian women and children for themselves. That is something that also must be remembered. But many acted exclusively because of conscience, and they need to be recognized.

Many Armenian, Syriac, and Greek towns and villages were renamed in Turkish. Now people are researching the old names and discovering that many are of Armenian or mixed origin, and the old names are being revived by locals.

There are mobile exhibitions portraying the lives of Armenians through postcard collections. "Armenians used to live here," the exhibitions say. The postcards are fundamental, because in the eastern parts of the country nothing Armenian remains any more, unfortunately. These mobile exhibitions of postcards go to various towns in Turkey, and people are amazed because they recognize the streets where they live in the postcards and they see buildings that do not exist anymore. So they start to think: "Yes, there were Armenians here, but where are they now?"

RELIGIOUS AND CULTURAL DIVERSITY

The fourth cluster of *memory works* involves religious and cultural diversity. Incredible things are happening in Turkish society. I mentioned the restoration of the synagogue of Edirne and the Armenian cathedral in Van, but there are many others, like the church of Surb Grigor Lusarovich in Kayseri, the church of Surb Vordvots Vorotmans that was renovated in Istanbul, Surb Giragos in Diyarbakır, little churches in the western parts of the country—Greek churches mainly—in Alanya and Bodrum; a Georgian church, Oshki, in Erzurum. Local people are interested now in refurbishing all these churches because they think that tourists will come. Twenty years ago, they would never have dared ask the state or the public authorities for permission to start collecting money to restore the dying church in the town. Now they dare. This is new, and very important. It means they are prepared to remember what happened 100 years ago.

Masses are now being celebrated in many of these churches—not every day, but still, it is a step forward. In a famous Greek monastery, Sumela, by the Black Sea, the Greek Orthodox mass was celebrated by the Ecumenical Patriarch in 2010 for the first time in many decades. Now it is celebrated annually on August 15.

Architects in Turkey were mainly of Armenian and Greek origin. These days, exhibitions recall their outstanding achievements, and people are learning about them. For example, the famous Dolmabahçe Palace was built by the very important family of Armenian architects, the Balyans. For the first time an Armenian cemetery in Malatya, a city with an important Armenian past, is being restored. Usually, those who erase the memory of a community start by erasing the cemeteries. Now, what remains of the cemetery is being restored, although hardly any Armenians live in Malatya any more. A chapel has been erected in this cemetery—a first since 1915.

WHERE DO WE GO FROM HERE?

Where do we go from here? Will all these activities, all these events, all this recalling, help the state itself to acknowledge the Armenian Genocide? I think we are still far from it. Despite the fact that it is not the same political class that is in charge, the state has its own habits, its own reflexes, and its own rigidities. Even the political Islamists, the ruling AK Party—despite the fact that they have been quite liberal with regard to non-Muslims and the *memory works*—stop short of acknowledging the realities of the past in the name of the state. It is not because they are unwilling. There are some very sincere people among them; it is for other reasons. This state, which is, after all, the official successor of the Ottoman state, is the one which organized all the massacres, and it would never recognize the full extent of its genocidal deeds of its own accord.

In the Sèvres Treaty of 1920, the Turkish state, then perilously weakened by defeat in World War I, acknowledged some of its deeds. But with the Lausanne Treaty of 1923, which followed Ataturk's consolidation of his rule over the Turkish state, everything was reversed, and everything could be forgotten. This is a major impediment, which in my opinion can only be challenged if the healthy *memory works* that are taking place in Turkish society go so deep as to challenge the official narrative. There is no other way.

Challenging the official narrative will not be easy. The organizers of the Armenian deportation and the genocide found jobs with the Kemalist regime after 1923. For example, a man called Şükrü Kaya, who was one of the top members of the so-called Young Turks who orchestrated the genocide, became Mustafa Kemal's Interior Minister. Thus, there was not only legal, but also personal continuity between the Ottoman state and the Turkish Republic. We also have to bear in mind that many people were bought off by the state with property confiscated from the Armenians, Greeks, and others. Large quantities of land, houses, and monuments were distributed by the state to many people as a part of a new system of political patronage. The authorities used this method very effectively with politically loyal Kurds.

Overall, people are now starting to think about the past more than ever. People have started to address the fate of the Armenians. They are also learning about the Balkan Muslims, who were slaughtered and expelled after the Balkan Wars of 1912–1913, and about the Bulgarians and the Greeks. The nineteenth century is full of stories of ethnic and religious cleansings; historians know about them, but at the level of society these stories are largely forgotten. Talking about the Armenian Genocide also enables us to talk about the expulsion of Muslims from the Balkans and the Caucasus. This is another untold story—how the Russian Empire expanded throughout the eighteenth and nineteenth centuries, with many local Muslim people being pushed out of the way. Despite the many challenges to this process I believe the *memory works* will continue in Turkey. The genie is out of the bottle, and it can never be forced back in.

NOTES

1. See Horizon Weekly, "Genocide Memorial Faces Opposition from Swiss President," *Horizon Weekly*, December 16, 2014, https://horizonweekly.ca/en/55723-2/.

2. Louis Fishman, quoted after Ayla Jean Yackley, "Turkey unveils Great Synagogue as Jewish population fades," *Reuters*, March 25, 2015, http://www.reuters.com/article/us-turkey-jews-idUSKBN0ML1LH20150325.

3. Initially, the conference had been scheduled to be held in May 2005 at Istanbul's Bogaziçi University, but had to be canceled due to pressure from Turkish government officials. Despite ongoing efforts by Turkish nationalists to prevent the conference from taking place, it was eventually held in September 2005 at a private university. For further background on this, see Arend Jan Boekestijn, "Turkey, the World, and the Armenian Question," *Turkish Policy Quarterly* 4, no. 4 (Winter 2005).

WORKS CITED

Boekestijn, Arend Jan. "Turkey, the World, and the Armenian Question." *Turkish Policy Quarterly* 4 no. 4 (Winter 2005).

Cetin, Fethiye. *My Grandmother—An Armenian-Turkish Memoir.* Translated by Maureen Freely. New York: Verso, 2012.

Horizon Weekly. "Genocide Memorial Faces Opposition from Swiss President." *Horizon Weekly.* December 16, 2014. https://horizonweekly.ca/en/55723-2/.

Kévorkian, Raymond. *The Armenian Genocide: A Complete History.* London: I.B. Tauris, 2011.

Yackley, Ayla Jean. "Turkey unveils Great Synagogue as Jewish population fades." *Reuters.* March 25, 2015. http://www.reuters.com/article/us-turkey-jews-idUSK-BN0ML1L H20150325.

Chapter 12

Saudi Regional Interventions in the Middle East: Consequences for Local Societies

(*Zurich, October 27, 2015*)

Madawi Al-Rasheed

Recently I have been looking at what has happened in the Arab world since the Arab uprisings. I have been focusing specifically on the role Saudi Arabia has played in either thwarting or supporting them, and the consequences for local societies. The Arab uprisings varied, but had one focus in common: regardless of how they started, they differed from every other protest the Middle East has witnessed by being mass protests. It was the mass character of the protests that distinguished these Arab uprisings from previous demonstrations of unrest.

In North Africa, where it all started—in Tunisia, Egypt, and then Libya— there was a lot of hope at the outset. I am one of the people who thought we were witnessing something fundamentally different from the coups masquerading as revolutions that happened in the 1950s or 1960s. Even in the Arabian Peninsula, usually a calm and quiet region, there were serious protests in Bahrain, and even Oman witnessed some demonstrations. Yemen did too, but this was not unusual in the country. Yemen has distinguished itself by having a strong society and a weak state. Yemenis have always challenged central authority. But in Syria there is an ongoing conflict. In the past, many Arab leaders—from Gaddafi to Gamal Abdel Nasser of Egypt and Saddam Hussein—have challenged the Saudis from the standpoint of Arab socialism or Arab nationalism. In the 1960s, the Saudi regime felt especially challenged by the mass protests that coalesced around these ideologies. Yet the mass protests we have witnessed since 2010 are extremely different from these earlier attempts to change the status quo in the Arab world.

In places like Tunisia and Egypt what emerged immediately was the demand for justice, dignity, and economic prosperity. We all know what has happened when the Arab masses were given the opportunity to elect their governments in what were regarded as open elections: they elected Islamists—in Tunisia the Ennahda Party, and in Egypt the Muslim Brotherhood. We can speculate why the Islamists won: they are more organized than other groups, they catalyzed enthusiasm for change, and represented a protest vote against the status quo.

But the Saudi regime worried about the loss of loyal allies in the Middle East, particularly in Egypt. Saudi Arabia felt threatened by the loss of Mubarak in Egypt, and could not imagine the Arab world without its closest ally. As a conservative absolute monarchy, Saudi Arabia, like most monarchies, abhors change that cannot be controlled. Its initial response was to condemn the uprisings; the Saudis used the word *fitna* in Arabic to describe them, which means sedition, rebellion, and civil strife. The Saudi regime feared the transformative potential of these uprisings inside Saudi Arabia itself. One thing that made the uprisings so different in their impact from previous challenges was the advent and proliferation of images and narratives on social media. The Saudi population is one of the most connected populations in terms of social media. A whole generation that had never seen peaceful protests in the Arab world became familiar with events that were taking place almost every day from December 2010.

The main objective of Saudi Arabia was to preserve the monarchy. The loss of allies such as Mubarak in Egypt and Ben Ali in Tunisia, whom Saudi Arabia relied on for intelligence and political support, worried the Saudis. The opening of the Egyptian public sphere immediately after the revolution was feared in Riyadh. Protests against Saudi Arabia took place in Egypt that would never have happened during the Mubarak regime, because Mubarak would not have allowed it. Egypt may not have any resources, but it is the most populous Arab country, and the Saudis fear it.

Throughout the twentieth century, Egypt has been the source of three trends in the Arab world: modernity—Egypt was the outstanding pioneer in spreading modernity through literature, cinema, art, and so on—Arab nationalism, which Saudi Arabia has always perceived as a threat, and finally, Egypt itself provided the key ideologues for the Islamist movement, from Hassan al-Banna and Sayeed Qutb to Ayman al-Zawahiri. Saudi Arabia could not anticipate what might come out of a post-Mubarak Egypt. Perhaps it would be democracy, and that was extremely worrying for the Saudi regime. Hence all their efforts were directed at reversing the trend.

SAUDI INTERNAL STRATEGIES

At home, Saudi Arabia used multiple strategies to prevent any kind of domino effect. They mobilized the religious establishment—that is, the Salafi–Wahhabi establishment—to provide *fatwas*, religious opinions, against peaceful protest. In Saudi religious discourse, civil disobedience and peaceful protests were criminalized. Activists who mobilize people to demonstrate were not simply committing a political dissident act, but above all were committing a sin against God and the King. The clerics, the *ulama,* emphasized that obeying God, the Prophet, *and* the King were on an equal footing. Both protesters and civil rights activists are sinners before they are dissidents. As a result of the repression, the protest moved from the street to the internet, and online hashtag activism gained in popularity in Saudi Arabia. One of the hashtags during the first months of the Arab uprising was #al-Ratb_La_Yakfi, which means: The salary is not enough. The Saudis immediately increased the salaries of their citizens, and since more than 60 or 70 percent find employment in the public sector, this was a good way to reward the population for submission. Saudis are told every day that it is better to be grateful for the security and wealth that they have rather than to want change, because change is uncertain.

SAUDI STRATEGIES IN THE REGION

The Saudi regime used three regional strategies in response to the Arab uprisings. The first was containment: the regime tried to limit the impact of the uprising in Egypt specifically. One may wonder why a country like Saudi Arabia that claims to rule according to God's law and claims to be an Islamic state would object to the Muslim Brotherhood gaining power in Egypt. My interpretation is that the Muslim Brotherhood demonstrated that they were willing to follow the rules of the democratic process. They were also willing to form political parties, engage in elections, and come to power democratically. Obviously, Saudi Arabia could not tolerate the example of Islam and democracy being combined. In fact, kingship does not exist as a political system in Islam, so the Saudis are particularly sensitive about asserting their monopoly with regard to Islam. The regime claims legitimacy from its assertion of being the only Muslim state in the world and the only one that fully applies shari'a. To have a country as important as Egypt, both demographically and intellectually, finding a way to marry Islam and democracy must have threatened the Saudi monopoly on Islam.

Containment meant, initially, starving the Egyptians. The aid that Egypt used to receive from Saudi Arabia and other Gulf countries was suspended when the Muslim Brotherhood came to power and only after the al-Sisi coup was it resumed. Egypt has a long history of vibrant media, suppressed under various dictatorships, but with the potential to create some kind of openness in the Arab world that would have vibrated across the region. So the Saudis tried to contain Egypt first through withholding aid and then pouring in resources to enforce change after the coup and stabilize the military regime.

The second strategy was counterrevolution, and the first place this happened was Bahrain. Again, the Saudi interest was to preserve the monarchy as a viable and durable political system, at least in its own backyard. The Saudis could not afford to see Bahrain falling into the hands of democratic forces, and therefore immediately sent troops—under the umbrella of the Gulf Cooperation Council—to support the Bahraini monarchy. The uprising in Bahrain was peaceful, and was not initially the work of a particular sectarian group when it started. Bahrain had a long history of activism throughout the twentieth century: it had an active civil society and trade unions. The Bahraini protest movement was driven by youth who wanted serious change and political participation; they also wanted an elected government and a real constitutional monarchy. Initially the protesters included Sunnis alongside people from the Shi'ite community, who were the majority. But the Saudis felt threatened by these mass protests only 15 kilometers away from Saudi Arabia. Then, after February 14, 2011, the uprising spilled over to Saudi Arabia, especially among the Shi'ite community in the eastern province, who started calling for equality with the Sunni majority and fair trials for Shi'ite political prisoners. Their demonstrations for these demands and in support of their Shi'ite brothers in Bahrain prompted Saudi Arabia to act as a counterrevolutionary force.

The Saudi obsession with preserving monarchies extended also to Morocco and Jordan, where Saudi Arabia promised financial support to monarchical regimes facing mass protests. More importantly, Saudi Arabia proposed that the Gulf Cooperation Council be enlarged to include Jordan and Morocco. This did not happen, but Saudi financial support to the two monarchies continued.

As a counterrevolutionary force, Saudi Arabia used diplomatic channels to influence the Yemeni uprising; this was counterrevolution disguised as negotiated transfer of power. Saudi Arabia, together with Qatar and other Gulf Cooperation countries, went into the Yemeni situation, which was not unusual for Saudi Arabia, as Saudi Arabia has always interfered in Yemen. In fact, the interference goes back to the 1930s, when Saudi Arabia meddled in Yemeni politics either by supporting tribal chiefs against each other or against the government, or supporting the government against other groups. The main purpose was to keep Yemen weak, and they kept it so weak that it generated more trouble than would have been possible to contain. So, counterrevolution was disguised as negotiation, which resulted in Yemeni president Ali Abdullah Saleh being removed from power, but also being given immunity from prosecution. After he was attacked physically, he escaped to Saudi Arabia, where his injuries were treated; then he returned to Yemen, armed with his immunity, to continue to meddle in Yemeni politics. The present tragic situation in Yemen is a consequence.

The third Saudi strategy is, perhaps surprisingly, revolution. The Saudi regime has acted as a revolutionary force, selectively and in specific cases. The most important case is Syria. The conservative Saudi monarchy, with no democracy, elections, or parliament, supported the Sunni-dominated Syrian rebellion in the effort to depose the Alawite Bashar al-Assad. The reason is very straightforward: Syria has become a proxy area for a regional war between Saudi Arabia and Iran. Saudi Arabia used to support the Assad regime; the two only fell out during the Israeli bombing of Lebanon after Hezbollah kidnapped Israeli soldiers in 2006, when Bashar al-Assad used provocative language against the Saudis, calling them "half men." In a patriarchal society, this is really very insulting: no man in the Arab world would like to be called half a man. But joking aside, the main thing is that Saudi Arabia has devoted resources since 2003 to limit Iranian expansion in the Arab world.

The Saudis see the increased expansion of Iranian power in Iraq after the American invasion as a threat. They are also troubled by their loss of control of Lebanon, especially with the rise of Hezbollah and the assassination of Rafiq al-Hariri. The Saudis can no longer count on a pro-Saudi government in Beirut. Syria became the bridge that linked Iran to Lebanon. Mubarak, before he was deposed, and the Saudi and Jordanian kings all started talking about a Shi'ite aggressor in the region. Saudi Arabia lobbied the United States to attack Iran, but Obama resisted. WikiLeaks published a letter from the Saudi king telling the Obama administration to "cut off the head of the snake,"[1] meaning Iran. But Saudi Arabia did not dare to attack Iran directly, so unfortunately for the Syrians, Syria became the battleground where several regional powers—Iran, Turkey, Saudi Arabia, and other Gulf countries—have played a very destructive role. One must also mention American, European, and Russian involvement—all have failed to deliver the beginning of a peaceful resolution to the Syrian crisis.

The intervention of the Saudi regime with its vast oil resources led to the increasing militarization of the Syrian uprising. To say this is not to deny the atrocities committed by the Assad regime against people in Syria, who began as peaceful protesters, copying the Egyptians in Tahrir Square. The moment the Syrian regime opened fire at the protestors, it ushered a long civil war. The Syrian uprising rapidly turned very bloody, and it continues so until the present day. The death toll is incredible, and so is the scale of the refugee crisis which has resulted. Saudi–Iranian rivalry has proved to be extremely detrimental to Arab society.

Saudi regional intervention has also taken the form of diplomacy; there were many international conferences in which Saudi Arabia participated, including those of the so-called Friends of Syria Group, Geneva I, II, and III. The Saudi goal was to rally the Arab regimes and the international community against the Syrian regime. Saudi Arabia has also of course been sponsoring rebel groups.

CONSEQUENCES OF INTERVENTION: MILITARIZATION

What have been the consequences for countries where the Saudis have intervened, either diplomatically, financially, or militarily? First, there was suppression of peaceful protests and the demise of democratic forces. There is no doubt that in Egypt, Bahrain, and other places, there is no room today for democratic forces, because the context has become so polarized and so sectarian that those who had democratic ideas have been sidelined or marginalized completely.

Islamist groups, who are part of the fabric of Arab society, include moderates willing to engage with democracy in some way or another. They are not liberal democrats, but they might be religious conservative democrats. There are some Saudis who want some kind of personal freedom and limitations on the power of the religious authorities to interfere in their personal lives. However, these Saudi "liberals" are hardly the mainstream; they do not constitute a very big cohort of activists. In terms of the Islamists, they range from the most radical and violent to the radical and non-violent. In a democracy, we would imagine there would be spaces for those radicals who are not violent; but after what happened in Egypt, that trend has fragmented, and perhaps some of its members have moved closer to violence.

Thus, Saudi intervention has encouraged the rise of the militant Islamists who are now filling a vacuum. There is no room any more for peaceful protest; those who have the means of coercion, who can terrorize populations, are gaining ground—and the classic example is the Islamic State in Iraq and Syria. If you have no means of coercion, you are not listened to; whereas if you flex your muscles, use weapons, you can actually gain territory and force people to obey.

SECTARIANIZATION

The most sinister impact of this intervention is the sectarianization of the conflicts in Bahrain, Syria, and Yemen, in addition to other countries. Saudi officials, especially the religious establishment, saw the Bahraini uprising as a Shi'ite conspiracy backed by Iran against the Sunnis. An uprising that started with calls for democracy, respect for human rights, dignity, and justice was characterized in Saudi official discourse as a Shi'ite uprising. It did not help when some sections of the Shi'ite population started raising the Iranian flag and brandishing photos of Iranian scholars in the streets of Bahrain.

In Syria, what started as a democratic movement for rights and dignity was turned into a sectarian war. The Saudis see it as a religious struggle by oppressed Sunnis against the Alawites, regarded as a Shi'ite minority that has ruled the Sunnis (even though the Alawites are not mainstream Shi'a, and definitely not like the Iranian Shi'a). In this perspective, there is no room for any kind of political discourse about rights, civil society, elections, representation, and so on. The battle has become a religious war between sectarian groups.

Like other Arab countries, Yemen is diverse at the level of ethnic and religious sects, but it is not as polarized as other Arab countries; sectarianism has never been a major issue in Yemen. Today, however, the intervention of Saudi Arabia in Yemen through the air strikes that have been taking place since March 2015 is seen by some Saudi religious scholars as a war by Sunnis against the Houthis, who are Zaidi Shi'ites. Zaidis are not the same as the Iranian Twelver Shi'a, but for Saudi scholars, that is beside the point; they view all these groups as the same thing—namely, as Shi'a.

POLARIZATION

The Saudi intervention has also prolonged military conflict: the classic case is Syria, where war started in 2011. Without foreign intervention from many sides, the Syrian people, living under the threat of war, might have found ways to compromise. But once you had regional powers deciding the outcome, and outsiders, particularly the Saudis, making it clear they will accept nothing less than the deposition of Bashar al-Assad, the chance for negotiation and diplomacy was lost. Politically too, the Arab world has become more polarized. No one can be neutral in the Arab world anymore. For example, if someone sympathizes with people who died in an Islamic State attack on an Isma'ili mosque in southern Saudi Arabia in October 2015 (Isma'ilis are regarded as Shi'a, but again, they are different from Shi'a in Iran or Iraq), he or she is immediately told, "Well, what about the Sunnis who are dying in Syria?" Even to show normal human emotions runs the risk of being perceived as being biased. The situation is so polarized that everyone has to take sides in a struggle represented as sectarian.

ECONOMIC CONSEQUENCES

Economically, very weak and impoverished Arab economies have become worse. Even more disastrous is the increased dependence of many Arab regimes on aid from Saudi Arabia and other countries in the Gulf—aid that is only forthcoming if regimes loyally support Saudi Arabia and the Gulf. Since it started its campaign of air strikes on Yemen, Saudi Arabia has been very interested in getting Egypt to send troops to Yemen. General al-Sisi has taken a lot of aid from Saudi Arabia, but has so far resisted sending masses of troops. Saudi Arabia gives aid under the pretext of helping other Muslims or helping other Arabs, but there is always a cost, and loyalty to the Saudi regime and loss of independence become critical issues.

In conflict zones, the destruction of infrastructure is massive. It will probably take generations to rebuild the economies of Syria and Yemen and their infrastructure. Unemployment was already an extremely difficult issue in the Arab world, which had one of the highest rates of unemployment in the world, and that situation is worse now. There is also what I call the "lost generation," especially Syrian refugee children, many of whom have fled to Lebanon. Many refugee Syrian children in Lebanon work as porters in supermarkets carrying people's shopping to their cars in order to get 2,000 Lebanese pounds, which is almost nothing. Those children have no schooling at all. What will happen in ten years' time to those who stopped school at age 7 or 8, or never even started? In the 1950s, all governments in the Arab world introduced mass education, and illiteracy began to decline, but now we have a lost generation, and these hundreds of thousands of children will be illiterate adults in the twenty-first century.

IMPACT ON GENDER INEQUALITY

It is extremely important to see the impact of Saudi expansionism on gender and gender inequality. The historical Saudi model of gender segregation—having women take the back seat in terms of empowerment, employment, and education—is now the common model in the Arab world. It is promoted as the true Islam. But it is Saudi Islam that has become popular in other Arab countries as a result of satellite channels and religious education books sponsored by the Saudis and distributed around the world. The Saudi model has a very specific cultural and geographical context; it is a minority sect based in the Arabian Peninsula. It has, however, become the norm, and any other way of being Muslim has become difficult to exercise. You either follow the Saudi model, or you are branded as a bad Muslim, or even a non-Muslim.

The harassment and marginalization of women who dare to challenge these gender norms and inequality have increased as a result. In fact, the societies where the Saudi model has penetrated are not used to this kind of gender inequality—in Tunisia or Egypt, for example, women had to work in order to earn a living; it was a necessity, not a luxury. But with the prevalence of the religious discourse that the right place for a woman is at home, of course we see more harassment of women in the streets.

INTOLERANCE OF DIVERSITY

There is today much greater intolerance of social diversity and pluralism. One of the unique features of the Middle East was its ethnic and religious diversity. I am not simply being nostalgic for a romanticized past where Christians and Muslims lived together and married each other and everyone was happy—that would be a historical error. Obviously there have been massacres, purges, and moments of tension. What is different now is the virulence of sectarianism. Political conflicts that would previously have been resolved politically have now become religious conflicts. And that is leading to an entrenched divide between the two branches of Islam, Sunni and Shi'a. Some people think Sunnis and Shi'ites always hated each other, from the seventh century onward. But that is not true. There were moments when their religious identity was politicized to gain some kind of equality or benefit. But now you can only promote your cause by being Sunni or Shi'ite. There is an intolerance of other religious minorities too.

Saudi Arabia has always been predominantly Muslim. The only Christians living there are immigrants from other parts of the Arab world, Asia or the West, and their practice of their religion is severely restricted. In London several years ago, I visited a shelter for Filipino women who had escaped from their Saudi employers in London. First, with the assistance of lawyers and human rights activists, they needed to get their passports back, because of course the employer retains the passports of domestic workers. One of them told me she hid her cross in her suitcase because if her employer saw it, he would destroy it. I also heard stories about what happened to poor Christian migrant workers if they were unfortunate enough to die in Saudi Arabia. Very poorly paid domestic or manual workers whose families could not raise the money to repatriate the body, and whose embassies would not help, are buried in unmarked graves in the desert by their friends. This is done without any kind of religious ceremony. This is an inhuman situation that needs to change.

Religious difference is not a lived experience for many Saudis. The only religiously different person will be a migrant, whom they encounter only in the context of work. The indigenous population is not at all a religiously diverse society, and therefore, from the Saudi point of view, the native religious diversity common to most of the Arab world is extremely difficult to understand.

The last decade has seen increased migration of religious minorities from the Middle East to the UK—Palestinian Christians under Israeli occupation,

Lebanese and Syrian minorities, and Iraqi Assyrians. Why do they end up in London? Assyrians for instance have had vibrant communities in Iraq for centuries, but today they are mostly gone—a loss to the Arab world. Today if you are different, whether you are religious or not, you are criminalized. Religious differences are reluctantly tolerated. Muslims are under pressure to become homogeneous on the one hand, and reject different religious groups on the other hand.

RIVALRIES, BOTH REGIONAL AND INTERNATIONAL

A lot of damage has been done to the Arab world by the rivalry between Saudi Arabia and Iran. Saudi Arabia alone cannot be blamed for this, because Iran is also a player in this regional conflict. But in order to understand what happened to the Arab uprisings, and why the Arab world has degenerated into such a pronounced state of chaos and bloodshed, we have to understand this rivalry. This conflict takes place in the international context of rivalry between the United States and Russia, which further entrenches polarization. Saudi Arabian foreign policy has changed: for the first time, the Saudis are directly intervening with air strikes in Yemen instead of operating through proxies. After decades of being armed by various Western powers, the Saudis are directly employing the technology, training, and weaponry they have acquired from the West.

When we questioned the UK government about why they were still selling arms to the Saudis, we got the reply that if the UK did not sell, the French would. It is an open market, they say. Perhaps there is scope for a global solution to the arms sales that are creating this chaos in the Arab world. This is necessary because months after the Saudi regime began bombing Yemen— the poorest Arab country—we have not seen the prospect of any kind of solution. In fact, the country is more polarized. It has no functioning infrastructure and has a serious humanitarian crisis, including famine.

The Saudi model of government, its religious outlook, and its social and cultural norms have been enhanced as a result of support from its Western allies. In the Arab world, there is increased polarization that has prevented the emergence of democratic forces for the immediate future. I see no possibility for change as long as the Saudi regime possesses the economic resources that enable it to project its power and ideas beyond Saudi Arabia. Any real change will have to happen in Saudi Arabia itself.

And perhaps we will see the beginning of some kind of change across the region. The increased dependency of local economies on Saudi wealth has important consequences both for the countries themselves and for the region. With falling oil prices, Saudi Arabia is going to face a serious problem that will have implications for domestic spending. The Saudi regime might not be able to maintain subsidies. There is also a growing number of educated young people who need jobs. Whether the Saudis are able to maintain domestic spending at current levels while financing wars abroad remains to be seen.

The rise of religious nationalism that we are seeing is extremely dangerous. Secular nationalism in the Arab world tried to homogenize people from different ethnic and religious groups. It was a complete disaster, because it was linked with dictatorship: you cannot force people to unify under dictatorship. The first victims of the current religious nationalism are religious minorities and those who do not conform to the Saudi model of Islam. Even if you are Sunni, if you do not practice like the Saudis you will have problems. You do not have to be Christian or Yezidi to have problems in the current climate of religious intolerance. Nobody is safe. In a globalized world, with increased movement of people, we may have the same kind of tensions arising in places that are not Arab, principally in Europe and elsewhere.

NOTE

1. WikiLeaks, "Saudi King Abdullah and Senior Princes on Saudi Policy toward Iraq," *WikiLeaks*, April 20, 2008, https://wikileaks.org/plusd/cables/08RIYADH649_a.html.

WORK CITED

WikiLeaks. "Saudi King Abdullah and Senior Princes on Saudi Policy toward Iraq." *WikiLeaks*. April 20, 2008. https://wikileaks.org/plusd/cables/08RIYADH649_a.html.

Chapter 13

Can Religious Pluralism Survive Sectarian War in Syria and Beyond?

(Zurich, March 14, 2016)

Fabrice Balanche

Can religious pluralism survive in the Middle East? Today this question is more relevant than ever. Five years after the Arab uprising, we see that it was not the democratic and secular revolution that we, and a lot of the media, thought it was. On the contrary, we now see it as a "green uprising," an Islamic uprising. Christian communities in the region are concerned about efforts to make shari'a, Islamic law, the main source of legislation. It was tried in Tunisia and in Egypt, it was successful. In Syria, the Christian minority fears an Iraqi scenario that would require them to leave the country or take refuge in protected zones, like Iraqi Kurdistan or what might become an Alawite country.

At the beginning of the twentieth century, there were a lot of religious minorities: in Turkey and what is now Syria and Lebanon. In what became Syria and Lebanon, one-third of the population was Christian. In the course of the past 100 years, most of the Christian minorities have disappeared from these former lands of the Ottoman Empire. The twentieth century was an era of nation-building on the ruins of the Ottoman Empire, and it was the force of nationalism that ended up weakening the Christian minorities in many Muslim countries. For most Arab nationalists, their identity was fundamentally Muslim, not secular. The recent Arab uprisings have confirmed that Islam, not secularism, is the most powerful political force in the Arab Middle East.

The Middle East is at the center of what we call the arc of crisis, a term that dates from the Cold War and the rivalry between the United States and the former Soviet Union. The arc of crisis remains with us today. There is great competition between Iran, Saudi Arabia, and Turkey for domination of the region. We also have two others, Qatar and Israel; however, I regard them as minor actors. The three important players are Shi'ite Iran and what we call the Sunni axis—that is, Saudi Arabia and Turkey. Russia partners with the former, while the United States backs the latter. But the real regional confrontation in Syria and, of course, also in Iraq and Lebanon is not fundamentally between Russia and the United States; it is between Iran, which is the Shi'ite power in the area, and Turkey and Saudi Arabia, the major Sunni powers. Neither Russia nor the United States are strong enough to impose a settlement. Any agreement between Russia and the United States can be undone by the regional actors Saudi Arabia, Turkey, and Iran. Religious minority communities are prisoners of these opposing forces.

In the Muslim world, the Sunnis are dominant: about 90 percent of Muslims are Sunni, and only 10 percent are Shi'ite. The latter are concentrated in Iran, Iraq, Bahrain, and Lebanon, though there are also small pockets of Shi'ites in Yemen, Saudi Arabia, and Syria. Shi'ites are deeply divided into sub-sects: The Twelver Shi'a, Alawites, Druze, Isma'ilis, Zaidis, and many other small communities that are scarcely recognizable as Muslim. For instance, the Alawites—the minority in Syria who are the community of Bashar al-Assad—believe in reincarnation; this belief is hardly the hallmark of Muslim orthodoxy, be it Sunni or Shi'ite.

In the mind of the most traditional Sunnis, Sunni Islam ought to reign supreme. The caliph (*khalifa* in Arabic) is the legitimate successor of Mohammed, and the caliph must be Sunni. There is no caliph now. True, there is the self-proclaimed caliph of the recently formed Islamic State, Abu Bakr al-Baghdadi. But there has been no official caliph since 1924, when Turkey became a republic and Ataturk abolished the caliphate. Yet orthodox Sunnis in the former Ottoman lands think that their rulers must be Sunni Muslims, otherwise they are not legitimate. Even in the officially secular Turkish Republic, the assumption among many traditional Sunni Muslims is that the president of the Turkish Republic must be a Sunni Muslim, that he must belong to the *umma*, that is to say, the Sunni community. They do not recognize any possibility for Christians, Alawites, or Druze to rule or exercise real authority.

Although in some countries, like Iraq, Sunnis are a minority, the traditional Sunnis nevertheless think that the Sunni minority should rule there because they are the majority in the Muslim world; they are the *real* Muslims, and others are heretics. While Jews and Christians are recognized as people belonging to the Holy Book, they are not regarded as full citizens; they are what in Arabic we call *dhimmi*: they are protected by Islam under conditions of submission, but do not have the same rights as Muslims.

If one looks at the map of the religious demography of Anatolia and the Levantine territories of the late Ottoman Empire, an interesting pattern is evident. Sunni Muslims were the dominant community: the caliph in Istanbul was a Sunni, and the governors of the various provinces were also Sunni. The dominant Sunni population tended to live in the cities and in the fertile plains.

The minorities—the Maronites, Druze, Shi'a, and Alawites—were concentrated in the mountains. The mountains were not very rich, and controlling them was not interesting for the authorities. So they let the minorities live in the mountains largely unmolested.

This distribution of the population is still fundamentally the distribution that you find in Syria and Lebanon today, allowing of course for modern migration from the countryside to the city: in the city today you find Alawites, Maronites, and Druze. But the original distribution of the population was minorities at the periphery, the Sunni majority in the center. What does "the center" mean? The city. The city was the true place of power, and it was prohibited for some religious minorities like the Alawites to live in the city. They had a lower status as infidels than Christians and Jews, the so-called People of the Book. Alawites in Syria only started to live in the city during the French Mandate; beforehand, this was forbidden. They started, as Sunnis often describe it, to "invade" the city in the 1960s, after the Ba'athist Revolution. Most of the Ba'athist leaders were Alawite. When they took power, they brought their families and their supporters into the city in order to control it. The Alawite Mountains, the original habitat of the Alawites, was not a wealthy area: it was characterized by small villages without water, growing only wheat and tobacco. One can understand why Alawites support the Assad regime in the Syrian civil war; as many Alawites say, "We do not want to go back to the mountains." The mountains, for them, signify poverty and discrimination.

The traditional city in the Middle East was a *divided* city. The map of Damascus at the beginning of the twentieth century shows three areas: Muslim, Christian, and Jewish. It is often said, "Damascus, in the past, was a mixed city." And yes, there were Muslims, Christians, and Jews there, but they did not live together. Everybody had their own neighborhood. There was only one mixed place, the *souk*, or market, where there were Muslim and Christian traders and shoppers. Economic life was one thing; private life another. In Syria and Lebanon these days, mixed areas are mostly wealthy: the richer you are, the more mixed your area; the poorer you are, the more sectarian your neighborhood. When you see mixed weddings among the middle class, it is a sign—an important sign—of religious pluralism. But when the middle class starts to be destroyed, and becomes more sectarian, it is a negative sign for a society. In the 1990s, I saw the Syrian middle class start to disappear and become more sectarian, and I thought at the time this was bad news for Syria.

Today, the Christian minorities in the Middle East are very small. In Iraq, you have fewer than 300,000 Christians—less than 1 percent of the population. They are concentrated in the north. In Syria in 1945, 20 percent of the population was Christian. In 2010, it was 5 percent, and today it is about

3 percent. There are about 6 million refugees outside Syria, 80 percent of whom are Sunnis, of course, because the Sunni community is about two-thirds of the Syrian population. But Christians make up 9 percent of the refugees. Why is this? Because the Christian community in Syria does not control territory like the Alawites or the Druze. The Syrian Christians are very weak, and they lack the armed militias that other sectarian communities have established to defend themselves. If Christians survive at all in Syria today, it is because they have a militia—like in Hasakah in the northeast, or the militias created by the Syrian Social Nationalist Party in the region around Homs—that looks after their community.

Why did the Christian population in Syria go from 20 percent in 1945 to 5 percent in 2010? It is not mainly because of discrimination. Since the collapse of the Ottoman Empire, Christians in Syria have not been discriminated against, neither in the French Mandate nor in the Republic. The Ba'athists certainly did not discriminate against Christians. The decline can be accounted for as a natural demographic trend. The first factor in this trend is that Christians in Syria have the advantage of a very good education, thanks to the Protestant, Catholic, or Russian Orthodox missions that flourished in the nineteenth and early twentieth centuries. If you are well-educated, you usually have fewer children. If you can speak French or English, you can emigrate more easily than others. The second factor has to do with what we call the demographic transition: the birth rate remains very high, the mortality rate decreases very fast, and for a short period the population increases very rapidly. The Christian community went through its demographic transition in the nineteenth century; in the twentieth century, this process was finished, because the fertility rate of the Christian community became very low.

By contrast, the Muslim society went through its demographic transition during the twentieth century. That is why there is a difference between the population growth of Muslims and Christians in many countries in the Middle East. But if the Christians had a short demographic transition, Shi'ite-related minorities like the Alawites also went through the transition very quickly. The same is true of the Druze. Their fertility rate is very low compared to the Sunnis. In the Sunni-dominated area of Dara'a, the fertility rate is around eight children per woman; in Idlib and in Raqqa, it is also about eight children per woman; whereas in the Alawite and Druze areas, it is only two or three. Among Syrian Christians, it is under two children per woman. So the Christian minority that was 20 percent of the Syrian population in 1945 was down to 5 percent by 2010. One finds similar demographic patterns in Lebanon.

Minorities in the Middle East were manipulated by French and British imperialism after the defeat and breakup of the Ottoman Empire. France took over what became Syria and Lebanon, and Great Britain took what became Jordan and Palestine. They divided the area into small states. In Syria, France created an Alawite state of 300,000 people on the coast, where the Alawites were two-thirds of the population. They created a Druze state of only 50,000 people. Lebanon at this time had a population of less than one million. It was a state that served the interests of the Christian majority. Arab nationalism was then a growing force, and France believed that if it created states for certain minorities, the minorities would feel obliged to support France and would not press for the establishment of a Greater Syria, including Lebanon and Palestine, because they would be afraid of Sunni domination. However, the powerful elements within the religious minorities thought secular Arab nationalism could be a safe alternative to Sunni domination; thus they agreed to belong to the new state of Syria. In Lebanon, it was the national agreement between the Sunnis, the Christians, and the Shi'ites that produced the foundation of the new state. Arab nationalism, encompassing all religious communities, emerged to challenge European colonialism.

When the new states of Syria and Lebanon became independent, the fight against French colonialism ended, and the fight for power inside these countries began. One tendency was secular and was represented by the Ba'ath and Syrian Social Nationalist Parties. Both were founded by members of minorities. The other tendency was a Muslim-oriented Arab nationalism, as espoused by Nasser in Egypt. We have to understand that in the Middle East, ideologies are, in fact, smokescreens for sectarian interests. Why do minorities belong to this or that party? It is usually because one party seems to offer better protection against Sunni domination. Why do Sunnis belong to this or that party? It is usually because they feel that one party or the other will promote their sectarian interests. The Communist parties in Lebanon and Syria were founded by people from the Greek Orthodox community. Why? Because the Greek Orthodox had a special relationship with Moscow. Before the Bolshevik Revolution, the Greek Orthodox in the Levant enjoyed the protection of the Czar of Russia. After 1917, Orthodox Christians still tended to lean toward Moscow, and they do so up to today, because Russia—regardless of the ideology of its rulers—has protected the Orthodox of the region.

The Soviet Union used the Orthodox community everywhere in the Middle East as partners, as allies. At the beginning of the 1990s, the Communist Party in Syria exploded. One branch was still pro-Soviet, even though the Soviet Union did not exist anymore. Another branch was more Euro-Communist, like Berlinguer in France. But actually, the division was between Khalid Baqdash and the Kurds, and Yusuf Faysal and the Christians. When the Communist Party in Syria exploded, it exploded along sectarian lines. The ideological pretext was just that—a pretext. So it is important always to have a sectarian view of political movements in the region, because sectarianism is the basis of society. Denial of sectarian realities leads one down blind alleys.

When the Syrian uprising started, most observers seemed to think it was a revolution for Western-style democracy—that people were fighting against dictatorship. Very few people said: "Be careful, it is really a sectarian war!" Christians, Alawites, and Druze tended to stay away from the uprising; the Kurds protested, but they also stayed away from the Arab opposition, because they have their own agenda, which is a Kurdish state. As a result, there was no unity between the Kurds and the Arab opposition, which does not want to give any autonomy to the Kurds. Today, the Kurds are not members of the Syrian National Coalition.

Sectarian realities are crucial for understanding the uprising of 2011. The coastal province of Latakia is the Alawite heartland of Syria. It is from there that the Assad family comes. The provincial capital, also called Latakia, has an Alawite majority, but a large Sunni minority. Christians make up about 10 percent of the city. When the uprising began, the Western media focused primarily on events in the overwhelmingly Sunni area around Dara'a, in the south. But there were also protests in the countryside around the predominantly Sunni town Baniyas in Alawite-dominated Latakia. Protests erupted only in Sunni areas; in the Alawite areas, there were no protests. While the Western media focused on Deraa, few paid any attention to Baniyas. The uprising in Baniyas was clearly sectarian; the population was vengeful against Alawites who surrounded them. The open displays of Sunni sectarianism did not conform to the narrative put out by Western supporters of the Syrian opposition; hence the media paid little attention to what was happening in Baniyas.

In spring 2011, I was in Syria, and I saw the protests in Latakia. The city of Latakia has a few mixed areas such as the South Corniche, a wealthy area close to the sea. The uprising was very violent in al-Ramel al-Falastini and al-Ramel al-Janubi, poor areas in the Sunni neighborhood of the city. Protesters came from this neighborhood and tried to invade the center of the city. Sunni middle class people had been protesting too, but when they saw poor Sunnis invading the city, the middle class went back home. They did not want to protest with the poor. It was a sectarian uprising, but it was also clearly a social uprising, and Sunni businessmen I spoke to in Latakia told me they would rather support Assad, because he had liberalized the economy and they were very happy with the new economic policy in Syria. They were afraid the uprising would destroy the country—which of course has happened. This class-based reality in Latakia demonstrates that the war in Syria is not exclusively sectarian; it was also a socioeconomic uprising, supported by the poorer Arab Sunni population and rejected by many of the more prosperous Sunnis.[1]

Why did the Alawites not join the uprising? First, because of their fear of Sunni domination; and second, because 90 percent of Alawites work for the state: they are in the army, in the civil service, they work in national-ized industries. Over the course of 20 years, the Alawites went from being marginalized, illiterate peasants living in very poor conditions in the moun-tains, to being middle class, thanks to their promotion by the regime. They do not have massive wealth, but their transition from the terrible conditions they experienced before to the middle class has been a huge step, and that is why they are loyal to the government. They do not want to go back to being poor, persecuted peasants in the mountains. Since so many of them work in the army, the secret service, and the administration, the Syrian army and the rest of the state did not disintegrate like, for instance, happened in Libya. As soon as the Libyan uprising began, the Libyan army splintered. But the Syrian army has stayed unified. There have been a lot of deserters, of course, but very few officers have left the army. Some journalists reported that 50 generals left the Syrian army in 2011–2012. The people who left were close to retirement age, they were Sunnis, their commands were not very strategic, and Qatar and Saudi Arabia gave them a lot of money to join the Free Syrian Army. Some Alawite intellectuals decided to join the Syrian Revolution, but they are very few in number, and they are mostly in France: they did not stay in Syria, and they have no social base in the country. Alawites know that the victory of the majority, the Arab Sunnis, would mean the re-Islamization of society and their exclusion from Syrian state institutions.

Alawites support Bashar al-Assad not because they love him, but because they do not have any choice. Christians and Druze are in the same position. The only other choice they have is to leave the country. Christians tend to leave because they do not have a stronghold, a territory, where they can remain with security. They also leave because they mainly live in the cit-ies, and this is an urban war. Take the city of Homs. It has Alawite and Christian areas. It also has a mixed wealthy area. The center of Homs was largely destroyed by the fighting. The rebels invaded the center and expelled most of the Christian community. Some of the displaced Christians left the country immediately; if they had relatives in Lebanon, they went there and applied for visas for Canada, France, and elsewhere. Others took refuge in Wadi al-Nasara, meaning "Valley of the Christians," a mountainous area where many urban Christians already had houses they used during summer holidays. Some took refuge in towns with Christian inhabitants, like Sadad or al-Qaryatayn, but when Islamic State attacked both villages in 2015, these people had to move again.

The difficulty for Christians in Syria is that they were a small community who are widely dispersed. It is more difficult to be protected when you are in a small village in the midst of Sunnis than when you are in the midst of another minority like the Druze or the Alawites. In Aleppo, the fighting was also in the center of the city. There you had the Armenians, who make up about half of the Christian community of Aleppo. Most of the Armenians from Aleppo have left Syria for Armenia. I was in Yerevan, the capital of Armenia, in 2015, and I met many people from Aleppo: they have opened shops and restaurants, and they do not intend to return to Syria, even though there are severe economic problems in Armenia. Some are waiting for visas to Canada or the United States. Many people said they would never go back to Aleppo, because they were afraid of the future; there could be peace tomorrow, but in 10 or 20 years' time, there could be another hostile, sectarian uprising.

The demographic trends are clear: I do not think the fertility rate of the Christian minority will increase fast enough to rebalance the demography of Syria. In areas like the north of Syria, most of the minorities will probably disappear. In a Christian area like Wadi al-Nasara, Christians might be able to survive because it is in the Alawite Mountains, and no threat is to be expected from the Alawite community.

I have in mind a church building in Tartus that dates from the Crusades in the Middle Ages. When the Crusaders left Tartus in the thirteenth century, this church was transformed into a mosque, but now it is a museum. It is built like a fortress; the Crusaders built it to serve as protection. I think this church illustrates the situation of Christians in the Middle East: they think of themselves as besieged in a fortress, surrounded by a generally hostile Muslim world. Religious pluralism will be hard-pressed to survive in the region. The Christians are just one set of victims. What happened to the Yezidi minority in Iraq is likely to happen to the Druze and the Alawites in Syria, too.

When speaking about the plight of the religious minorities, we should not forget that secular Sunnis are also victims of the jihadism that runs rampant in Syria today. For example, in Damascus I met a lawyer from Raqqa. He, like all the other lawyers in Raqqa, was obliged to leave the city because they were considered to be enemies of the Islamic State. In the eyes of these radical Islamists, such lawyers were specialists in the secular law of the Syrian Republic, not shari'a law. This was the only reason for them being classified as enemies.

Religious diversity is threatened in Syria and the rest of the Middle East by the jihadist movement, by fundamentalism. This movement also poses a grave threat to secular Sunnis. In Syria and Iraq, religious pluralism can be maintained for the time being by authoritarian states that protect minorities. Alawites are a minority in Syria, but the Alawite Bashar al-Assad protects all minorities, not just his own. In Iraq, the Shi'ite majority now dominates the state. Since the overthrow of Saddam Hussein, state-building in Iraq has actually become *Shi'ite* state-building. Arab Sunnis have little space in this new state. The prime minister is Shi'ite, and of course he gives the power and the jobs to the Shi'ite community. Arab Sunnis are marginalized in the new power structure. The Kurds prefer to build up their own state, and right now, Kurdistan is quite independent from Baghdad. The Kurdish desire for independence is supported neither by the United States nor Iran, but Iraqi Kurds do not need formal independence; they *are* independent.

The Middle East is in a new Thirty Years' War, as Europe experienced in the seventeenth century. The Thirty Years' War started in Prague, with a problem between Calvinists, Catholics, and Unitarians. France, a Catholic country, supported the Protestant princes in Germany, because she wanted to fight against the Habsburgs. Sweden intervened, and an internal religious sectarian problem in Central Europe became an international problem. A comparable situation exists in the Middle East today. The socioeconomic and sectarian problems that gave rise to the 2011 uprisings are being manipulated by regional powers that want to expand their influence at a time when the United States' influence in the region is diminishing. This conflict could destroy many states in the Middle East. It is difficult to imagine that Iraq and Syria will remain unified.

Ralph Peters, an American researcher, has drawn a map of a possible new Middle East that gives us an indication of what could happen in the region after 20 or 30 years of war: namely, the destruction of existing states and the creation of new states from ethnic and religious territories.[2] In Iraq now, there are three distinct territories: Shi'a, Arab Sunni, and Kurdish. In Syria, at a minimum, there will be a Kurdish territory in the north and, if the Assad regime falls, there could also be an Alawite state on the coast and a Druze state in the south, as there was during the French Mandate period. Ethnic cleansing is happening very extensively: there are no more Christians or Shi'ites living in Islamic State and al-Nusra Front areas—that means most of the rebel-controlled areas of Syria. The small Druze communities close to Idlib were obliged to convert to Sunnism if they wanted to survive. Many Sunnis have taken refuge in government-controlled parts of Damascus, Homs, and Latakia, because there is greater security there. Whether they are secular Sunnis or religious people, they believe in religious diversity and not in fundamentalism. But the coexistence between religions that they espouse is challenged by the rise of the fundamentalist movement.

Is appeasement an option? Many people say: "If we just let the Syrians live together, we could have a peace agreement." This is not realistic. Syria is not an island, and its neighbors Turkey, Saudi Arabia, and Iran will never let a Syrian deal hold because the war in Syria is also a proxy war between these three powers. So unfortunately, minorities, and particularly the Christians in the Middle East, are the victims, and they will remain the victims during decades of conflict. What is really happening now is that minorities are either migrating or, if they can control a large enough territory, building up their own de facto states. I am very pessimistic about religious diversity in this area.

NOTES

1. Also see my article "Géographie de la révolte syrienne," *Outre-Terre*, no. 29 (2011): 437–58.
2. See Ralph Peters, "Blood borders. How a better Middle East would look," *Armed Forces Journal*, vol. 144, no. 2 (June 2006).

WORKS CITED

Balanche, Fabrice. "Géographie de la révolte syrienne." *Outre-Terre*, no. 29 (2011): 437–58.
Peters, Ralph. "Blood borders. How a better Middle East would look." *Armed Forces Journal*, vol. 144, no. 2 (June 2006).

Chapter 14

ISIS, Christians, and National Identity in the Middle East

(Boston, April 7, 2016)

Joshua Landis

I want to make an argument that I hope will explain a little bit about what is going on in Iraq and Syria and where ISIS comes from. I will talk about identity and national formation—that is, nation-building—and ignore many other issues that are very important to understanding Syria: socioeconomic and economic issues, country versus city, and so on. All these aspects are crucial to understanding the dynamics of the Syrian civil war, ISIS, and what is happening to Christians in the region, but I am going to focus on identity because I think it is one of the key elements.

Let me make a comparison between what happened in Central Europe during and after World War II and what is happening in the Levant states today. First of all, if we look at the map from Poland to Palestine, we notice that all of these nation-states were created in 1919 at the Paris Peace Conference, out of multiethnic, multireligious empires that were destroyed. World War I was the empire-destroying war: the Russian Empire, the German Empire, the Austro-Hungarian Empire, and, of course—most important for our story—the Ottoman Empire. These were lands that did not lend themselves to national borders based on ethnicity or religion.

In Central Europe before World War II, Poland was 64 percent Polish; by the end of World War II, it was 100 percent Polish. Czechoslovakia: 32 percent of the population was minorities before World War II; by the end of the war, all those minorities were gone. And that is the way it was throughout Central Europe. The borders did not change so much as the people were changed to fit the borders. There were giant waves of refugees. We know about the six million Jews that were exterminated as this "Great Sorting Out,"[1] as I call it, took place. After World War II ended, between 1945 and 1947, 12 million Germans were ethnically cleansed from Central Europe. 3 million Sudeten Germans in Czechoslovakia: all gone. The Polish Germans, an even bigger population: all gone. Half a million Germans in Romania and Yugoslavia: all ethnically cleansed. Even little Crimea had a population that was 5 percent German. Hitler occupied it, and used those Germans as a collaborative elite to help him rule; when Stalin retook Crimea, all those Germans were either marched to Siberia, or killed, or they fled. Their situation was similar to that of the Palestinians in Kuwait. When Saddam invaded in 1990, there were some 300,000 Palestinians, some of whom were used as a collaborative elite. As soon as Saddam was driven out, the Kuwaitis kicked out all the Palestinians; they ended up mainly in Jordan. So the Great Sorting Out in Europe, long and bloody, has constant parallels elsewhere. For minorities, such processes are always a zero-sum game. One could even perhaps argue that what is going on in Ukraine right now is the end of this Great Sorting Out in Europe: nation-building in the ruins of multiethnic, multireligious empires.

How did the sorting out happen in the Ottoman Empire? In the Levant especially, it had a particular coloration. In every one of what became the Levantine states—Syria, Iraq, Jordan, Lebanon, Israel–Palestine—minorities were given a leg up by the colonial powers. Britain took what became Iraq, Jordan, and Palestine. France took what became Lebanon and Syria. Britain and France practiced divide-and-rule by promoting the minorities, and when they left at the end of World War II, minorities either grabbed the state or got the lion's share of power in every one of the Levantine states. I would argue that, in part, the "Arab Spring," the continuing consequences of the American invasion of Iraq, and, earlier, the civil war in Lebanon, amount to the majority population trying to throw off minoritarian rule and re-adjudicate the sectarian or communal balance of power in these societies.

I am often accused of embracing primordial identities. But I argue that what we are witnessing is a new phenomenon. Nationalism and nation-building are historically quite new phenomena! It starts with the French Revolution, then the American Revolution, and comes like an earthquake, reorganizing the map of the world. Before this, there were no nation-states as we know them today. The world had bishoprics, emirates, caliphates, empires, clans, tribal entities, free cities—all sorts of political arrangements, but not nations. All these earlier structures were destroyed in the modern period. If one asks what represents modernity in international relations, the answer has to be the nation-state. Today there are 193 states represented in the United Nations. The world has been chopped up with a nation-state cookie cutter, and that is the way it works today. Governments represent their people. Before this, there were sovereigns who ruled over their subjects. But under the concept of nationalism brought in with the French Revolution, sovereignty lies with the people. The subjects are now the rulers, and we call our government's public servants, servants of the people. This is a radical change, and it was bound to cause major upsets and revolutions. Most of the wars we have seen in the last 200 years are wars about borders: which people are in, constituting the sovereign people, and which people are out.

Anatolia (today's Turkey), at the head of the Ottoman Empire, was 20 percent Christian in 1914, before World War I. By the end of the Turkish national revolution, in 1923, there were no more Christians in Anatolia. 3 million Christians had been exterminated or ethnically cleansed. We know about the Armenians, who of course were accused of being a fifth column and helping the Russians in World War I; the Turks exterminated them, or marched them out to Syria. Some of them survived in Aleppo and elsewhere, but most of them died. At the end of World War I, Greece thought it could conquer Anatolia and rebuild the Byzantine Empire, presumably converting Anatolia back to Christianity. This experiment ended in disaster: Mustafa Kemal Ataturk built a Turkish army and rekindled Turkish nationalism, and as his army marched through Anatolia, all the Greek Orthodox who had lived there for 2,000 years were driven out. A million and a half went to Greece, many fled to Syria and elsewhere, and 800,000 Muslims from the former Greek provinces of the Ottoman Empire were transferred to Anatolia. At the time, there were only four million Greeks to begin with. One out of every four Greeks today is actually of Anatolian descent, which is why the enmity between Greece and Turkey is still so bitter. Turkey is still trying to digest the Kurds. (Turkey claims they are simply mountain Turks and so forth). Thus, the nation-building process in Anatolia is not yet complete.

Before 1973, Cyprus was a mosaic of Muslims and Christians living side by side in villages. After the Turkish invasion in 1973, we have the Great Sorting Out. Now all the Muslims live in the north, all the Christians live in the south, and there is not any mixing whatsoever.

Lebanon is the Noah's Ark of the Levant. The last census ever taken in Lebanon was in 1932, and it showed the Christians as a slight majority. Based on that, the French colonial power was able to give the Maronite Christians, the Catholics, the lion's share of power. According to Lebanon's 1943 "National Pact," the President and the army chief of staff have to be Maronite, and 6 out of every 11 members of parliament have to be Christian. By 1975, when the Civil War began in Lebanon, the population had become majority Muslim, and they demanded one person, one vote—in other words, democracy. In the name of democracy, they wanted to push the Christians off their privileged perch. Fifteen long and bloody years of war was ended by the Taif Accord, which established 50–50 division of parliament—for every Christian, there is a Muslim. At that point, Lebanon had 4.5 million people: a third Christian, a third Shi'ite, and a third Sunni. Today there are a million plus Syrian refugees, the vast majority of whom are Sunni. They are not going to go home. This will change the balance of power, in the same way that the 1948 Palestinian refugees upended the balance of power and helped kindle the Civil War in 1975. The Lebanese story is far from over.

In Iraq, when the British created the state and installed King Faisal, they put the Sunnis at the top. Sunni Arabs are roughly 20 percent of the population, Shi'ite Arabs 60 percent, and the Kurds in the north 20 percent. Sunnis had had the lion's share of power in the region under the Ottomans, and they simply continued to. Saddam Hussein was a Sunni, leading the Ba'ath Party in a single-party state that was in fact an instrument for enshrining Sunni power. The Iraqi army was an instrument of Sunni domination, with much of the officer corps being Sunnis from Tikrit, like Saddam.

When America swarmed into Iraq in 2003, in the name of promoting democracy and power-sharing, what they did, in essence, was to cast the Sunnis from the top of society down to the bottom, and catapult the Shi'ites from the bottom of society to the top. Saddam was hunted down, the Ba'ath Party was made illegal and its members criminalized, and the army was disbanded. The army and the state were to be rebuilt under Maliki and others—in other words, around Shi'ites. Sunnis in Iraq, completely disenfranchised and pushed to the margins of society, turned to al-Qaeda. America helped to destroy al-Qaeda in Iraq, but as soon as they left in 2010, the Shi'ites drove out what Sunnis had remained, as a result of which Sunnis were radicalized again. When ISIS swept in in 2014, it barely fired a shot in order to take Fallujah and all the Sunni cities and reoccupy that area. In essence, America today is arming the Shi'ites to kill and drive out the Sunnis. We say, "We are going to do power-sharing and build a new Iraq, with everybody joining in," but that is not what is happening. The Kurds have de facto independence, and the Sunnis are being destroyed. It's a long and bloody zero-sum game for minorities.

Israel–Palestine: the Jews today are a majority, but in 1850, about 5 percent of Palestine was Jewish. In 1914, the figure was 15 percent; by 1948, when the British left, Jews constituted about one-third of the population. Palestinians were two-thirds of the population, and believed they would be able to dominate and rule over the Jews, but the 1948 war ended in a terrible disaster for the Palestinians: 800,000 people, two-thirds of the entire Palestinian population, fled or were driven out and became refugees, never to be allowed back.

The Jews are the only minority in the Middle East that has been able to turn themselves from a minority into a majority. But that is, of course, because Jews have been sorted out, not only in Europe, where six million were killed, but also throughout the Muslim Middle East. In Baghdad in 1914, the largest single religious community was the Jewish community. Damascus and Aleppo had thriving Jewish quarters. The mother of the American comic Jerry Seinfeld is from Aleppo. America was a recipient of emigrants coming from the Great Sorting Out of Jews from the Arab world. But so was Israel. Palestinians lost the zero-sum game, and have been fighting ever since 1948 to get a share of Palestine. They probably will not—but I do not know. Maybe there will be a two-state solution, but it does not look very likely. Again, it is a zero-sum game for minorities, a Great Sorting Out, long and bloody.

In Syria, the important minority are the Alawites, about 10–12 percent of the Syrian population. (The last census that recorded religion was in 1960; we are all basing our figures on the 1960 census.) Syrians are not allowed to ask about religion in a census. The Alawites are a Shi'ite heterodox sect who previously experienced very radical demographic segregation. Before the French occupied Syria in 1920, the Alawites lived in no village larger than 200 people. All the cities of the coast—Latakia, Jableh, Baniyas, and Tartus—were Sunni cities with a small Christian minority, but no Alawites. The Alawites were servants and so forth, but they lived in strict segregation up in the mountains and, like the Druze and Isma'ilis, were not considered true Muslims.

In an American context, we would think the comparable sect are the Mormons. The Alawites had a book, they had a prophet, and a liberal would say: "Fine. They are Muslims." The Alawites say: "We believe in the Qur'an, we believe in Mohammed, we are Muslim." But fundamentalists do not agree.

In Syria, Hafez al-Assad, an Alawite, had installed himself as president in 1970. In 1973, he tried to change Article 3 of the Constitution, which says that the president has to be a Muslim. The result was giant demonstrations from Aleppo down to Damascus, led by the Muslim Brotherhood. Assad ended his attempt to change the Constitution, but said, "I am a Muslim, and anybody who says I am not, will be shot." That is the way it was in Syria ever since, until the "Arab Spring," when almost all the rebel groups felt free to call the Alawites *Nusayri*, a pejorative name for Shi'ites. *Majusi* is another favorite pejorative (*magi*, the Persian kings from the east that visited Jesus, has the same origins). *Majusi* means pre-Islamic Persians, and to use it in relation to Alawites is to associate them with non-Arab, non-Islamic, Zoroastrian Persians.

When the French took control of Syria, the Alawites were the poorest of the poor. They got to the top because the French drafted them into the military. The French needed to create an army in order to suppress the Arab nationalist movement that was led by Sunnis from the city in the 1920s. Who went into this French army? Men from the minorities: Armenians, Druze, Isma'ilis, Alawites, plus Sunnis from the countryside who were willing to shoot at urban notable nationalists in the cities. When the French left, the Alawites were a big minority in the army, and by 1955, 65 percent of the non-commissioned officers were Alawite. Syria was very unstable; there were a lot of coups until 1970, and the Alawites moved up the ranks very quickly as others at the top were purged.

Since 1970, the Alawites have ruled through the Ba'ath Party. When Hafez al-Assad died in 2000, the presidency passed to his son Bashar al-Assad. The vast majority of top generals are Alawite. The Ba'ath Party became an instrument for minorities; now they also help the Christians. Many other minorities—Isma'ilis, Druze, and Kurds—were given a leg up under the Assads. In the current civil war, the minorities tend to support Assad. The Syrian rebel militias are Sunni Arab, and largely from the countryside rather than urban centers. The split between minorities and the Arab Sunni majority is one of the characteristics that define this revolution.

This Great Sorting Out has hit Middle Eastern Christians hard. In Egypt in 1910, the Copts were more than 15 percent of the population. Today they are a little bit less than 10 percent, we believe. In Syria, Christians have gone from being about 15 percent in 1945 to probably less than 5 percent. Palestine: the Christians have gone. Iraq: when the United States invaded in 2003, there were probably about a million and a half Christians; today, there are 400,000 or 300,000 Christians in Iraq—less than a third of the number before the invasion. Christians are being driven out in this Great Sorting Out, just as Jews were before them. But there are many other minority groups in Iraq that have almost disappeared as well. It is well known that when ISIS took over its present territory, Yezidi women were enslaved, many men were killed, and the rest were driven out. In Mosul, when ISIS took over, 60,000 Christians fled in one day and lost all their possessions on the way, because their rings and any other valuables they were carrying were taken off them at roadblocks.

In Syria today the government-controlled area is the Alawite heartland and the coastal cities. Probably about 65–70 percent of the current population of Syria lives in the government-controlled area. Non-ISIS rebel militias are concentrated in Aleppo, Idlib, Homs, Dara'a, and al-Suwayda provinces. The Kurds control pockets of territory along the border with Turkey. ISIS has the big desert region along the Euphrates, from Raqqa, their capital, all the way through Deir ez-Zor and down through Iraq. The Sunni parts of Iraq all opened their doors to ISIS, and ISIS took over in one summer, with almost no shots fired. Their advance was stopped by the Shi'ites and by the Kurds, both in Syria and in Iraq. On the government-controlled coast, there is a mixed population of Alawites and Christians, but also many Sunnis. The wealthier upper-middle-class Sunnis, worried about losing their possessions and their privilege, have by and large stayed with Assad. The uprising is led by poor Sunnis from the countryside.

Let me repeat: The United States is helping the government in Baghdad, a Shi'ite sectarian government, to destroy the state and cut it in two, while maintaining the fiction of internationally recognized borders. Meanwhile, Russia is helping Assad's very sectarian heterodox Shi'ite government destroy its Sunni opponents, ISIS as well as the rebel groups. People are being moved so that the borders, which are UN-mandated and legally fixed, do not have to be shifted; the international community does not want to have to carve up the Middle East again and recognize new states. The big Sunni population between Baghdad and Aleppo is stuck between two bookends of Shi'ites who are getting international support to crush the Sunni attempt to become an independent nation, and the Sunnis are getting smashed in the process. In Ramadi, which was conquered by the Iraqi army early in 2016, not one house was left standing after America had bombed and the Iraqi militias and military had gone in. That might not technically be ethnic cleansing, but it is very close.

ISIS represents a radical interpretation of Islam that appeals to Sunnis and characterizes Shi'ites as non-Muslims, as evil. There is demonization by both sides, because Shi'ites call the Sunnis jihadists, terrorists, Saudi fifth colum-nists—every bad name in the book. The new national identities are religiously based instead of ethnically based, as they were in Europe. Religious identity is putting itself forward: Jews against Muslims, Alawites and Shi'ites against Sunnis, Christians clinging to the coat-tails of dictators, and other minorities who are fearful of getting driven out as the elephants fight each other.

I do not know how this will all work out. What can Washington really do? What can American power do? We have seen American power save Yezidis from complete destruction and drive back ISIS; we can tweak around the edges, do a little bit here, do a little bit there. Still, the United States failed in its major effort, which was to create democracy in Iraq. We foolishly thought that we would get Iraqis to embrace each other and treat each other as equals, that we could destroy a very tyrannical state. It turned out that that state was holding the country together, and regime change to promote democracy at the end of a whip has not worked. Think of Libya, think of Yemen: we negoti-ated out the leader of Yemen; we bombed and left in Libya. We occupied and tried to rebuild in Iraq; we did the same thing in Afghanistan. But we have not had success, in part because in this Great Sorting Out process we have launched terrible civil wars that we do not understand and we cannot control. We still think we can rebuild Iraqi nationalism, that we will be able to get Kurds, Shi'ites, and Sunnis to live together. It just seems improbable. Can Humpty Dumpty be put back together? America presumes that it can: that there will be a political solution. That Assad will probably leave, but the Alawites will stay and the military will stay. But will they embrace the Sunni rebels and somehow live together in a unitary state? It is not at all clear how that can be achieved.

I think Obama has been wise to keep the United States from further inter-vention in Syria. He called for regime change, and then he thought better of it. He thought that Assad would fall on his own and that he would be on the right side of history, without having to do much. But once it became clear that only America would be able to get Assad out, he got cold feet. He said: "I do not want to own Syria, because then I would have to destroy all these different militias and groupings and build a new state. This will be a very costly enterprise." There are 1,500 militias in the rebellion, according to the CIA.[3] One would have to unify all these different tribes and militias, many of which are fighting each other as well as fighting Assad. We tried to do that in Iraq, and it is very expensive. Obama said the United States is not going to do it. It is a bad deal, as Trump would say. We are going to stay at home and build the middle class, not the Middle East.

NOTES

1. Also see my guest commentary, "The Great Sorting Out: Ethnicity & the Future of the Levant," *Qifa Nabki*, December 18, 2013, https://qifanabki.com/2013/12/18/landis-ethnicity/.

2. Just like America: we do not know how many Muslims or Jews there are in America. We can guess, but we do not know from the census.

3. As estimated by the then Director of National Intelligence, James R. Clapper, in 2014. See James R. Clapper, "Current and Future Worldwide Threats to the National Security of the United States, delivered to the Senate Armed Services Committee," *Public Affairs Office—Office of the Director of National Intelligence*, February 11, 2014, http://cryptome.org/2014 /02/dni-14-0211.pdf.

WORKS CITED

Clapper, James R. "Current and Future Worldwide Threats to the National Security of the United States, delivered to the Senate Armed Services Committee." *Public Affairs Office—Office of the Director of National Intelligence*. February 11, 2014. http://cryptome.org/2014/02/dni-14–0211.pdf.

Landis, Joshua. "The Great Sorting Out: Ethnicity & the Future of the Levant." *Qifa Nabki*. December 18, 2013. https://qifanabki.com/2013/12/18/landis-ethnicity/.

Chapter 15

The Persecution of Christians in Today's Middle East

(Zurich, May 4, 2016)

Daniel Williams

On the eve of the American-led invasion of Iraq in 2003, John Paul II sent an envoy to Washington, Cardinal Pio Laghi, to explain what would happen to Christians and other religious minorities in Iraq if Saddam Hussein was overthrown. It is not that the Pope liked Saddam Hussein, but he understood the dynamics of Iraq. He was gravely concerned for the future of Iraqi Christians and their country. President George W. Bush showed scant interest in the papal message. One of the President's aides turned to the papal envoy as he was being ushered out of the meeting and said, "Do not worry; it is going to be all over in a trice. And listen, we are with you on the issue of abortion." During the invasion and occupation, the Bush administration never responded to the needs of the Iraqi Christians or any of the other religious minorities— the Yezidis, the Sabeans, etc. All of these ancient religious communities were ignored.

Fast forward to March 2016. US Secretary of State, John Kerry, then declared that Christians and Yezidis in Iraq and Syria were victims of genocide. This would have been encouraging, except for one important detail: in almost the same breath, Secretary Kerry said that the United States would do nothing much about it. These are the kinds of events that made me entitle my book *Forsaken* (New York and London: OR Books, 2016). Christians and other minorities in the Middle East have been abandoned to a terrible fate, while Washington and other powers pursue destabilizing interventionist policies under the cover of slogans like "transition to democracy." Vulnerable religious minorities have no means to protect themselves and no guardians on whom they can count. Their future is grim across what was the homeland of Christianity.

Take the conflict areas of Iraq and Syria. Christians have no reliable defenders in Iraq. I was reminded of this when I was recently in the north of the country. I asked many Christians about their commitment to remaining in the Middle East. After all, the bishops urge their people to remain in the land stretching between Iraq and Egypt since it is a Christian "holy land," and stress the importance of bearing witness there. The answer of one brave Catholic priest summed up the consensus view. First he told me that he had been kidnapped several years ago in Baghdad. As happened to many priests and ordinary Christians, he was held for ransom. When it began to look as if he would not be ransomed, his kidnappers took a hammer and broke his nose, broke his teeth, and broke his back. And they refused him water for four days. You can do without food for four days, but four days without water would normally kill you. He is a tough guy and survived, and eventually his parish in Baghdad got 85,000 US dollars together and paid the ransom.

Following his release, this priest went back to his home town Mosul. Today, since all the Christians have been driven out of Mosul, he tends to Christian refugees at a church in Erbil, Kurdistan. I asked him, "Should Christians stay?" He answered, "Stay—to prove what? What is it to remain if you cannot worship, if you are forced to pay special taxes, if you cannot live in dignity? Our bishops are fooling us, and themselves, by urging people to stay. If we have to live the same life in Mosul and the villages around as before, we will remain enslaved. Iraq is not for Christians anymore." And he is right. Iraq is no longer for Christians. In the 13 years since Washington launched Operation Iraqi Freedom, the Christian population has plummeted from over one million to roughly a quarter of that figure. Most of those who remain see no future for themselves and their families in their homeland and want to leave.

Syria looks more and more like war-torn Iraq. Much of the country is occupied by various anti-government militias; most are also anti-Christian. Virtually all of these rebel-controlled areas are now devoid of Christians and other religious minorities. In Syria, they have a protector of sorts, the government, but it is an advocate that is embroiled in a very vicious civil war. Is the government of Syria concerned about the fate of Christians? Perhaps. But the war in Syria has been so catastrophic, it is hard to imagine that Christians should have any illusions about their future, no matter what the outcome of the war is.

It is not only in war-torn Syria and Iraq where Middle Eastern Christians have grave problems. In Egypt, Christians are persecuted even though the country has not been at war for many years. They are subject to mob rule and corrupt police. Persecution is not government policy, but what I found in my long experience (I lived for 10 years in Egypt) is that the state does not actually protect Christians. They suffer persecution by omission. The police do not defend them. You can kill a Christian, take his property, burn down his house or his church, and you can do all of these things with impunity.

When a church in Alexandria was bombed on New Year's Eve 2010–2011, what was Mubarak's response? He said, "Oh, some crazy people did this." This is always the response from Egyptian authorities: anyone who attacks Christians is simply mad; it has nothing to do with Islamic radicalism. The Egyptian government is reluctant to prosecute Muslims for crimes against Christians, and the police tend to sympathize with Muslims. In any case, Egypt is not a country of the rule of law, neither under Nasser, nor Sadat, nor under Mubarak, and finally, not under his successor Abdel Fattah el-Sisi. Equality under the law was one of the demands of the young Coptic Christians who were involved in the Tahrir Square demonstrations in the early days of the "Arab Spring." Safety, not to mention equality, does not appear to be on the horizon.

So it is in Palestine. Christians in the Occupied Territories are also under great pressure from hostile forces. The population has been decreasing over decades because of economic issues produced by the endless conflict with Israel, the isolation of living under occupation, the desire of parents for their children to be educated somewhere else as a way of moving forward, and so on. These are chronic issues for the Palestinians in what remains of historic Palestine. These concerns have now been aggravated by fears that the Islamic State, and related ultra-conservative Islamic movements—the Salafis, the Wahhabis—have infiltrated the Palestinian movement.

Hamas is a branch of the Muslim Brotherhood and has controlled the Gaza Strip since 2007. Since then it has been blockaded by Israel and Egypt. This has caused great hardship for all the people of Gaza. But for Christians, this distress has been compounded by persecution coming from Hamas. Since Hamas seized power in Gaza, girls and boys should not attend class together; girls are not allowed to ride on the back of motorcycles, and so on. These strictures also apply to Muslims, but they especially impact Christians, who do not believe in segregation, even those who belong to the most conservative Palestinian churches. In addition to the Hamas rulers of Gaza, there are a growing number of Salafis in Gaza who do not think Hamas is Islamic enough, and demand more restrictions on Christians. In 2008, there were 3,000 Christians in the Gaza Strip; today, there are around 1,500 Christians left, despite the strict Israeli restrictions on leaving the Hamas-controlled area.

The former leader of the Palestine Liberation Organization (PLO), Yasser Arafat—for all his many faults—was pretty clear that the Palestinian national movement, as a part of a broader Arab national movement, should be secular and include Christians. I was once at a press conference with Arafat, and he got very angry when someone suggested that the future Palestinian state would not be secular. "We are not Lebanon," he said. But by the year 2000, at the start of the so-called Second Intifada, Hamas outflanked the PLO in terms of violently opposing Israel and claiming to battle corruption and campaigning for an Islamic Palestine. The PLO, having lost much of its popularity, began to embrace Islam as a focal point of the Palestinian movement.

The Second Intifada was called the al-Aqsa Intifada, after the mosque adjacent to Jerusalem's Dome of the Rock shrine. Arafat created a group called the al-Aqsa Martyrs' Brigades, a Muslim guerrilla and suicide band. For Palestinian Christians, this was a danger signal. Suddenly, a secular movement, once the revolutionary home of all the Palestinians, was turning into a sectarian movement. Palestinian Christians felt shoved aside. They wrote letters of protest to the PLO, saying, "What is all this al-Aqsa stuff? We are in Bethlehem, we are in al-Bira, we are in Ramallah" (all towns and areas with majority Christian populations before 1948). "We are Christians, and we support the Palestinian Revolution," they proclaimed. But they were brushed off. After that, Christians grew alienated from the national movement.

It is striking to see in PLO-controlled Bethlehem men in Salafi outfits, the white tunic with the pantaloons that are slightly above the ankle and a certain kind of beard, and women wearing full-length, veiled niqabs. I had never seen this before in Bethlehem, in all my years of working there. Of course, Palestinian Christians notice this, and it has made them fearful. This has not been the primary cause of the current migration from Palestinian areas, but is an added factor. If you are a Palestinian Christian in the Occupied Territories sitting around the kitchen table having coffee, you might say to your relatives: "Well, the economy is not so good, we are not allowed into Jerusalem, the Israelis do not let us do this or that. And that hill over there is full of Salafis, so maybe George or Michael should emigrate." That is the conversation. You do not hear this from PLO officialdom, you do not read it in the media, but if you spend enough time with Palestinian Christians, that is what they say to you.

I covered the Middle East for many years as a reporter for American newspapers and then as a researcher for Human Rights Watch. During these two decades, I came across Christian persecution, but did not understand that this was a broad, pan-Middle East issue until the "Arab Spring" in 2011 in Egypt. It was then that I understood that there was a common ideology at work—one that explains the persecution of Christians in Syria and Iraq, Egypt, Palestine, and beyond. It is the ideology of a supremacist Islamism, which in its extreme manifestation morphs into violent jihadism and terrorism.

This ideology is not the sole cause of the persecution of Christians. It has to be acknowledged that the West itself has some responsibility for the intensified and accelerated persecution of Christians. The US-led invasion of Iraq was a watershed event in our times and unleashed waves of anti-Western and anti-Christian feelings. The West has also been tolerant of certain governments in the Middle East that share responsibility for fomenting sectarian hatreds. Corrupt dictatorships have only pretended to protect Christians and other minorities. They have done nothing to nourish true equality. Neither should one ignore the poverty that creates vast frustration among the masses of people, Muslim and Christian, in the Middle East.

All these factors are relevant to the growing phenomenon of the persecution of the Middle East's Christians. But it is also important to focus on the nature of the Islamist ideology that drives the persecution of Christians today.

Critics of Islam attribute the persecution of Christians and other minorities in the Middle East to Islam as a whole. Defenders of Islam say it has nothing to do with Islam, that such actions are alien to the beliefs and traditions of Islam. They are both wrong. There is no question that under traditional Islam, Christians were conquered, then subjected to institutionalized discrimination, and were sometimes violently persecuted. However, they were not always persecuted and oftentimes prospered. Not infrequently, they played a very important role in the politics of the Islamic Middle East.

But in recent decades, two closely related branches of Islam have fueled much of the persecution of Christians: Salafism and Wahhabism. Salafism is a puritanical branch of Sunni Islam that contends that Muslims must live as the Prophet Mohammed and his companions lived. This branch strictly follows texts of the Qur'an and the hadiths, the words and practices attributed to the Prophet Mohammed. Wahhabism is related to Salafism, but has a special relationship to the House of Saud, which now reigns over the Kingdom of Saudi Arabia. The House of Saud united most of the Arabian Peninsula by means of violent jihad.

Jihad means "holy war" or "struggle." It can refer to non-violent spiritual endeavors, but it more often refers to the use of force, either in defense of, or for the expansion of, Islam.

The predominantly Christian lands of the Middle East from Iraq to Egypt were conquered in the AD seventh century by holy warriors from Arabia. The early Muslim conquerors did not want to destroy what they were conquering, nor obliterate the majority Christian population in such important cities as Damascus, Alexandria, Aleppo, and Antioch. There was wealth and expertise in these cities, along with plenty of Christians. So Christians survived, though not as equal citizens. A system of social and political control was devised whereby the Muslim overlords would protect the lives, property, and religious practices of the People of the Book—Christians and Jews—in return for submission, the payment of taxes, and an extensive set of social disadvantages. Traditional Islamic law classifies these disadvantaged Christians and Jews as *dhimmis,* meaning "protected people." If the *dhimmis* accepted their disadvantaged status, they were entitled to receive the protection of their rulers. Over the centuries, *dhimmis* experienced a range of treatment, both harsh and tolerant and everything in between, but were never equal in Islamic law.

Despite their disadvantaged status, Christians were nonetheless part of the political, social, and moral fabric of the Middle East, even as minorities. In modern times, as the *dhimmi* system weakened under Western influence, Christians took part together with Muslims in anti-colonial movements. Christians in Egypt in the nineteenth and twentieth centuries campaigned against British rule. Some became major figures in the nationalist party of Egypt. Palestinian Christians produced leaders to combat the Zionist project. There is no secret about this. George Habash, who more or less invented airline hijacking, was from the Palestinian Christian community, although he did not act in the name of his religion. The founder of Ba'athism, a pan-Arab nationalist movement, was Michel Aflaq, a Christian. Such Christians were acting as citizens of a wider Arab world that fought against European imperialism.

But there were other traditions that undermined the status of Christians. One tradition that the Caliph Umar had established as a legal framework for the *dhimmis*, called the Pact of Umar, evolved in the early centuries of Islam. There is no unity among historians of Islam about the exact contents of the pact. But Salafists regard the strictest version as valid: Christians were forbidden to build new places of worship or repair old ones, to place crosses on churches, to speak loudly during the prayer time of Muslims, or to dress like Muslims, etc. Christians were also obliged to show deference to Muslims. Salafi legal scholars regard this understanding of the Pact of Umar to be the virtual equivalence of sacrosanct Islamic law—the shari'a—although it is just a treaty, not something handed down from God. A strict understanding of the Pact of Umar has been incorporated into the modern Salafi-inspired Islamist ideology. Radical Islamists also cherry-pick verbatim sacred texts to defend harsh restrictions on Christians and Jews. They may distort the texts, but they are not inventing them, and defenders of Islam are wrong to suggest radical thought has nothing to do with religion.

How did the extreme Islamist ideology gain such power in our times? The Arab defeat by Israel in the war of 1967 dealt a fatal blow to the inclusive ideology of Arab nationalism that gained ascendancy in the aftermath of the First World War and the collapse of the Ottoman Empire. Islamism began to fill the ideological void. Its proponents maintain that Arab Muslims can reclaim past glories by adhering to Salafist understandings of Islamic law and practice.

One of the most influential of the modern ideologues was Sayyid Qutb, a prominent member of the Muslim Brotherhood in the 1940s and 1950s. Qutb, an Egyptian, visited the United States and spent time in Colorado. Based on his experiences in Colorado, not considered the most Sodom-and-Gomorrah part of the United States, he wrote a damning report on Western decadence.[1] He also wrote about Christianity. Qutb believed that the Pact of Umar's most discriminatory practices against Christians should be revived.

Al-Qaeda expanded on Qutb's ideas: the behavior of People of the Book "must be clothed in humiliation and submissiveness" to the laws of Islam. Christians must be forbidden from openly proclaiming their religion, and prohibited from charging interest on capital, engaging in fornication, and other alleged sins. Their very presence among Muslims is bad. The al-Qaeda ideologue Ali al-Aliyani prescribed the eventual solution: "Oh Allah, destroy the Jews, the Christians and polytheists, and whoever has befriended them or helped them in any way against your servants [meaning Muslim believers]."

More recently, a Sunni Islamist ideologue in Syria named Mustafa Abdul Kader Setmariam extended the threat against Christians. Setmariam's nom de guerre is Abu Musab al-Suri, and he is one of the brains behind the Islamic State. Among his innovations is the idea that to carry out jihad, you do not need orders from some higher authority. Wherever an individual Muslim is, he can perform jihad. This is a break with Islamic tradition, which actually puts restrictions on who can order jihad. Al-Suri declared that Christians and Jews are in league with the enemies of true Islam, in particular with the government of Bashar al-Assad. Al-Assad belongs to the Alawite offshoot of Islam, which many Sunnis consider heretical. Al-Suri lumps Christians in with its long roster of enemies, including Jews and lapsed Muslims.[2] Al-Suri's influential interpretation, combined with Islamic State's view that Christians should be the target of jihad, means it is open season on Christians.

The heart of the radical jihadist idea is that Christians have no place in the Middle East. Can anything be done to defend Christians in this landscape of rising violence and intolerance? It appears that there is no political will in the Western world to help Christians live in peace and dignity in their homelands. Certainly, promiscuous foreign military interventions, like the invasion of Iraq, have helped neither Christians nor other minority communities thrive.

If Christians are to have a future in the Middle East, a solution must also come from the region's Muslim communities and leadership. Most Muslims recognize the wrong of what persecution does. And Muslim liberals, at least, understand that anti-minority violence soon spills over onto Muslims who do not agree with the jihadist ideology. Both al-Qaeda and the Islamic State have declared tolerant Muslims heretics who can be punished or killed with impunity. While I was interviewing Christians in Erbil, one refugee received an Instagram from a Muslim friend who had pretended to be the owner of the Christian's furniture store so that Islamic State would not confiscate it. He was beaten for his troubles—the note was accompanied by a photograph of the Muslim's back, crisscrossed with whip marks. In another instance, in early 2016, 300 Iraqis in Mosul were executed and thrown into a mass grave.

It is dangerous for workaday Muslims to speak out. If you are a Sunni Muslim in Syria, are you going to stand in your grocery store at prayer time and say, "Sorry, I do not have time to pray right now"? Are you going to oppose the Islamic State in Raqqa because you see Christians beheaded? You would have to be very brave to do that. The jihadists' killing and expulsion of Christians tell Muslims, "We can do whatever we want."

In Egypt, Salafis who have been practicing mob persecution against Christians are making it clear that Egypt's many liberal Muslims are next in line. Women are especially targeted, sometimes by groping in the street. If you look at Egyptian movies from the 1950s, you see women in Alexandria playing beach ball in bikinis. On the beaches today, if women are in the water at all, they are wearing niqabs. There is a famous old Egyptian beach west of Alexandria, with little villas. Egyptian women there used to put on a sarong to go shopping and wear no veils; they cannot do that anymore. Screens were put up on the beach, so that men cannot gape at the women bathing.

There are Muslim liberals, and some of them speak out, but they have no political weight and you do not see them on TV. Recently, I saw a woman from Pakistan speaking on TV against the Salafis, their extreme version of Islam, and so on—but she lives in Canada.

In the 1990s, an Egyptian called Nasr Hamid Abu Zaid taught at Cairo University; he was a liberal theologian, and he told his students that relying on thirteenth-century Islamic texts for guiding your activities or beliefs today was not rational. Other professors at Cairo University went to court in 1995 to denounce him as an apostate and to force the annulment of his marriage to his Muslim wife—Muslim women cannot marry heretics, they argued. He went into exile in the Netherlands.

Similarly, Ahmed Subhy Mansour, a professor in al-Azhar, the leading Islamic university in the Middle East, proposed that violent teachings should be expunged from Islam. Al-Azhar scholars declared him an enemy of Islam. The Egyptian government imprisoned him for two months. In 2002, he was granted political asylum in the United States, where he continues to write and organize. In 2011, he protested the killing of two dozen Coptic Christian demonstrators outside the state TV building in Cairo. He writes that churches should be built freely in Egypt, and that it should be against the law to preach violence in mosques.

Intolerant regional voices have, by way of contrast, flourished. Saudi Arabia, where Wahhabism is the state religion, has spread intolerant, anti-Christian Wahhabism on satellite television throughout the Middle East and into Europe, where they fund numerous mosques. I am mystified by the fact that Muslim non-Salafi, non-Wahhabi religious leaders rarely speak out against their preachings.

It is hard not to think of persecutions past and the reluctance of people in the West and in the Middle East to speak out forcefully. In the West, at least, everyone knows the poem written by Lutheran pastor Martin Niemöller in the 1930s that condemned Nazism. But it has almost become a cliché without force: "First they came for the communists, and I did not speak out—because I was not a communist." Then Jews and so on, he wrote. Niemöller concluded with the famous line: "Then they came for me, and there was no one left to speak for me." Is there anyone to speak up consistently and forcefully for Christians and other minorities? I do not see it.

At a minimum, the United States and Europe as a matter of urgency ought to grant political asylum to Christian refugees from the Mosul area. This should not be done on the grounds that they are Christians, but because their communities qualify for special treatment on human rights grounds. Under international law, anyone with a well-founded fear of persecution on the grounds of religious belief has the right to apply for political asylum. Iraqi Christians and Yezidis certainly qualify.

In any event, I am not optimistic about Christianity's future in the home of its birth. Imagine what Syria will look like if its civil war goes on for another 10 years. In Egypt, the Copts' numbers are large enough for them to survive, and they have a certain amount of influence—but they depend on a dictator for protection, and in the past, no dictator has proven capable of defending minority rights. Palestinian Christians tell me: "Yes, everyone tells us to stay, but we are leaving anyway." So Palestine will be a museum of dead Christianity. Pilgrims will go to the Church of the Nativity and the Church of the Holy Sepulcher, but they will not find Palestinians worshipping there.

I am confident that this dire trend in the region will continue; there will be no turning back, no affirmation of tolerance and equality. Dignified Christian life is pretty much dead in the Middle East. Christians, in their shrinking numbers and reduced influence, have become observers of their own demise.

NOTES

1. Sayyid Qutb, "The America I Have Seen: In the Scale of Human Values" (1951), in *America in an Arab Mirror: Images of America in Arabic Travel Literature, 1668 to 9/11 and Beyond*, eds. Kamal Abdel-Malek and Mouna El Kahla (Basingstoke: Palgrave Macmillan, 2000), 9–27. Qutb's text was first published in the Egyptian magazine *Al-Risala* (vol. 19, 1951).

2. From a jihadist training video, August 2000. Cited in Paul Cruickshank and Mohannad Hage Ali, "Abu Musab Al Suri: Architect of the New Al Qaeda," *Studies in Conflict & Terrorism* 30, no. 1 (2007): 1–14.

WORKS CITED

Cruickshank, Paul and Mohannad Hage Ali. "Abu Musab Al Suri: Architect of the New Al Qaeda." *Studies in Conflict & Terrorism* 30 no. 1 (2007): 1–14.

Qutb, Sayyid. "The America I Have Seen: In the Scale of Human Values" (1951). In *America in an Arab Mirror: Images of America in Arabic Travel Literature, 1668 to 9/11 and Beyond*, edited by Kamal Abdel-Malek and Mouna El Kahla, 9–27. Basingstoke: Palgrave Macmillan, 2000.

Williams, Daniel. *Forsaken. The Persecution of Christians in Today's Middle East.* New York and London: O/R Books, 2016.

Chapter 16

The Challenges of Social Pluralism in Post-Revolutionary Egypt

(Zurich, June 14, 2016)

Mariz Tadros

In the space of four years, Egypt has had four different political leaders. After the February 2011 revolution, the Supreme Council of the Armed Forces, led by Field Marshal Tantawi, took office. It was an interim arrangement agreed to by the young revolutionary forces and others until a democratically elected parliament could take over. A year later, Egypt had President Morsi from the Muslim Brotherhood. He held office from June 2012 until he was ousted 12 months later. Then there was another interim president. He was the Head of the Supreme Constitutional Court: namely, Adly Mansour, who held office for almost a year. Then the Minister of Defense, General Abdel Fattah el-Sisi, came to office, and he continues as president to this day. Between 2011 and 2014, there were two major uprisings, the first ousting President Mubarak, the second ousting President Morsi. It has been a rapidly changing political situation in Egypt, and now a military-based government appears to be firmly in the saddle.

The main question that I will address today is whether the drive for greater social pluralism, which was so powerfully evident during the late revolutionary upheavals, has now reached a dead end. In answering this question, I will focus less on the words and deeds of the political elites, and more on what I see happening within society and the sub-elite level. I will start with the cases of two women. Each case involves issues of religious pluralism and gender equality. Both cases also feature appalling instances of sexual violence. But in recounting them, I do not wish to suggest that the acts of sexual violence are mainly the result of repressed sexuality, or anything of that sort. I am interested in what these two incidents elicited in terms of social responses and reactions, and what they do to our understanding of democracy and rights.

The first story concerns a Muslim woman who participated in a peaceful protest against the military in December 2011. She was dressed in a black

157

abaya—that is, a gown that covers the entire body, and a headscarf; her face was not covered. In an incident that was famously captured on video and in photographs, soldiers dragged her across Tahrir Square, removed the veil from her head and undressed her, exposing her blue bra. She became widely known as the blue bra woman.

Why was the blue bra woman stripped of her clothes? This assault happened at a time when the future of social pluralism in Egypt was being vigorously contested. There was then an alliance between the Muslim Brotherhood and the army. The revolutionary youth movement and others were challenging that alliance. Through this act of sexual violence, the authorities sent a clear message to women generally: "Enough protests, enough taking to the streets! Accept that we are in power, and accept your place at home. You thought that because you participated in the revolution against Mubarak, you would continue to be allowed to express your voice and protest—well, think again."

My second story took place not long ago, in a poor village in Upper Egypt, an area that is associated with high levels of poverty and political, economic, and social marginalization. A 70-year-old Christian grandmother, Soad Thabet, was grabbed in the street by several men who completely removed her clothes and dragged her along the ground. That same day, five houses in her village belonging to Copts were torched.

Why was this 70-year-old grandmother stripped and abused in public? Her troubles began because she was the mother of a Christian man who was rumored to have engaged in a relationship with a Muslim woman—a grave offense against the sexual and sectarian norms of traditional shari'a law. Soad received death threats because of the rumors about her son's behavior, and reported them to the police; but she was left unprotected. Thus, this elderly woman was stripped naked in the street.

The sexual abuse of Soad Thabet was a message aimed more at the Coptic community than at her: "Know your place in society. We can get back at you. We will teach you to 'walk next to the wall,'" as the saying goes in Egyptian Arabic. In other words: "Do not assume that you will be protected if we, as the dominant community in the village, turn against you."

Neither the story of the blue bra woman nor Soad Thabet ended with the humiliation of sexual violence. These crimes, contrary to the intentions of the perpetrators, became a catalyst for positive change.[1] The abuse of the blue bra woman generated the largest ever women's protest in the history of Egypt since women rose against British colonialism a hundred years earlier. I was at the protest in Tahrir Square. It was packed. There were a lot of men, there were women of every age and social class, and there was a strong sense of moral indignation. The mood was not, "Oh, this poor woman, this victim." Rather, there was a powerful collective feeling that the military should be ashamed of themselves, and that the woman herself was a heroine. She became iconic of the struggle for liberty.

The case of Soad Thabet also generated a sense of unity among different political forces in Egypt. An exceptionally large number of Muslims showed sympathy for Soad Thabet and took up her case. Many members of the Muslim intelligentsia campaigned for her on Facebook, saying that what happened to her happened because she was a Copt and a woman, and that this was outrageous. There was widespread recognition of two kinds of injustices: gender injustice—that is, the way in which political struggles are happening on women's bodies—and, secondly, religious unfairness—that is, the way in which Copts are being threatened and terrorized by mobs in their own communities. Christians, Muslims, and freethinkers pressed for accountability from the governor of Minya, the province where Soad Thabet lives. They pressed the Ministry of the Interior to explain why the police had failed to protect the threatened woman. The case went as far as parliament, and an inquiry was set up to investigate why the authorities had failed in their duty to protect her.

I wanted to tell the story of the reaction to these two incidents because when we think about the Middle East these days, we no longer think first and foremost of ordinary people rising up in defense of human dignity and in resistance to oppression. We tend to think mainly of the successful measures of repression—there was an Arab revolt, now there is an Arab winter, and people have accepted many encroachments on their rights. There is not much acknowledgment of the fact that people are still resisting all kinds of violations of their rights in very powerful ways. They need solidarity. They need to feel that the international community is aware of and is celebrating their struggles for liberty and social pluralism.

In terms of justice outcomes, in the case of the so-called blue bra woman, Field Marshal Tantawi apologized—the only time he did so during his 20 years as head of the military. He issued an apology to all Egyptian women. In the case of Soad Thabet, President al-Sisi also made a public apology to her. He appeared on national television and said that what had happened to her was unacceptable. The rule of law should apply, he said, and he apologized to her and to all Egyptian women for what she had been subjected to. The initial response to the sexual abuse of Soad Thabet from al-Azhar University, which represents the highest center for Islamic learning in the Sunni world, was to say, "Let us get together, shake hands, and have a reconciliation session."

Apologies and gestures of reconciliation may be a positive step toward getting people to recognize that wrongs have been done, but the danger is that both are used in lieu of taking the perpetrators to court and seeking justice. Apologies are not the same as justice. The military personnel who stripped the blue bra woman were never brought to trial. The men who attacked Soad

Thabet and the policemen who failed to protect her after she reported threats are not being adequately held to justice. Yet, despite the lack of justice, the apologies and conciliatory gestures from the authorities do reinforce the notion that the use of sexual violence to punish women and Christians is not acceptable. Pursuing the struggle for gender and religious equality can have an impact on a country's political order, even in a non-democratic context.

A question immediately arises: Would the struggles for women's equality and for religious pluralism—not only for Copts, but also for Baha'is, the Shi'a, and atheists—have fared better if the Muslim Brotherhood had stayed in power? After all, President Morsi and the Muslim Brotherhood came to power through elections. I think not. The fact of a party having achieved an electoral majority does not necessarily mean that it will advocate for an inclusive political order. My argument is that the situation would have been even worse for religious minorities and women if President Morsi and the Muslim Brotherhood had still been in power.

What we saw during the Muslim Brotherhood's year in office was a severe encroachment on gender equality and religious pluralism, a pronounced circumscribing of space. The discourse on sexual harassment worsened. A lot of Muslim Egyptian women who wore a headscarf but may not have worn the more conservative kinds of veil were socially stigmatized. They were regularly pushed around on the streets of Egypt and told to adopt more conservative attire. It was much worse for Coptic women, especially in poor areas. Not only were they stigmatized because they were not veiled at all, but they were told, "Just you wait. We will veil you, we will get you to conform to our Islamic system." There were no laws about this—President Morsi did not make a speech or announce a formal policy. Yet women were subjected to regular harassment on the streets of Egypt, in particular in rural and poor urban areas. Around 40 percent of the Egyptian population is poor, so we are not talking here about a minority of women.

When the Muslim Brotherhood and other Islamist groups—that is to say political forces promoting the transformation of Egypt into a shari'a-based state—were asked why they did not participate in the mass protest in Tahrir Square against the stripping of the blue bra woman, their attitude was: "Well, what was she doing in Tahrir Square in the first place?" Or they said, "She may have been wearing an abaya, but why was she not wearing more clothes underneath? Did she want to expose her underwear?"

The ideology of a regime matters. From the "Arab Spring" uprisings until this day, Egypt has not become a democratic country. There have been elections, but they were not democratic elections, because "democracy" without substantive rights, without the rights of the most vulnerable members of a community being protected, is not really democracy. But there are variations in authoritarianism, strands, if you like, of different colors, which have a huge impact on gender equality, religious freedom, social pluralism, and so forth. During President Morsi's tenure, there was a great deal happening at grass-roots level that was never either triggered by or reflected in public statements, official policies, and laws, but that was felt every day in the lives of people.

For instance, there were no laws issued during President Morsi's tenure that discriminated between Christian and Muslim citizens. However, every day people had experiences that gave them the sense of suddenly living in a country that did not belong to them. Day after day, one would hear, "Just you wait, you Copts; now that we are in power, we will show you who is in charge." Partly this happened because Copts did not on the whole vote for President Morsi; the majority of Christians opposed Islamist rule because they had had experience of Islamist political movements creating division in their communities—suddenly you go to a vegetable seller and he or she says, "We do not sell to Christians." I am not saying that religious discrimination has not existed in Egypt for a very, very long time, or that it suddenly emerged under the Muslim Brotherhood—certainly not. It has long historical roots; but it got much worse during Morsi's year in power.

It is interesting that the number of Egyptians who went out against President Morsi's regime on June 30, 2013, was far larger than anything that happened in the heyday of the "Arab Spring" uprising. In 2011, there were something like 40 BBC correspondents and stringers in Tahrir Square, but in 2013, nobody really asked who these millions were and what they wanted.[2] There is a need to understand why people rose up all over the country only one year after President Morsi came to power. So in 2014, my research team and I sought an answer. We carried out a survey, based on a sample of 2,400 people who had risen up against Morsi. They were about 80 percent Muslim, 20 percent Christian, 50 percent rural, 50 percent urban, men and women.

When we asked why people rose up, the number one answer—supported by 35.8 percent of respondents—was *akhwanat al-dawla*, meaning "the Brotherhoodization of the state." What does this mean? People saw a monopolization of political, social, and economic power in the hands of the Muslim Brotherhood, and they had not expected this. When they elected Morsi as president, they had expected him to create an inclusive political and social order. The second most popular reason people gave for the uprising was the deterioration in the economic situation. The Muslim Brotherhood had created very high expectations among the Egyptian people: "You will all have jobs, you will all have homes," and so forth. When people did not see anything happening, they were frustrated. The third reason people gave was lack of security—they did not feel safe. The variation between Christians and Muslims was very minor; in other words, these were the top three reasons for both Muslims and Christians.

The issue of security is partly a question of social cohesion: Do you feel that you are part of a community and that the community will stand up for you? The Islamist discourse that said, "Now we are in power, we will rule; we will show you what an Islamist state looks like; we will tell you how to live," ruptured social cohesion, even among Muslims, some of whom were devout but did not follow the Muslim Brotherhood. That is a really important point to raise when thinking about religious pluralism and gender equality, because there are always members of the majority faith who themselves do not want to be dictated to: artists, Muslims who do not want to practice Islam in a certain way, atheists, and Muslims who belong to leftist or revolutionary movements.

Of course, there is another narrative that says, "Okay, we recognize that millions of Egyptians rose up against the regime. But they did not want it to be out of power, they just wanted it to be reformed." However, the majority of people in our survey denied this. We recorded 69 percent of our respondents saying that when they went out on June 30, 2013, they wanted Morsi to step down as president. It is true that, in our questionnaire, we did not ask, "Did you want al-Sisi to come to power?" But I think it is extremely important to recognize that Egyptians were expressing—just as they had in 2011—their rejection of a leader that they felt had lost legitimacy.

Among the variety of political, religious, judicial, and other forces that agreed on the ousting of Morsi were the Patriarch of the Coptic Orthodox Church, the head of al-Azhar, and Mohammed al-Baradei, the Nobel Prize winner who took part in the negotiations to oust Morsi and who did—this on record—agree for Morsi to step down. These forces agreed on a road map that provided for parliamentary elections and then presidential elections. One of the major mistakes made in Egypt after Morsi's ouster was to reverse this order. Presidential elections came first, then parliamentary elections.

Following the ousting of President Morsi, there were exceptionally serious physical attacks on Christian places of worship, schools, orphanages, and bookshops. There have always been sectarian attacks, but to lose 64 places—torched or looted or both—in 72 hours was exceptional. We probably lost about 3 percent of Christian establishments in 72 hours. This was initiated by the Muslim Brotherhood and the pro-Morsi group in retaliation for state security's excessive use of violence against their demonstrations in Raba'a Square. Some demonstrators there were armed, but the police used excessive violence in response, as a result of which hundreds of Muslim Brotherhood members and supporters lost their lives. The churches and other Christian institutions that were attacked had not mobilized in any way against the Muslim Brotherhood, so it was difficult to understand why the attacks happened. The instruction given to Copts from Christian leadership was not to leave their homes, not to try to stop the torching of the churches, and not to get drawn into armed engagement; I think that was important in preventing a great deal more violence across the country.

What does all of this mean for the situation post-2013? There has been a reversal of the Brotherhoodization trend, but the Salafization of society continues. There is concern that al-Azhar is not supporting inclusive politics; for instance, they failed to issue a statement condemning the attack on the blue bra woman in 2011. Some Egyptian Muslims have been trying to hold al-Azhar accountable, but they have not been given their due space by the institution.

The situation today is one where there are still severe encroachments on religious pluralism. Blasphemy laws work like a McCarthyite witch hunt: people are constantly accused of having said something against Islam, even if there is no evidence, and the judiciary is complicit in this. The absence of the rule of law is a major issue.

There is, however, improved social cohesion.[3] Let me give you one example. In 2012, I interviewed a very poor day laborer who works on the land in Minya. He was telling me in tears—and it is not common for elderly Egyptian men to cry in the presence of women—that what upset him most about Brotherhoodization was that previously, at break time, he would have his meal with the Muslim laborers in the fields, that everybody would sit together. By 2012, he said, they were no longer eating together—and that had broken him. In 2014, however, when I went back to him, he said they were eating together again, without anything having been said. People had simply gone back to being field laborers together, rather than Christians and Muslims. That does not mean, I emphasize, that discrimination does not persist, as we see in the case of the stripping of Soad Thabet. But it does say that, at least in terms of everyday life, people are remembering what brought them together in the first place.

On women's equality, we now have the largest number of women representatives in the history of the Egyptian parliament, around 14.9 percent. In 2012, only 3 percent of the Muslim Brotherhood and Islamist-dominated parliament were women. Yet we do not want women to be there just filling seats. I think the difference is that the women who were in parliament in 2012 were very much not advocating for a pro-women's rights agenda; yes, they voted in favor of a law that would give female-headed households more economic rights, and that was very commendable. But that law was initiated by the feminist movement three or four years previously, and anything else that had to do with women's empowerment—in other words, challenging the gender hierarchy—they did not promote (at the time, we were very worried that female genital mutilation would be decriminalized). In contrast, a significant percentage of the women who are now in parliament have actually been promoting women's rights. They brought the case of Soad Thabet to parliament and they insisted on a parliamentary inquiry.

Sexual harassment continues, but the incidence has decreased dramatically, I think partly because there is more security on the streets, partly because the Brotherhood is no longer in power. Women are no longer being told to such a high degree, "Cover up!" Does this mean that suddenly Egyptian society has become progressive, in favor of women's rights, believing that women should wear anything they want to? Absolutely not. Patriarchy is still strong; there is still a great deal of discrimination against women. But at least the rhetoric that says, "You do not have the right to the street if you are not complying with us," has been weakened dramatically—although, of course, not entirely.

What does all of this mean for Egypt and for the broader region—for Syria, for Yemen? The first thing to say is that ideology does matter. It is important to stay true to the ideals of a civil state, a non-military state; and "civil" should also mean "non-theocratic." Theocracy can also have a devastating impact on the quality of democracy, even if it comes to power through the ballot box.

The second thing is that the mistake of assuming that elections and democracy are the same thing must not be repeated. We do, of course, need elections. But elections have to be held at the right time, in secure conditions where people are not terrorized. Political order needs to be agreed by consensus, so that whoever comes to power does not engage in the tyranny of majoritarian democracy. There need to be substantive rights for artistic expression, for religious freedom, for minority rights, and so on.

The third thing to talk about is the danger of regional power configurations. The situation in 2011 was very different from what it is now. One of the issues is the Western critique of the human rights record of the current Egyptian government. There are human rights violations issues that have to be addressed, but this critique does not include a recognition that average Egyptians, non-armed civilian Egyptians, are being exposed to terrorist acts. They are the people who are getting blown up, and they are asking, "Why is it that when people get blown up in the West, there is sympathy; but when we get blown up, nobody cares?" They think they live in daily terror from terrorism, and nobody cares. There are very strong terrorist networks operating between Libya, Yemen, Syria, and Iraq; it is not just ISIS. In the May 2016 *IDS Bulletin* of the Institute of Development Studies at the University of Sussex, available online, a very distinguished Islamist writer who was part of the jihadi movement, Ali Bakr, describes how these intricate networks have been able to establish a very strong base in the region since 2011.[4] As long as these threats persist, security will unfortunately sometimes trump issues of human rights. What we need is balance for both, so that we have pluralism and respect for rights on the one hand, but also recognition for the rights of all on the other.

One of the missing links in this puzzle is the role of al-Azhar University. Al-Azhar is influential in the whole of the Sunni world, not just in Egypt, and when we talk about a counter-narrative to the radical narrative of ISIS and other Islamist movements, I do not think it is good enough anymore simply to say that ISIS does not speak in the name of Islam. We need to take that a step further and say we no longer recognize them as Muslims. There has been a reluctance to take that step, but I think we should expect it of al-Azhar. Equally, in the case of the women who are being stripped, we should expect al-Azhar to come out and say, "We are against any measure by any actor that takes away from women's dignity and bodily integrity, whether you are Copt or Muslim."

Something very interesting did happen in Egyptian society in 2011 and 2016. In 2011, the woman who became known as the blue bra woman was celebrated in graffiti as a heroine. This is extremely unusual—a woman who had been stripped of her clothes, which, in Egypt's traditional patriarchal society, is a source of shame and of dishonor to herself and her family, was suddenly celebrated as a heroine. The slogan I heard in the protests that I went on, sung by men as well as women, was, "Raise your head high; you are more honorable than any of them!" I think this shows a social transformation—that men and women were saying they would not allow themselves to fall into the trap of endorsing conservative political struggles on the bodies of women. This is the kind of resistance movement that I think is very powerful, because it comes from the bottom up. It is not the *blah blah blah* of elitist conferences; it is the Egyptian people themselves.

In 2016, there were attempts by some Islamist-leaning individuals to say in relation to Soad Thabet, "Well, let us not exaggerate; the Copts are always trying to cause divisions in society." But many Muslims united with Christians to say, "This is unacceptable and shameful for the Egyptian people; we want justice for this woman." Soad Thabet was given the honorable title "Sayed of Minya"—our Lady of Minya—and instead of being known as the stripped woman of Minya, she became the Lady of Minya. And so, in the midst of all the turbulence and chaos, there are real and successful struggles for equality and civility.

NOTES

1. For further background on this development, see my article that I published shortly after presenting this paper: "Disembodying honor and exposing the politics behind it," *openDemocracy*, July 5, 2016, https://www.opendemocracy.net/5050/mariz-tadros /disembodying-honour-and-exposing-politics-behind-it.

2. These millions of people were of course not all Copts, because Copts constitute just 10 percent of the population.

3. Also see my publication "Decrypting Copts' Perspectives on Communal Relations in Contemporary Egypt through Vernacular Politics (2013–14)," *IDS Working Paper*, no. 456 (May 2015).

4. See Ali Bakr, "A Panoramic Perspective on Islamist Movements in the Middle East," *IDS Bulletin* 47, no. 3 (2016): 77–98.

WORKS CITED

Bakr, Ali. "A Panoramic Perspective on Islamist Movements in the Middle East." *IDS Bulletin* 47 (2016): 77–98.

Tadros, Mariz. "Decrypting Copts' Perspectives on Communal Relations in Contemporary Egypt through Vernacular Politics (2013–14)." *IDS Working Paper* no. 456 (May 2015).

———. "Disembodying honor and exposing the politics behind it." *OpenDemocracy.* July 5, 2016. https://www.opendemocracy.net/5050/mariz-tadros/disembodying-honour -and-exposing-politics-behind-it.

Chapter 17

Saddam Hussein, Operation Iraqi Freedom, and the Islamic State: Can Religious Pluralism Survive the Onslaught?

(Zurich, October 25, 2016)

William Warda

Christian Solidarity International's series of talks on the future of religious minorities in the Middle East comes at a time when more and more media attention is focused on the violence directed at these vulnerable communities, without, I must add, inducing noticeable improvement in their precarious situation. The term "minority" itself is very problematic, not least because it connotes, in addition to its objective meaning of being less numerous, a subjective sense of cultural inferiority and of unimportance. Yet this connotation is far from an accurate depiction of reality.[1] To take only one example, the Assyrians, one of the main Christian communities in the region, have a long and rich history, spanning several millennia. They have contributed significantly to the social, political, and cultural development of their homeland in present-day Iraq. Thus, when referring to the existential threat faced by minorities in Iraq, we are not discussing the disappearance of a marginal element of Iraqi culture—it is the very heart of the country that is on the verge of extinction.

The bitter plight of minorities in Iraq, such as the Assyrians, Chaldeans, Yezidis, Turkmens, Shabaks, or Mandeans, is nothing new; it is the result and extension of centuries of massacres, discrimination, and marginalization. Contrary to the hopes of the religious minorities, the formation of the Iraqi state in the first half of the twentieth century did not bring such practices to an end. In 1932, independent Iraq acceded to the League of Nations. Its accession was contingent upon a declaration by the nascent state of a commitment to the protection of its minorities.[2] But only a few months later, in August 1933, over 3,000 Assyrians were massacred and more than 60 villages destroyed in the area surrounding Simele in northern Iraq, epitomizing well the disjunction between discourse and practice regarding minorities. Such disjunction still continues to characterize Iraqi politics today.

SADDAM HUSSEIN'S RUTHLESS DESPOTISM

The accession of Saddam Hussein to the Iraqi presidency in 1979 ushered in a period of severe and deliberate repression of all elements of Iraqi society, driven by a relentless pursuit of ever more absolute power. One of the fiercest resistances encountered by the autocrat stemmed from the Kurdish-dominated territories of northern Iraq, and Saddam brutally crushed their attempts at rebellion and yearnings for independence. The most notoriously brutal of his repressive campaigns against Iraqi citizens was the genocidal al-Anfal ("spoils of war") campaign in 1988 against the Kurds. The campaign witnessed a combination of aerial bombardments with mass deportations and even chemical warfare. It was not only the Kurds who were victims; other communities were caught in the crossfire. 120 Assyrian Christian villages were destroyed, producing mass displacement. Dozens of churches and monasteries, some dating back to the earliest days of Christianity, were turned into ruins, and some prominent Christian clerics were assassinated on suspicion of disloyalty to Saddam. Many Yezidis were also killed and their villages and temples were rendered uninhabitable.[3]

During Saddam's presidency, Iraq was involved in two conflicts with major regional consequences—namely, the eight-year-long war with Iran and the invasion of Kuwait. Thousands of young Christians were drafted to the front, and it is estimated that over 50,000 disappeared, either taken prisoner or killed.[4] The experience of war (*tajrubat al-harb*) became an additional, ever more central, tool in Saddam's arsenal of weapons to control the Iraqi population. Manipulating it craftily, the dictator successfully instituted a pervasive climate of existential fear, which induced the Iraqis to focus on survival rather than political reforms. Death, suffering, and paranoia ruled.[5]

The suffering caused by Saddam Hussein's barbarism was compounded by the imposition of unjust and cruel UN economic sanctions on the Iraqi people, as a form of collective punishment for the actions of the very dictator who was strangling them. Saddam exploited the increasingly dire economic situation of his country to further strengthen his rule, and the draconian economic sanctions strengthened his hold on power. On the one hand, he used the sanctions to absolve himself of any responsibility for the deterioration in the living conditions of the Iraqis. On the other, they served as the perfect justification for the introduction of ever more repressive measures. As he would often repeat, "Make your dog hungry and he will follow you."

Even though the ideology of the ruling Ba'ath party was ostensibly secular, the 1980s and especially the 1990s witnessed a distinct Islamization of politics. Arab nationalism was then in decline and the Islamic resurgence was gaining momentum throughout the Arab world. In 1991, Saddam Hussein added the phrase "Allahu akhbar" to the Iraqi flag and in 1993, he launched the Return to Faith campaign (*al-Hamla al-Imaniya*). The latter capitalized on the desperation that was driving many Iraqis toward religion as a source of comfort and security. In addition to enjoining the population to piety and closeness to God, the campaign also led to the shutting down of various social spaces, such as discotheques and social clubs, as well as to the prohibition of public consumption of alcohol. Children, but also governmental and military employees, were automatically enrolled in Qur'anic classes.[6] At the same time, Saudi Arabia, with its expansive conception of its religious *mission civilisatrice,* was taking advantage of the poverty in the areas of Iraqi Kurdistan to sponsor the construction of mosques and Islamic centers there. These practices paved the way for an increase in sentiment against non-Muslims, which was to soar after the overthrow of Saddam in 2003.

POST-2003: THE NIGHTMARE CONTINUES

Launched in the spring of 2003, Operation Iraqi Freedom was expected to improve the situation in Iraq and lead toward a more democratic and inclusive country. Some were even hopeful that the presence of the coalition forces—coming, after all, mostly from Christian-majority countries—would contribute to greater protection for religious minorities, a view that was widely reported in the media at the time. However, this was far from being the case: not only was minority representation marginal in the new government, but discriminatory practices and attacks against members of religious minorities, rather than abating, continued unchecked.

In various parts of the country, properties belonging to Christians and Yezidis were illegally seized, sometimes with the justification that what is owned by non-Muslims constitutes *ghana'im*—that is, "just spoils." The issue acquired enough visibility for a special committee to be formed to oversee the restitution of seized properties, but often victims were reticent to come forward, fearing retribution in a climate where abductions and killings of Christians were all too common. Extortions of minority-owned local businesses were also frequent, and failure to pay "taxes" could result in their closure, if not physical destruction. In some cases, attacks against religious minorities were so systematic as to lead in effect to the cleansing of non-Muslims from some neighborhoods, even at the height of American military occupation. For instance, the neighborhood of al-Dura was virtually emptied of Christians, and in other neighborhoods of the capital, such as New Baghdad, al-Mansur, Zayouna, or al-Mashtal, the percentage of Christians plummeted from 80 percent to 20 percent during the occupation.[7] Overall, the Christian population of Baghdad declined from half a million to less than 150,000.[8] Similar trends were observed in other cities, such as Diyala, Ramadi, and al-Habbaniyya, where there remain hardly any Christians today.

Even in Iraqi Kurdistan, Christians and Yezidis were the targets of attacks, despite the Kurdish Regional Government's (KRG) strong claims that they were providing a safe haven for minorities. For instance, in December 2011, Kurdish extremists burned down stores, hotels, casinos, clinics, and other facilities belonging to Christians and Yezidis in Dohuk, Zakho, and Simele. These attacks, by the very fact that they were occurring in a part of the country thought to be safe, prompted tens of families to emigrate.[9] Operation Iraqi Freedom and its aftermath did not bring any respite to religious minorities, who, owing to the coalition's *laissez-faire* policy in these matters, were left even more exposed not only to religious extremists, but also to anti-Western elements, who were quick to frame minorities as fifth columnists. The international community remained passive and silent. Minorities were simply not part of their political equation and security concerns.

THE ISLAMIC STATE OF IRAQ AND SYRIA

The overthrow of Saddam Hussein and his autocratic regime in 2003, accompanied by a process of thorough de-Ba'athification at all levels of Iraqi administrative, political, and social institutions, left a political vacuum which enabled local governments and militias to operate with ever more latitude, often in a form of de facto independence from Baghdad. It was in this context of increasing regionalization, compounded with an upsurge of fundamentalist readings of Islam, that the Islamic State of Iraq and Syria (ISIS) could declare its caliphate in the summer of 2014.

I do not want to present here numbers to quantify what happened to Christians, Yezidis, Shabaks, Kaka'is, and other groups at the hands of ISIS. The American government and Pope Francis have rightly described what is happening as genocide. Thousands went missing or were killed, large numbers of women—in particular Yezidis, but also tens of Christians women—were captured to serve as sex slaves, and millions left their homes in Mosul and the Nineveh plains and surrounding areas to escape death and forced conversion.[10] In the territories controlled by ISIS, no church, monastery, or temple was left intact. It is hard to imagine that in what used to be a predominantly Christian territory, no church bell has been heard in over three years. That religious minorities, and in particular Christians, are on the verge of extinction

in Iraq and severely threatened in other countries of the Middle East is a fact
and not the result of mere conjecture. In Iraq alone, the numbers of Christians
declined by 70 percent between April 2003 and December 2015. In addition
to emigration, according to the statistics of the Hammurabi Human Rights
Organization, more than 881 Christians were killed in Iraq in that period, of
whom 16 percent were highly skilled workers, 1.6 percent clerics, 14 percent
women, 4 percent children, and 4 percent elderly.[11]

The combination of armed violence, terrorism, discriminatory policies,
a decline in employment opportunities, and a reluctance to marry and start
a family has created an almost unbearable sociopolitical environment for
minorities in Iraq, so much so that emigration is often seen as the only viable
solution.[12] Some forces are pushing minorities to remain in the country, to
resist a while longer, but how can anyone deny the right of those communities
who have suffered so much to consider emigration?

ISSUES OF REPRESENTATION

On the political level, a major challenge facing minorities in Iraq—and the
wider region—is that of true representation. Part of the issue is that the term
"religious minorities" encompasses a wide range of groups which are far
from homogeneous. Competing interests and internal power struggles impede
constructive dialogue toward the formation of a unified voice to advocate for
the rights and protection of minorities. This internal dissension is an obstacle
not only to local advocacy, but also to voicing the concerns of religious
minorities at the regional level. In a context of continuously increasing hostility toward minorities, these shortcomings are particularly detrimental.

As for external support, Sunni, Shi'ite, and Kurdish politicians who claim
an interest in minority issues do so mainly out of a desire for greater political
legitimacy, especially vis-à-vis the international community. The few members of religious minority communities who, on the basis of their merit and
endurance, have obtained governmental and political appointments, are then
used to mask the continuing structural discrimination against their communities by those in power. As such, true representation is stolen from minorities
by those who purport to be their "patrons," and the appearance of support
further undermines the efforts of minorities to ask for greater assistance from
the international community, which so far has shown only limited concern
for their plight.

Finally, the tensions between the central government and the KRG,
already sowing the seeds of the next conflict in the country, leave minority groups particularly exposed and vulnerable. The territorial dispute
between the two entities concerns in part areas predominantly inhabited by

religious minorities, who find themselves caught in the crossfire without being able to voice their opinion. For Baghdad as well as for the KRG, minorities are an inconvenience that ought to be contained, co-opted, or simply eradicated.

The lack of self-representation, the political hypocrisy and hostility of Kurds, Shi'ites, and Sunnis, and the passivity of the international community have contributed in effect to the silencing of minority voices, deprived of real access to the political sphere and as such unable to enact change in spite of numerous claims of "concern" and "support" by external actors. One of the clearest illustrations of this powerlessness is the continued existence of discriminatory pieces of legislation in post-2003 Iraqi laws, such as article 26 of the Iraqi National Identity Card Law, which states that if one parent converts to Islam, the children who have not reached the age of majority automatically become Muslims.[13]

The ideal solution for minorities in Iraq would be the establishment of a decentralized state, one in which the rule of law would be upheld, human rights respected, and all its population granted equal citizenship. Such a state needs to be pluralistic, acknowledging the fundamental cultural, religious, ethnic, and political diversity that characterizes Iraq. A monolithic government can only lead to further discrimination against minorities.

When striving toward change, it is tempting to assume that the best strategy would be to start with a complete overhaul of state institutions, leading to the creation of an entirely new political, governmental, and administrative system. Yet such an approach did not lead to positive results in 2003, nor did it in 1932 at the end of the British Mandate, when Iraq gained independence. It is therefore doubtful that such a measure would work in the present case. It would then be better to operate, at least initially, within the current administrative framework and to implement reforms progressively. Crucially, for the changes to be truly beneficial to minority communities, this reforming process has to be deliberate and decisive in giving greater attention to minorities at all levels of governance.

THE CASE OF THE NINEVEH PLAINS

With the ongoing military campaign to retake Mosul and the surrounding territories from the control of the Islamic State, there has been much discussion about what will follow and about how to tackle the many challenges ahead, three of which I want to address here. Firstly, there is a significant risk that the various groups who joined forces against ISIS will, subsequent to the defeat of their common enemy, turn against each other, thereby producing more violence. The only way to mitigate this is through the general disarmament of combatants on all sides. To prevent further bloodshed, the "liberated" areas must be placed under the protection of external leadership, at least for a certain limited time, sufficient to allow for re-settlement, create security, and build peace, a point to which I will return shortly.

Secondly, the return of the displaced population should be carefully prepared, with the awareness that it will take time. The example of the Sinjar Mountains is particularly telling: this predominantly Yezidi region was retaken over a year ago, and yet so far less than 5 percent of the displaced Yezidis have returned to their villages. A similar phenomenon can be expected for the Nineveh plains, as long as the third challenge, the long-term stability and political future of the area, is not adequately addressed. In this respect, it is certain that there can be no restoration of the status quo ante: there has been too much death and destruction. Further, the emigration of many Christians irrevocably affected the social configuration of the population of the Nineveh plains. Before the Islamic State conquered the Nineveh plains, the Christians were estimated to represent 22 percent of the population there. Today, they probably do not exceed 10 percent. This puts into question the appropriateness of the suggestion, which has attracted much international attention and support, to transform the Nineveh plains into a governorate for minorities—with the aim of empowering, on the political and administrative level, communities who were hitherto marginalized.

While I share great sympathy with this proposal, I doubt it would achieve its intended goal. With the aforementioned shifting demographics, even in such a governorate Christian voices would remain insignificant in the decision-making process. A variant of this idea would be the formation of a smaller governorate only for non-Muslim minorities, that is, mainly Christians and Yezidis. In theory, this would be better, but the implementation of such a project would be a very complex task, as the various communities of the Nineveh plains are so deeply intertwined geographically that the identification of borders suitable for such a governorate and agreeable to all would be nearly impossible.

Hence, if in the long term it might be possible to resolve the issue of how to design a governorate for minorities that truly serves those communities, at the moment it is better to focus on strengthening local institutions, especially city councils, including town, district, or sub-district councils. They should remain within the existing administrative structure, but with veto rights on decisions taken by higher authorities that would have direct and discriminatory consequences for their constituencies. Having elected city councils would further allow Christian and Yezidi towns and villages to preserve their unique religious, ethnic, and linguistic identity.

THE ROLE OF INTERNATIONAL POWERS

In any of the scenarios envisioned for the future of Iraq and of its religious diversity, the international community has an important role to play. On the one hand, Iraq would benefit from international assistance in the process of reforming its laws as well as its judicial system to ensure full respect for the rule of law in every part of the country and at all levels of society. On the other hand, the international community—be it through the UN or a group of countries—is the only possible source of guarantees for the protection of religious minorities, who are at present deeply mistrustful of the ability and willingness of either the KRG or the central government to fulfil this vital mission.

The international community ought to be more engaged, proactive, and consistent. In most cases, the various organisms of the UN and similar organizations act post factum, which significantly reduces their ability to offer solutions that are effective in the long run. The implementation of sustainable development policies, aimed at raising the standard of living of the local population while empowering it to take ownership of its own future, is one of the key strategies necessary to shift from a largely passive approach to one truly able to prepare for upcoming crises and thus alleviate their negative impacts.

The efficiency of the international community in addressing political and humanitarian challenges as well as security concerns is also gravely undermined by a fundamental lack of consistency. One of the most glaring examples of this in recent decades is the recurrent condemnation of terrorism and violent religious extremism by countries which continue to support groups espousing those very tactics and ideologies. These alliances are dubiously justified with claims that they help to prevent some greater evil. More importantly, they further the political ambitions of those in power. In a country such as Iraq, religious minorities have to face the direct consequences of such contradictions, of tactical alliances between Western powers and state and non-state actors that engage in violent religious extremism and terrorism. The same can be said about claims by many members of the international community, especially in the West, to be deeply concerned with ensuring that human rights are upheld globally. Yet how can a country such as the United States effectively advocate for the respect of human rights, when it fosters very close relationships with some countries that daily violate even the most inalienable of those rights?

The situation of religious minorities in Iraq is at the moment extremely bleak. If international actors do not assume their responsibility to protect, if the rule of law is not soon re-established over the whole country, if legal and judicial reforms are not implemented, if minorities are not empowered politically,

I fear that these communities which have inhabited the area for millennia will not survive the onslaught—a loss from which Iraq will never recover.

NOTES

1. Nīfīn 'Abd al-Mun'im Mus'ad, *al-Aqallīyāt wa-l-istiqrār al-siyāsī fī al-waṭan al-'arabī* [Minorities and political stability in the Arab world] (Cairo: Jāmi'at al-Qāhira, Kullīyat al-Iqtiṣād wa-l-'Ulūm al-Siyāsīya, Markaz al-Buḥūth wa-l-Dirāsāt al-Siyāsīya, 1988), v; Paul A. F. Walter, *Race and Culture Relations* (New York: McGraw-Hill, 1952), 21.See also United Nations Centre for Human Rights, *Minority Rights*, rev. ed., Human rights fact sheet 18 (Geneva; New York: Office of the United Nations High Commissioner for Human Rights, 1998); 'Abd al-Salām Ibrāhīm Baghdādī, *al-Waḥda al-waṭanīya wa-mushkilat al-aqallīyāt fī Ifrīqiyā* [National unity and the issue of minorities in Africa], 2nd ed. (Beirut: Markaz Dirāsāt al-Waḥdah al-'Arabīya, 2000), 83.

2. Similar declarations concerning the protection of their respective minorities were made by a number of States upon accession to the League of Nations, including Albania (November 2, 1921), Estonia (September 17, 1923), Finland (June 27, 1921), Latvia (July 17, 1923), Lithuania (May 12, 1922), Iraq (May 9, 1932). See Najilā Kan'ān, *Ḥimāyat al-aqallīyāt fī al-qānūn al-duwalī al-'āmm: Naẓra tārīkhīya wa-qānūnīya* [The protection of minorities in international public law: a historical and legal perspective] (Beirut: Dār Nilsun, 2009), 246; Muḥammad al-Sammāk, *al-Aqallīyāt bayna al-'urūbah wa-al-Islām* [Minorities between Arabism and Islam] (Beirut: Dār al-'Ilm lil-Malāyīn, 2002), 112.For Iraq specifically, see 'Awnī 'Abd al-Muḥsin Farsakh, *al-Aqallīyāt fī al-tārīkh al-'arabī mundhu al-Jāhilīyah ilā al-yawm* [Minorities in Arab history, from the Jahiliyya until today] (London; Beirut: Riyāḍ al-Rayyis lil-Kutub wa-l-Nashr, 1994), 397–399.

3. International Federation for Human Rights and International Alliance for Justice, *Iraq: Continuous and Silent Ethnic Cleansing. Displaced Persons in Iraqi Kurdistan and Iraqi Refugees in Iran* (Paris: AIJ—FIDH, January 2003), 40–42.

4. William Warda, "al-Ashūrīyūn fī al-'Irāq" [Assyrians in Iraq], *Majallat Dirāsāt 'Irāqīya* 9 (January 1999).

5. Ḥassan al-'Alawī, *al-'Irāq: Dawlat al-munaẓama al-sirrīya* [Iraq: State of secret organization] (Riyadh: al-Sharika al-Sa'ūdīya lil-Abḥath wa-l-Nashr, 1990).

6. William Warda, "al-Ḥimāya al-dūwalīya lil-aqallīyāt: Dirāsāt ḥālat al-ḥimāya al-dūwalīya lil-masīḥīyīn al-'irāqīyīn namūdhajan" [On the international protection of minorities: a case study of the situation of the international protection of Iraqi Christians] (Master's Thesis, Department of Political Sciences, University of Baghdad, 2013), 248.

7. Hammurabi Human Rights Organization (HHRO), *2011 Annual Report on the Situation of Iraqi Minorities* (Baghdad, 2012).

8. HHRO, *2009 Annual Report on the Human Rights Situation of Christians in Iraq* (Baghdad, 2009). See also HHRO, *2015 Annual Report on Human Rights Violations in Iraq with Concentration on Minorities* (Baghdad, 2016).

9. HHRO, *2011 Annual Report*, 19–21.

10. HHRO, *al-Taqrīr al-sanawī ʿan awḍāʿ al-ḥuqūq al-insān fī al-ʿIrāq khilāla ʿām 2014* [2014 Annual Report on Human Rights in Iraq] (Baghdad, 2015), 32–63.

11. HHRO, *2015 Annual Report*; HHRO, *2011 Annual Report*.

12. HHRO, *al-Taqrīr al-sanawī ʿan awḍāʿ al-ḥuqūq al-insān fī al-ʿIrāq khilāla ʿām 2016* [2016 Annual Report on Human Rights in Iraq] (Baghdad, 2017).

13. Republic of Iraq, "Qānūn al-baṭāqa al-waṭanīya (3) li-sana 2016" [National identity card law (3) of 2016], *al-Waqāʾiʿ al-ʿIrāqī* 4396 (February 2016).For more details, see HHRO, *2016 Annual Report*, 2; HHRO, *2015 Annual Report*, 5.

BIBLIOGRAPHY

al-ʿAlawī, Ḥassan. *al-ʿIrāq: Dawlat al-munaẓama al-sirrīya* [Iraq: State of secret organization]. Riyadh: al-Sharika al-Saʿūdīya lil-Abḥath wa-l-Nashr, 1990.

al-Sammāk, Muḥammad. *al-Aqallīyāt bayna al-ʿurūbah wa-al-Islām* [Minorities between Arabism and Islam]. Beirut: Dār al-ʿIlm lil-Malāyīn, 2002.

Baghdādī, ʿAbd al-Salām Ibrāhīm. *al-Waḥda al-waṭanīya wa-mushkilat al-aqallīyāt fī Ifrīqiyā* [National unity and the issue of minorities in Africa]. 2nd ed. Beirut: Markaz Dirāsāt al-Waḥdah al-ʿArabīya, 2000.

Farsakh, ʿAwnī ʿAbd al-Muḥsin *al-Aqallīyāt fī al-tārīkh al-ʿarabī mundhu al-Jāhilīyah ilā al-yawm* [Minorities in Arab history, from the Jahiliyya until today]. London; Beirut: Riyāḍ al-Rayyis lil-Kutub wa-l-Nashr, 1994.

Hammurabi Human Rights Organization. *2009 Annual Report on the Human Rights Situation of Christians in Iraq*. Baghdad, 2009.

———. *2011 Annual Report on the Situation of Iraqi Minorities*. Baghdad, 2012.

———. *2015 Annual Report on Human Rights Violations in Iraq with Concentration on Minorities*. Baghdad, 2016.

———. *al-Taqrīr al-sanawī ʿan awḍāʿ al-ḥuqūq al-insān fī al-ʿIrāq khilāla ʿām 2014* [2014 Annual Report on Human Rights in Iraq]. Baghdad, 2015.

———. *al-Taqrīr al-sanawī ʿan awḍāʿ al-ḥuqūq al-insān fī al-ʿIrāq khilāla ʿām 2016* [2016 Annual Report on Human Rights in Iraq]. Baghdad, 2017.

International Federation for Human Rights, and International Alliance for Justice. *Iraq: Continuous and Silent Ethnic Cleansing. Displaced Persons in Iraqi Kurdistan and Iraqi Refugees in Iran*. Paris: AIJ—FIDH, January 2003.

Kanʿān, Najilā. *Ḥimāyat al-aqallīyāt fī al-qānūn al-duwalī al-ʿāmm: Naẓra tārīkhīya wa-qānūnīya* [The protection of minorities in international public law: a historical and legal perspective]. Beirut: Dār Nilsun, 2009.

Musʿad, Nīfīn ʿAbd al-Munʿim. *al-Aqallīyāt wa-l-istiqrār al-siyāsī fī al-waṭan al-ʿarabī* [Minorities and political stability in the Arab world]. Cairo: Jāmiʿat al-Qāhira, Kullīyat al-Iqtiṣād wa-l-ʿUlūm al-Siyāsīya, Markaz al-Buḥūth wa-l-Dirāsāt al-Siyāsīya, 1988.

Republic of Iraq. "Qānūn al-baṭāqa al-waṭanīya (3) li-sana 2016" [National identity card law (3) of 2016]. *al-Waqāʾiʿ al-ʿIrāqī* 4396 (February 2016).

United Nations Centre for Human Rights. *Minority Rights*. Rev. ed. Human rights fact sheet 18. Geneva; New York: Office of the United Nations High Commissioner for Human Rights, 1998.

Walter, Paul A. F. *Race and Culture Relations*. New York: McGraw-Hill, 1952.

Warda, William. "al-Ashūrīyūn fī al-ʿIrāq" [Assyrians in Iraq]. *Majallat Dirāsāt ʿIrāqīya* 9. (January 1999).

———. "al-Ḥimāya al-dūwalīya lil-aqallīyāt: Dirāsāt ḥālat al-ḥimāya al-dūwalīya lil-masīḥīyīn al-ʿirāqīyīn namūdhajan" [On the international protection of minorities: a case study of the situation of the international protection of Iraqi Christians]. Master's Thesis, Department of Political Sciences, University of Baghdad, 2013.

Chapter 18

The Christians of Lebanon:
Surviving amidst Chaos

(Boston, November 9, 2016)

Marius Deeb

My theme in this essay is that the Maronite Catholic community and the Maronite Catholic church have been the defenders of Lebanon throughout its modern history, and other Christian communities have rallied around them. As crises have afflicted Lebanon, those who have acted as saviors of Lebanon have come from the Maronite Catholic community, whether they were from the political elite or the Lebanese Army. When there was a dearth of saviors, the Maronite Catholic church took over that role.

Lebanon produced the earliest nationalism in the Middle Eastern region, associated with the collective consciousness of the Maronites as a community and as a Christian church that had established links with Rome as early as the time of the Crusaders. At the outset, the Maronite Community and the Maronite Church were coterminous (not unlike the Armenian nation and the Armenian Church). This remained so until the early nineteenth century, when the whole of Mount Lebanon as the core of the Shihabi *Imarah,* or 'princedom,' became the focus of the Maronite Community and the Maronite Church.

There were two conflicts in the nineteenth century that resulted in the creation of an autonomous Mount Lebanon. The first conflict was social in character, and took place between the Maronite peasants, supported by the Maronite Church, and their feudal lords (*Muqata'jis*), who were primarily Druze, although some were Maronite, especially in the Kisrawan region. It was in this region that Tanyus Shahin, the leader of the peasants of Kisrawan, evicted the Khazins, the Maronite feudal lords, and took over their possessions. They also set up a Republican government in 1859, influenced by the ideas of the French Revolution. The second conflict was religious, as it took place between the Druze, supported by the Ottoman officials, and the

Christians. It resulted in the massacre of 11,000 Christians in Wadi al-Taym, al-Shuf, and in particular in Dayr al-Qamar, Zahleh, and Jizzin.[1]

This dual conflict led to the intervention of European powers, and the landing in Beirut of 7,000 French troops on August 16, 1860. The European powers, France, Britain, Russia, Austria, and Prussia, signed the statute known as the *Règlement Organique* in Istanbul on June 9, 1861, which established Mount Lebanon as a *mutasarifiyya*, that is, an autonomous region governed by an Ottoman *mutasarrif* who had to be a non-Lebanese Catholic.

This was a step in the development of the nascent Lebanese nationalism. Because of its role in Lebanon, France was viewed by the Lebanese Christians, and in particular by the Maronites, as their protector. They referred to France as "the loving mother (*l-Umm al-Hanun*)." It was not just the Catholicism of France that attracted the Christians, but also the ideas of the French Enlightenment and of the French Revolution. At the end of World War I, the Maronite Christians, and in particular the Maronite Patriarch, Ilyas al-Huwayik, who had made the arduous journey to Paris, urged the French government to "recognize Lebanon's independence."[2] He was prevented from addressing the Paris Peace Conference, but was able to submit his memorandum calling for the independence of Lebanon and "the return to its historical and natural boundaries, including the al-Biqa' region that Turkey had cut off from Lebanon."[3] As a result, the French High Commissioner in Syria and Lebanon declared the establishment of Greater Lebanon (*Le Grand Liban*) on September 1, 1920. The Christians were a majority in this new Lebanon, but did not have the dominant majority they had enjoyed under the *Mutasarifiyya* of Mount Lebanon.

According to the Lebanese statesman Taqi al-Din al-Sulh, "Until 1943, most Muslims and some Christians did not identify themselves as Lebanese. They worked to change the entity that was established in 1920, [that is, Greater Lebanon] by removing the regions in which Muslims were most numerous and annex them to Syria."[4] Many owed their allegiance to a Pan-Arab Nationalism and later to Pan-Syrian Nationalism as expounded by Antun Sa'adeh. Despite these efforts, the Grand Liban survived. In 1926, while France was still the mandatory power in Lebanon, a written constitution was drafted and remained in operation for 63 years until the Taif Accord of 1989. The constitution of 1926 was basically written by Michel Chiha (1891–1954), the leading Christian intellectual and ideologue of Lebanese nationalism at the time. He was a banker, an essayist, a journalist, and a poet.

When Lebanon became independent in 1943, many of the articles of the constitution had to be revised to accommodate the new reality. The independence of Lebanon was made possible by a consensus reached between the leading Christian and Muslim politicians, that an independent and sovereign Lebanon was worth having. The National Pact (*al-Mithaq al-Watani*) of

1943 was an unwritten agreement reached between the Maronite Christian President Bishara Al-Khuri and Sunni Muslim Prime Minister Riyad al-Sulh that Lebanon would not seek union with Syria, or with any other Arab country, and that it would not remain under French colonial rule. This was the first pillar of the National Pact, and again Michel Chiha played an important role in defining the terms of the agreement.

The second pillar of the National Pact was that all basic freedoms would be safeguarded, including freedom of the press, freedom of worship, freedom of speech, and free elections. This second pillar of the National Pact prompted the eldest daughter of Riyad al-Sulh, 'Alya' al-Sulh, to state in 1989 that Lebanon "cannot have except one master: freedom. This freedom gives the right to be different. Being Lebanese is not an accident of birth . . . but a vocation to be free, and a will for democracy."[5]

The third pillar of the National Pact was the equal partnership between Christians and Muslims in the cabinet, in parliament, and in the civil service. This was unprecedented in the Middle East. In all the Arab countries, Christians were then, in 1943, and are still today, regarded as *dhimmis,* so-called protected people, but in reality second class citizens. The executive post of the presidency was allotted to the Christians in 1943, not because they were a majority then, but to ensure that in Lebanon Christians were on equal footing with their Muslim compatriots.

The liberal democracy that was established as a result of the National Pact of 1943 was not a majoritarian democracy of the Westminster genre. It was what the Dutch political scientist Arend Lijphart called a consociational democracy, where ethnic and/or religious communities are always represented in a certain proportion in parliament and in the cabinet. Lijphart chose Lebanon and Switzerland as examples of this consociational democracy.

Michel Chiha was not only the main writer of the constitution of 1926 and the formulator of the National Pact, but also an ideologue of Lebanese nationalism. Chiha wrote that the basis of Lebanon was what he called the "interpenetration of the Mountain (Mount Lebanon) and the sea (the Mediterranean)."[6] What was unique about Lebanon according to Chiha was that "the sources of its wealth lay at the ends of the world."[7] The very basis of Lebanon depended on the activities of the Lebanese abroad and their interactions with the world. "Xenophobia in Lebanon is tantamount to a slow death, a kind of suicide,"[8] he wrote.

Chiha's conception of Lebanese nationalism is deeply rooted in history, and is inclusive. For him, Christians, Muslims, and Jews belong to the Lebanese polity, which has to be pluralistic, liberal, democratic, and open to the whole world. The Mediterraneanism emphasized in Chiha's ideas or in those of other Christian intellectuals—such as Michel Asmar of al-Nadwah al-Lubnaniyah, a forum for discussion of nationalist ideas—also meant that links to the West were vital for its survival. Lebanon's openness to its Arab hinterland was essential as well. I mention these matters because what Lebanon has been subjected to with the eruption of the civil war in April 1975, and what Lebanon has continued to be subjected to until the present time, is at loggerheads with what the founders of the Lebanese polity had in mind when Lebanon first became an independent country.

Prior to 1975, Lebanon faced two major crises. The first had to do with the issue of the presidency of Lebanon. According to article 49 of the Lebanese constitution, the President of the Republic shall be elected by secret ballot with a two-thirds majority of the members of the Chamber of Deputies on the first ballot, or by an absolute majority on the second ballot.[9] The president serves for a term of six years and cannot be re-elected for another term unless six years have passed from the time of the expiration of his presidency. The first president of independent Lebanon, Bishara al-Khuri, who was elected in 1943, decided to run for another term, and therefore had to amend the constitution for that purpose. Michel Chiha strongly opposed any change to the constitution that would allow President Bishara al-Khuri to be re-elected for a second consequent term. Despite his warnings that amending the constitution was neither popular nor prudent, the Chamber Deputies approved, on May 22, 1948, a provisional constitutional law allowing the incumbent President of Republic to be re-elected for another term of six years.[10] Opposition to the re-elected President Bishara al-Khuri gathered strength in the early 1950s, leading to a general strike. Eventually, the peaceful revolution known as the Rosewater Revolution succeeded when President al-Khuri resigned on September 18, 1952.

The new president, Camille Chamoun (1952–1958), was a capable politician and his presidency was marked by economic prosperity and the avoidance of regional crises until May 1958, when a mini-civil war took place, lasting one hundred days. The conflict was due more to the external intervention by Abdel Nasser United Arab Republic than to internal issues. In retrospect, the mini–civil war of 1958 had no lasting impact when compared to what happened to Lebanon from April 13, 1975, onward. Like the previous crisis of 1952, the role of the Maronite commander of the army, General Fu'ad Shihab, was crucial. President Chamoun was allowed to complete his term in office, the insurgents against him were contained, and the civil war ended with the slogan "No Victor and No Vanquished."

General Fu'ad Shihab was elected president in August 1958, and took over power after President Chamoun completed his term, on September 23, 1958. After a meeting was held between President 'Abd al-Nasir and President Shihab, in a location significantly chosen on the Lebanese–Syrian border, a modus vivendi was reached between the two countries that ushered in a period of peace and tranquility throughout Shihab's presidency. If there was ever a golden age in Lebanon, it was the period from 1952 until 1967. I can personally attest to this because that period coincided with my childhood and my youth when I grew up in Lebanon.

The Arab–Israeli war of 1967 had a deleterious impact on Lebanon, because soon after it, Palestinians began mounting attacks against Israel across the Lebanese–Israeli border. On November 2, 1969, Lebanon was forced to sign the Cairo Agreement with the PLO leader Yasser Arafat, which was brokered by the Egyptian President Abdel Nasser. Most of the Christians in Lebanon were against the agreement because it gave the PLO control of the Palestinian camps and control of a strip of land in southern Lebanon from which they could operate against Israel.

The conflict that began on April 13, 1975, was quite different from the mini–civil war of 1958. In the case of the latter, there was still hope, as the conflict did not last long, that things would settle down and the Lebanese would resume what they were doing before. The poet and politician Edward Hunain gave a lecture at al-Nadwah al-Lubnaniyyah in May 1961, significantly entitled "After the Storm," in which he reformulated the ideals of Lebanese nationalism. He maintained that the Lebanese sought "the habitual life, the everyday life, the familiar domestic life, the life that they live spontaneously, naturally, without exertion or fatigue, in secrecy and openly, in the market place and at home, in the field and in the shop, in the factory and on the beach, in the tavern and at church. They wished to work, to eat, to have fun or to pray, for the habitual life is the authentic love of the motherland, and the ideal humanistic patriotism. . . . To make a country live the ordinary life is to sponsor a continuous and tempered development, and to renounce the coup d'état and revolution."[11]

What happened to Lebanon from April 1975 onwards has been the negation of Edward Hunain's vision. What he had called the "habitual ordinary life" has been undermined for the vast majority of the Lebanese people. The armed struggle across the Lebanese–Israeli border that eventually led to the establishment of an Israeli security zone in southern Lebanon in June 1978, and the division of Beirut between various militias, was a far cry from what Edward Hunain and the founding fathers of Lebanon had envisaged for their motherland. Lebanon during its golden age was called the Switzerland of the Middle East, and its capital Beirut was depicted as the Paris of the Levant. Although the conflict in 1975 began as a conflict between the majority of the Muslims who had supported the military presence of the PLO in Lebanon and most of the Christians who were against it, the Syrian President Hafez al-Assad deceptively intervened in Lebanon, and Syria ended up being the dominant power in Lebanon by early 1977.

As in the previous crises of 1952 and 1958, a savior emerged, not from among the leading politicians like Camille Chamoun or from the Lebanese official armed forces like General Fu'ad Chehab, but from a Christian militia called the Lebanese Forces, headed by the young charismatic commander Bashir Gemayel (the younger son of the leader of the Kataeb Party Pierre Gemayel), who had allied himself to Israel to oust the PLO and Syria from Lebanon. He was elected president of Lebanon on August 23, 1982. His attempt at ending the war in Lebanon and across the Lebanese–Israeli border was nipped in the bud when he was killed on September 14, 1982, by a bomb planted by agents working for the Syrian President Hafez al-Assad. The successor of the assassinated President-elect Bashir Gemayel was his brother President Amine Gemayel, who tried for six years to reach an agreement with Syria but to no avail. Syria forced President Amine Gemayel to rescind the Lebanese–Israeli Agreement of May 17, 1983, brokered by the United States, that would have permanently pacified the Lebanese–Israeli border. After the withdrawal of the PLO forces from Lebanon in 1982, they were replaced by the militants of Hezbollah, an organization formed in June 1982 by Iran and Syria to serve their interests in the region, and to keep the Lebanese–Israeli border ablaze.

Before his term ended, President Amine Gemayel appointed the Commander of the Lebanese Army, General Michel Aoun, as Interim Prime Minister heading a military cabinet of six members. Syria then put pressure on the three Muslim members of the cabinet to resign. So on March 14, 1989, Aoun declared a War of Liberation against Syria. Here again a new savior emerged among the Maronite Christians to liberate Lebanon from Syrian hegemony. Because of his stand against Syria, Interim Prime Minister General Michel Aoun "struck a nationalist fiber, and 'reached across religious boundaries and into the hearts of many Lebanese.'"[12] The highest-ranking Sunni clergyman in Lebanon, Mufti Hasan Khalid, refused to condemn Aoun's confrontation with Syrian President Hafez al-Assad and had secret contacts with him. On May 16, 1989, Mufti Hasan Khalid was killed by a car bomb that exploded when his motorcade passed by.

President Hafez al-Assad decided to undermine the institution of the presidency in Lebanon, because Lebanon's presidents had consistently opposed Syrian domination. For that purpose, the Lebanese parliamentarians were invited to the city of al-Taif to "reform" the political system in Lebanon. The irony of meeting in al-Taif was in asking the representatives the longest existing democratic polity in the Arab world, Lebanon, to convene in the Kingdom of Saudi Arabia, which lacked both political and religious freedom. The document that was approved by 58 out of the 62 deputies who attended the meeting made changes in article 49 of the constitution that would undermine the presidency. Under the constitution of 1926, the president had been "the head of the executive branch of government."[13] In the Taif Accord the president became "the ceremonial head of state, the symbol of the nation's unity."[14] In the original constitution the president had been "the commander-in-chief of the Armed Forces," while in the al-Taif Accord the president became "the ceremonial commander-in-chief because the Armed Forces fell under the authority of the council of ministers."[15] The Interim Prime Minister Michel Aoun rejected the Taif Accord, and to forestall the election of a new president under these conditions, he issued a decree on November 4, 1989, dissolving parliament. As most of the Arab countries and the United States had supported the Taif Accord, the Lebanese parliamentarians convened on November 5, 1989, and elected a member of parliament, René Moawad, as president of Lebanon. The new president was too independent for the Syrian President Hafez al-Assad, and so, on November 22, 1989, the newly elected Moawad was on his way to attend the Independence Day celebration when a car was detonated on the route of his motorcade, killing him. A few days later, a hurried meeting of the Lebanese parliamentarians was held and a new president, Elias Hrawi, was elected.

It was not surprising that General Michel Aoun, who rejected the Taif Accord and defied the Syrian President Hafez al-Assad, became very popular indeed. "Spontaneous demonstrations by tens of thousands of people took place outside the B'abda presidential palace" in support of Aoun in 1990.[16] A visitor to the presidential palace noted the destruction there. "No glass, no lights, no chairs, no walls—everything was broken or destroyed."[17] General Michel Aoun operated from a fortified basement that was originally a kitchen and a shelter. On the other side of the destroyed presidential palace there were "tents, flowers, platforms, loudspeakers . . . and the pictures of General Michel Aoun and Lebanese flags everywhere. It was a surrealistic scene: the stones were a testimony to the disaster [which afflicted the place], and the people were living in a state of joy."[18]

What happened beyond the borders of Lebanon affected the fate of Aoun. Kuwait was invaded by Iraq on August 2, 1990, and the United States wanted the Syrian President Hafez al-Assad to join the coalition against Saddam Hussein. In order to get Syria's support, the Bush Administration allowed Syrian President Hafez al-Assad to oust General Aoun from the presidential palace. On October 13, 1990, Syria mounted an air and ground attack, killing around two hundred Lebanese officers and soldiers. General Aoun decided to take refuge in the French Embassy, and later was given political asylum in France. The Vatican issued a statement at that time to the effect that: "to resort to military force to solve a sensitive political domestic problem was unfortunate especially as a foreign state had intervened to impose a military solution."[19]

With General Michel Aoun in exile and the heir of Bashir Gemayel's Lebanese Forces Party, Samir Geagea, in prison, the Maronite Catholic church, in the name of its Patriarch Sfair, took the lead in mobilizing the Lebanese Christians. The memorandum issued by Patriarch Sfair on September 20,

2000, was a watershed. It described the suffering of the Lebanese people and in particular the Christians under Syrian domination. It stated that the political system had been undermined because of the Syrian domination of the state institutions. As the elections were rigged, Syria had nominated the politicians, the civil servants, and even members of the judiciary.[20] Syrian domination of Lebanon negated the National Pact of 1943, which asserted that neither West nor East would dominate Lebanon, that is, "neither France would stay in Lebanon nor Syria would stay in Lebanon." Patriarch Sfair maintained that Lebanon deserved to be independent and sovereign again, by returning to the principles of the National Pact.[21] Patriarch Sfair's memorandum resonated among the Christian communities, and on April 30, 2001, 29 prominent Christian politicians and intellectuals met in Qurnat Shahwan, the seat of the Maronite bishopric of Mount Lebanon. This group, later called the Qurnat Shahwan Gathering, issued a statement calling for the end of Syrian occupation and the restoration of Lebanon's liberal democracy with the basic freedoms that Lebanon had previously enjoyed.

Patriarch Sfair continued his campaign by visiting the southern regions of Mount Lebanon in early August 2001. The purpose of this journey to al-Shuf, Jizzin, and Aley was 'the reconciliation between the two religious communities, the Maronites and the Druze, who had founded Lebanon in the early eighteenth century. In this journey of uniting the Maronite and the Druze communities, Patriarch Sfair was in effect re-founding Lebanon based on its historical roots. An enthusiastic welcome greeted the Patriarch as he traveled through the towns and villages. In both Christian and Druze villages, roses were strewn and rice was thrown on his path. Statements of welcome and praise of Sfair's mission of "unity and love" were written on various placards that were displayed on the roads. One placard read, "The glory of Lebanon has been given to him." Another placard read, "Welcome to the Conscience of Lebanon." The Patriarch visited al-Mukhtara, the seat of the feudal Druze lord Walid Jumblatt, where a huge crown turned out to greet him. Jumblatt welcomed the Patriarch and declared that "the war in Mount Lebanon has gone and will never return; together we shall protect Mount Lebanon and together we shall protect Lebanon."[22]

Two important actions taken by the United States and France empowered the Lebanese opposition against Syrian domination. First was the signing into law, on December 12, 2003, by President George W. Bush, of the "Syria Accountability and the Lebanese Sovereignty Restoration Act" passed by Congress. Second was the landmark UN Security Council Resolution 1559, sponsored by the United States and France, that was passed on September 2, 2004. Resolution 1559 called for free presidential elections, the withdrawal of foreign troops from Lebanon, and the disarming of militias. Despite this resolution, Syria prevailed on the Lebanese parliament, which amended the

Lebanese constitution and extended the term of the incumbent President Emile Lahoud for three years on September 3, 2004.

The opposition to Syrian domination which had been led by the Maronite Catholic church and supported by the vast majority of the Christians gained momentum as it was joined by the foremost Druze leader Walid Jumblatt and the most prominent Sunni leader Rafiq al-Hariri, who had resigned as Prime Minister on October 21, 2004. The opposition leaders were campaigning to win the next parliamentary elections and to ask for the implementation of UN Security Resolution 1559, which stipulated among other matters the withdrawal of Syrian troops from Lebanon.

The Syrian President Bashar al-Assad, who had previously threatened Prime Minister Rafiq al-Hariri "to break Lebanon on his head," fulfilled his threat by using Hezbollah operatives to kill Rafiq al-Hariri on February 14, 2005. After al-Hariri's funeral, as Michael Young writes, "it was the Christians [again] and the Druze . . . who daily kept the flame of outrage alive." It took almost a month of anti-Syrian protests "for the Sunni community to go into the streets."[23] The protest movement culminated in the massive demonstration of March, 14, 2005, when 1.5 million people peacefully assembled in Beirut, calling for the withdrawal of Syrian troops, a free democratic polity, and the truth about the assassination of al-Hariri and all the other terrorist operations for the last three decades. In this demonstration, an unprecedented phenomenon was born, heralding a new era for Lebanon. This phenomenon, called the Cedar Revolution, is different from the other revolutions that took place in the region because it was a nonviolent revolution with strong adherence to democratic principles and political pluralism, which sought the support of the West and emerged as an antidote to militant Islam and terrorism.

The first achievement of the Cedar Revolution was the withdrawal of Syria's troops and its overt intelligence apparatus on April 26, 2005. This goal was achieved then because of the pressure exerted by the United States. On May 7, 2005, Michel Aoun returned to Lebanon after fifteen years in exile, and was received with tremendous popular enthusiasm. On May 18, 2005, Michel Aoun visited Samir Geagea in his cell in the Ministry of Defense. Michel Aoun expressed his admiration for Geagea's courage and "spiritual strength," and stated that keeping Samir Geagea in prison was unjust and that he should be released. Samir Geagea should have responded to Michel Aoun's grand gesture at that time by allying his party with Aoun's in the parliamentary elections, and by endorsing Aoun for the presidency, but he did not. I wrote three years ago: "All the leaders of the Cedar Revolution, like Samir Geagea, former president Amine Gemayel, Walid Jumblatt, and Saad Hariri, should have endorsed Michel Aoun for the presidency of Lebanon for he had earned it by being the pioneer in fighting Syria with his War of Liberation (1989–1990) and by playing a crucial role in the events that led to the

Cedar Revolution."[24] By alienating Michel Aoun, they pushed him to sign an agreement with Hezbollah in February 2006.

Major intellectual figures of the Cedar Revolution were targeted by its enemies—for instance, the intellectual and journalist Samir Kasir, who was assassinated in June 2005. His writings and activities were instrumental in mobilizing the rank and file of the Cedar Revolution. Gubran Tueni was assassinated in December 2005. He was a leading member of the Cedar Revolution in parliament and he was the publisher of the most prestigious newspaper in Lebanon, *al-Nahar,* whose columns had inspired the supporters of the Cedar Revolution. Later, Pierre Gemayel, the son of the former Lebanese president Amine Gemayel, was assassinated in November 2006. He was a leading figure of the Cedar Revolution in parliament and a longtime critic of Syria and Hezbollah.

At the behest of its two masters, Syria and Iran, Hezbollah provoked a war with Israel in July 2006 to turn the tables against the leaders of the Cedar Revolution. It was done on purpose as the summer season of 2006 was predicted to be the best tourist season since 1974. The war ended on August 14, 2006, with United Nations Security Resolution 1701 calling for the expansion of the already-existing United Nations Interim Force in Lebanon (UNIFIL) to 15,000 troops, and for the deployment of 15,000 Lebanese Army troops to southern Lebanon, where they had not been since 1968.[25]

As though the contrived and devastating war that Hezbollah provoked with Israel was not enough, Hezbollah began a sit-in in downtown Beirut on December 1, 2006, that lasted for eighteenth months, forcing the closing of hundreds of shops and businesses, and adding to the unemployment and economic woes of the country. The enemies of the Cedar Revolution further attacked the institutions of Lebanon when parliament was closed down for fourteen months from March 2007 to May 2008. This had never happened since the independence of Lebanon in 1943.

In 2007, President Bashar al-Assad sent a Sunni terrorist organization called Fatah al-Islam to the Nahr al-Barid Palestinian camp in northern Lebanon. This was the time when Syria was sending Sunni militants to its neighbors. It took the Lebanese Army 160 days (from May 20, until September 2, 2007) to defeat this terrorist organization. One hundred and sixty-three soldiers and officers died in that war. The fallen members of the Lebanese Army belonged to all the main religious communities. The triumph of the Lebanese Army boosted its commander General Michel Sulaiman who became the most popular figure in Lebanon.[26] When Hezbollah used military force, in early May 2008, against the media outlets of Saad al-Hariri (the heir of Rafiq al-Hariri's al-Mustaqbal movement) and strongholds of the Druze leader Walid Jumblatt in Mount Lebanon, it led to a major political impasse that was resolved in Doha under the sponsorship of the Emir of Qatar.

On May 25, 2008, all major Lebanese political leaders agreed in Doha that the popular Commander of the Lebanese Army, General Michel Sulaiman, would be elected president of Lebanon. On June 7, 2009, parliamentary elections took place and the results were like the previous parliamentary election of May–June 2005, with the Cedar Revolution coalition winning 71 seats out of a total 128. Both parliamentary elections were free except in regions where the Shi'ite movements Hezbollah and Amal (the latter of the Speaker of the House, Nabih Birri) dominated, because no political competition was allowed in those areas.[27]

The Special Tribunal for Lebanon, which was set up under Chapter VII by United Nations Security Council Resolution 1757 on May 30, 2007, was looming large and led Hezbollah to insist on receiving a veto power in the Lebanese Cabinet, by having 11 ministers out of a total 30 ministers. It thus took Prime Minister Saad al-Hariri 135 days of consultations to form his cabinet after the June 2009 elections. Saad al-Hariri's term was cut short on January 12, 2011 when 11 ministers resigned. This did not stop the work of the Special Tribunal for Lebanon. On June 30, 2011, it indicted four and eventually five Hezbollah members for the assassination of Rafiq al-Hariri. The most senior of these Hezbollah members, Mustafa Badr al-Din, was killed in May 2016, near the Damascus airport as he was leading Hezbollah fighters in Syria.

Since the formation of the Lebanese Cabinet headed by Prime Minister Tammam Salam (the son of former Prime Minister Saeb Salam) on February 15, 2014, a period of dialogue has been ushered in among all the major political movements despite their differences. Because of Lebanon's long history in democratic practice, reason, dialogue, negotiations, and compromise have, more often than not, prevailed. The indictment of members of Hezbollah in the assassination of Rafiq al-Hariri and the deep involvement of Hezbollah fighters in Syria has weakened the organization. The chaos that has engulfed Syria since 2011, and the rise of Sunni militants on the Syrian border with Lebanon, let alone the over one million Syrian refugees who have sought safe haven in Lebanon—all these factors have contributed to a continuous dialogue among the Lebanese. Samir Geagea, the leader of the Lebanese Forces Party, began a dialogue with Michel Aoun that led to an understanding being reached between the two leaders in January 2016. Eventually Samir Geagea, who was always close to Saad al-Hariri, convinced him that Michel Aoun is the only viable option as a presidential candidate, and that Michel Aoun will never depend on any external power or on Hezbollah to make his decisions. In the final analysis, Michel Aoun will always remain his own master.

President Michel Aoun, who was elected by parliament on October 31, 2016, will be able to accomplish a lot, in terms of both domestic issues and regional issues. He has already promised to fight corruption in the government, and to resolve the problems of power and water shortages and the collection of garbage. Beyond these mundane domestic issues, his relationship with Hezbollah would deter it from engaging in military adventures across the Lebanese–Israeli border. The best that could happen during President Michel Aoun's tenure in power is the re-establishment of a Lebanese polity characterized by peace and tranquility. It is a tall order to achieve but it is possible.

Two issues that concern the Christians of Lebanon are demography and identity. The Lebanese Republic has been conceived from the beginning of its formation as having two wings: one representing those who reside in Lebanon, and the other, those Lebanese who live abroad. In this sense, it is unique polity. To count the Lebanese Christians by counting only those who reside in Lebanon is totally unacceptable. Since the wealth of Lebanon, in the words of Michel Chiha, comes from the ends of the world, the Lebanese belong to Lebanon wherever they are in the world. A recent law passed in Lebanon encourages the numerous Lebanese all over the world to regain their nationality and participate in parliamentary elections. As the vast majority of the Lebanese abroad are Christian, including them would make them at least on par with their Muslim compatriots. This could be done, and I am certain the newly elected President Michel Aoun will be pursuing this course, because the Lebanese Christians constitute the *raison d'être* of Lebanon. Without them there will be no Lebanon.

The question of identity is of utmost importance. Most Lebanese Christians do not regard themselves as Arabs. Professor Franck Salameh pointed out in his scholarly masterpiece on Charles Corm that this Renaissance man had objected to the depiction of Lebanon in the National Pact of 1943 as having "an Arab face."[28] In the Taif Accord, Lebanon was depicted as Arab in character, but the Taif Accord was imposed on Lebanese Christians by force. A conference was held in March 1984 in Lausanne, attended by the major Lebanese politicians, to introduce changes to the political system. The identity of Lebanon was a topic of discussion. While the Lausanne Conference was in session, a meeting was being held in Beirut, attended by the Christian Lebanese Forces, represented by its then-commander Fadi Ifram and its secretary-general George Adwan; the Maronite Lebanese Order of Monks, represented by its president Abbot Bulus Nu'man; and the representatives of a large number of Christian organizations from the Maronite, Greek Orthodox, Syriac Catholic, Syriac Orthodox and Armenian Catholic communities. They issued a manifesto stating that "the Christians in Lebanon reject the Arab identity because it is at loggerheads with their own identity."[29]

Lebanese Christians live in a polity that they have fiercely defended over the last forty years. Despite the wars and the conflicts that have ravaged their homeland, they have always rebuilt their country and continued to have faith in a better future. It is not only the beauty and the splendor of Lebanon that have kept the Christians attached to their country, but also the freedom that they enjoy at all levels. The religious freedom that they enjoy is a model for the rest of the Christians of the Levant and of Egypt. They ring the bells of their churches loudly and display their crosses for the onlookers to see. They have Christian festivities where their Christians symbols are paraded in public without fear.

NOTES

1. See Kamal S. Salibi, *The Modern History of Lebanon* (New York: Frederick A. Praeger, 1965).

2. *Al-Nahar,* September 2, 2009.

3. Ibid.

4. Taqi al-Din al-Sulh, "Al-Nida' al-Qawmi 'Aqidatun wa-Nidalun," in *'Ahd al-Nadwah al-Lubnaniyya: Khamsuna Sanat min al-Muhadarah, Les Années Cénacle* (Beirut: Dar al-Nahar, 1997), 255.

5. Quoted after Marius Deeb, *Syria's Terrorist War on Lebanon and the Peace Process* (New York: Palgrave Macmillan, 2003), 166.

6. Michel Chiha, "Presence du Liban," in *'Ahd al-Nadwah al-Lubnaniya, Khamsuna Sanat min al-Muhadarah, Les Années Cénacle* (Beirut: Dar al-Nahar, 1997), 244.

7. Ibid., 252.

8. Ibid., 249.

9. See *The Lebanese Constitution,* prepared by the Department of Political Studies and Public Administration, American University of Beirut (Beirut: Khayats, 1960), 20.

10. See ibid., 34–35.

11. Edward Hunain, "Ba'd al-'Asifah," in *'Ahd al-Nadwah al-Lubnaniyyah, Khmsuna Sanat min al-Muhadarat, Les Années Cénacle* (Beirut: Dar al-Nahar, 1997), 420.

12. Marius Deeb, *Syria's Terrorist War on Lebanon and the Peace Process* (New York: Palgrave Macmillan, 2003), 158, quoting Nora Boustany, "An Old War Claims New Victims," *The Washington Post*, April 12, 1989.

13. *The Lebanese Constitution,* 20–23.

14. Marius Deeb, *Syria's Terrorist War on Lebanon and the Peace Process* (New York: Palgrave Macmillan, 2003), 170.

15. Ibid., 170–171.

16. Marius Deeb, *Syria's Terrorist War on Lebanon and the Peace Process* (New York: Palgrave Macmillan, 2003), 173.

17. Karim Pakradouni, *La'nat Watan: Min Harb Lubnan ila Harb al-Khalij,* 'Abr al-Sharq Press, Beirut, n.d., 21; quoted in Marius Deeb, *Syria's Terrorist War on Lebanon and the Peace Process* (New York: Palgrave Macmillan, 2003), 173–174.

18. Karim Pakradouni, *La'nat Watan: Min Harb Lubnan ila Harb al-Khalij*, 'Abr al-Sharq Press, Beirut, n.d., 21; quoted in Marius Deeb, *Syria's Terrorist War on Lebanon and the Peace Process* (New York: Palgrave Macmillan, 2003), 174.

19. Ibid., 178.

20. See ibid., 218–219.

21. See ibid., 219.

22. Marius Deeb, *Syria, Iran and Hezbollah: The Unholy Alliance and Its War on Lebanon* (Stanford: Hoover Institution Press, 2013), 10–12.

23. Michael Young, "The general out of his labyrinth," *The Daily Star*, June 14, 2005. Quoted in ibid., 18.

24. Ibid., 21.

25. See ibid., 27–28.

26. See ibid., 33–34.

27. See ibid., 22, 40, and 58.

28. Franck Salameh, *Charles Corm: An Intellectual Biography of a Twentieth-Century Lebanese "Young Phoenician"* (Lanham: Lexington Books, 2015), 105.

29. Marius Deeb, *Syria's Terrorist War on Lebanon and the Peace Process* (New York: Palgrave Macmillan, 2003), 99.

WORKS CITED

al-Sulh, Taqi al-Din. "Al-Nida' al-Qawmi 'Aqidatun wa-Nidalun." In *'Ahd al-Nadwah al-Lubnaniyya: Khamsuna Sanat min al-Muhadarah, Les Années Cénacle*. Beirut: Dar al-Nahar, 1997.

Boustany, Nora. "An Old War Claims New Victims." *The Washington Post*. April 12, 1989.

Chiha, Michel. "Présence du Liban." In *'Ahd al-Nadwah al-Lubnaniya, Khamsuna Sanat min al-Muhadarah, Les Années Cénacle*. Beirut: Dar al-Nahar, 1997.

Deeb, Marius. *Syria's Terrorist War on Lebanon and the Peace Process*. New York: Palgrave Macmillan, 2003.

———. *Syria, Iran and Hezbollah: The Unholy Alliance and Its War on Lebanon*. Stanford: Hoover Institution Press, 2013.

Hunain, Edward. "Ba'd al-'Asifah." In *'Ahd al-Nadwah al-Lubnaniyyah, Khmsuna Sanat min al-Muhadarat, Les Années Cénacle*. Beirut: Dar al-Nahar, 1997.

American University of Beirut, Department of Political Studies and Public Administration. *The Lebanese constitution. A reference edition in English translation*. Beirut: Khayats, 1960.

Pakradouni, Karim. *La'nat Watan: Min Harb Lubnan ila Harb al-Khalij*. Beirut: 'Abr al-Sharq Press, n.d.

Salameh, Franck. *Charles Corm: An Intellectual Biography of a Twentieth-Century Lebanese "Young Phoenician."* Lanham: Lexington Books, 2015.

Salibi, Kamal S. *The Modern History of Lebanon*. New York: Frederick A. Praeger, 1965.

Young, Michael. "The general out of his labyrinth." *The Daily Star*. June 14, 2005.

Chapter 19

Social Pluralism, Religious Cleansing and "Hybrid Warfare" in Contemporary Syria

(Pembroke, Oxford, November 22, 2016)

John Eibner[1]

The violent conflict that has ravaged Syria since the "Arab Spring" uprisings of 2011 has led to extensive religious cleansing and the erosion of social pluralism. Much of the territory stretching from Syria's northeastern Mediterranean coast all the way to the outskirts of Baghdad in neighboring Iraq is now a *de facto* Sunnistan, virtually devoid of non-Sunnis. The religious cleansing of this region is not just a by-product of the ravages of this war, which features a host of state and non-state actors. It is largely a consequence of a form of, to use NATO's (North Atlantic Treaty Organization) terminology, "hybrid warfare," which is conducted by a Washington-led coalition. In his 2014 West Point address, President Obama described this coalition as a network of "alliances unrivaled in the history of nations," with the United States as its "hub."[2] This imperial configuration includes not only liberal western democracies, but also Sunni Islamist states and non-state actors, which, in turn, include violent jihadists. This U.S.-led network of alliances instrumentalizes Sunni jihadism as a weapon of war against the dictatorial regime in Damascus, the political base of which is made up primarily of non-Sunni minorities and progressive, secular-oriented, non-Islamist Sunnis. By empowering and utilizing forces dedicated to the imposition of Sunni supremacy in the region, the United States' practice of hybrid warfare in Syria has accelerated the religious cleansing process.

SOCIAL PLURALISM IN SYRIA

The modern Syrian state's fleeting flirtations with political pluralism have repeatedly failed to lay solid foundations for democracy. Since independence

193

in 1946, governments in Damascus have been overthrown eight times by means of military coups, the last being the seizure of power by the Alawite Hafez al-Assad in 1970. Since then, Syria has been governed by an iron-fisted dictatorship, with Bashar al-Assad succeeding his father as the country's president in 2000. The Syrian state was and is dominated by a tough and elaborate security service. Brutal means have customarily been used to crush political dissent from whatever quarter it arises. This was the case in the early 1980s, when Hafez al-Assad suppressed a Muslim Brotherhood-led insurrection. But despite the lack of political pluralism, modern Syria has been more socially pluralistic than any other Sunni Arab majority state in the Arab Middle East.

Before the "Arab Spring" uprisings of 2011, Syria was only on the periphery of my professional consciousness. For decades, my Christian Solidarity International (CSI) colleagues and I had focused on conflict zones where vulnerable religious minorities were endangered. This was not the case in Syria. At the beginning of 2011, I was concerned mainly with Iraq, and not its apparently tranquil Levantine neighbor. At that time, Iraq's Christian community and other non-Muslim minorities were being targeted for eradication, mainly by a violent insurgency whose aim was to restore the political supremacy of the country's Sunni minority, which had been violently terminated by the overthrow of Saddam Hussein in the course of the U.S.-led Operation Iraqi Freedom in 2003. Between 2003 and 2011, Syria had become a place of refuge for approximately one million displaced Iraqis. They included Sunnis, Shi'ites, Christians and others. The Georgetown-based historian Joseph Sassoon has produced valuable documentation of this mass Iraqi migration to Syria.[3] I spoke with many Christians who had fled to Syria from Iraq. Virtually all had positive things to say about the social and economic conditions they encountered there compared to those prevailing in "liberated" Iraq.

But after the start of the 2011 uprising in Syria, I began to encounter displaced Iraqi Christians who had fled their "liberated" homeland, only to be forced to return to Iraq as the "Arab Spring" uprising in Syria morphed into a violent sectarian conflict. Soon thereafter, my attention turned to Syria.

For centuries Syria had been a mosaic of different religious communities. They did not always coexist happily, and certainly not on the basis of equality. For most of the period between the Islamic conquest of Byzantium's predominantly Christian Syria in the 7th century and the end of the Ottoman Caliphate in 1918, the spirit, if not always the letter, of discriminatory Shari'a governed relations between the Sunni ruling class and the non-Sunni population. The lot of Syria's religious minority communities was characterized by institutionalized legal and social disadvantages, coupled with episodic waves of violent persecution under Sunni rule and periods of greater tolerance. Under the prevailing system of social and political control based on Shari'a law, the conquered Christians and Jews of Syria survived as *dhimmis*—the status assigned to "Peoples of the Book," or non-Muslim religious communities that nonetheless adhere to scriptures which Muslims consider to be genuine (if distorted) divine revelations. Provided that Christians and Jews accepted Muslim rule and the disabilities assigned to their religious caste, they were entitled, at least theoretically, to protection from threats emanating from external powers and from within the politically superior community of Sunni Muslims. But other non-Muslim minorities, among them the Alawites,[4] were not entitled to protection. They lived as *kufar* (infidels) entirely outside the protection of Islamic law.

In the 19th century, European powers intervened in the Ottoman Caliphate to promote western-style reforms and to "protect" the region's Christians and Jews. But this did not succeed in producing religious equality. After the Ottomans' defeat in World War I, Syria was awarded to France as a "mandate," and its French rulers enforced the constitutional concept of the equality of all citizens, regardless of religion, and freedom of religious observance and education.[5] Under the independent Syrian state, the Assads maintained continuity with this aspect of the French Mandate, and based their political system largely on the support of religious minorities, non-Islamist Sunnis and other secularized people.

Reliable statistics are hard to come by, but on the eve of the "Arab Spring" uprisings, roughly 75 percent of Syrians were Sunnis. Christians and Alawites made up about 8 percent and 12 percent of the population respectively. Shi'ite Twelvers, Isma'ilis and Druzes are among the smaller minority communities. Wherever the Syrian government rules, religious communities have extensive space in society for expression of their beliefs and traditions, provided they do not stray into the realm of opposition politics.[6] This social freedom extends beyond religious communities, and encompasses liberated women and secular people who do not identify with the belief system of any religious community. Before the current war, Syria had a well-earned reputation for providing more social pluralism than any other Sunni Arab majority country in the Middle East, not to mention respectable health services and educational opportunities. Since the early 1970s, the guarantor of this pluralistic social system has been the Assad dictatorship.

As Alawites, the late Hafez and his heir Bashar have always had a strong interest in protecting the country's religious minority communities against the revanchist forces of Sunni supremacism, which have long represented the most powerful opposition movement in the country. This protection was acknowledged by President Obama at a meeting of Middle Eastern church leaders in September 2014.[7] The Assads have therefore largely based their rule on the support of the religious minorities, non-Islamist Sunnis and other secularized people. The main instrument for ensuring the stability of this system has been its Alawite-dominated network of intelligence and security agencies. But today, social pluralism is in retreat in much of Syria. It is being destroyed by the peculiar form of warfare that has been waged there since 2011.

"A KIND OF THIRTY YEARS' WAR"

There are important aspects of the current conflict in Syria that are unique to our times and point to the future development of warfare. But there are also those that also harken back to the distant past. In 2014, the former Director of the CIA and Defense Secretary Leon Panetta spoke of the conflict in Syria as "a kind of Thirty Years' War" of the sort that devastated Central Europe in the 17th century, destroying one third of the population of Germany in process.[8] Panetta was not far off the mark. There are some striking similarities. Among them are the interventions of Great Powers, the multitude of armed forces, the use of proxies, including mercenaries, and the apocalyptic magnitude of death and destruction. Not since the Mongol invasions of the 13th century has warfare been more grisly for the Syrian people and ruinous for its economy and infrastructure. Reliable death statistics are hard to come by, but the figure produced by the Syrian Center for Policy Research is 470,000—just off half a million.[9] Half the population of 22 million has been displaced. Seven million of the homeless have found refuge inside Syria—overwhelmingly in government-controlled areas—while four million have sought refuge abroad. What I have seen on the ground confirms a UN report's conclusion that the war in Syria has produced the "world's largest humanitarian crisis since World War II."[10] With the country's economy and infrastructure in ruins, there is little hope for an early end to this catastrophe for the Syrian people.[11]

As in Europe's Thirty Years' War, the violent power struggles in Syria have taken on a markedly sectarian character. This was already apparent by the summer of 2011. It was a major factor in CSI's autumn 2011 decision to issue a "genocide warning" for the region.[12] The alert fell largely on deaf ears. However, nearly five years later, Secretary of State John Kerry issued a genocide determination. Kerry's statement expressed abhorrence at the religious cleansing committed by the Islamic State in Iraq and Syria, which he declared was inherent in its ideology. Kerry identified the victimized communities by name: "Yezidis, Christians, Shia Muslims," while also noting that others, in particular Sunni Muslims and Kurds, were also victims of "crimes against humanity." One of the important factors that led to this genocide determination was Washington's desire to legitimize its military operations in Syria and Iraq—operations that, by their very nature, also kill, maim and displace civilians. Kerry wanted the world to know that these U.S.-led military actions were, as he said, "fully warranted" by the Islamic State's genocidal deeds.[13]

Secretary Kerry's statement was correct, insofar as it went. But he neglected to draw attention to the fact that the religiously cleansed areas of Syria extend far beyond the borders of Abu Bakr al-Baghdadi's Caliphate. There are other large pockets of religiously cleansed territory in northern, central and southern Syria, such as in Aleppo, Idlib and Dara'a provinces and the Douma suburb of Damascus. Forcibly displaced minorities have been able to return where the Syrian Army and its allies have recovered territory. This has happened in the Armenian town of Kassab near the Turkish border, the old city of Homs, Sadad, Ma'aloula, al-Qaryatayn and Palmyra. In the case of the Khabur valley villages in Hasakah Province, the displaced Assyrian Christian population was able to return in the wake of occupation by Kurdish militias.

Syria's religiously cleansed areas are coterminous with territory that is, or has been, conquered and controlled by anti-government Arab-dominated Sunni armed forces. They range from the Islamic State and al-Qaeda to those groups called "moderate" and supported by the United States, Europe and Sunni Islamist states in the region, in particular Saudi Arabia, Qatar and Turkey. In northern Syria, a jihadist-dominated rebel coalition called Jaish al-Fateh, backed by Washington and its allies, seized control of Idlib province from the Syrian government in 2015, and religiously cleansed it. Jaish al-Fateh also controlled much of religiously cleansed east Aleppo city. Jaish al-Fateh's strongest components were the Salafist militias the Nusra Front (an al-Qaeda affiliate), Ahrar al-Sham and Jaish al-Islam, but it also included the Free Syrian Army (FSA). Jaish al-Islam (the Army of Islam) is the strongest force in key districts in Damascus.

Washington publicly touts the restriction of its support to "moderate" rebels. But the collaboration of these "moderates" with al-Qaeda, in formations like Jaish al-Fateh and in many other cases, shows how little this term really means. There are even prominent figures in the United States, such as former CIA Director General David Petraeus, who advocate arming allegedly "moderate" elements within the ranks of al-Qaeda.[14] What defines a "moderate" rebel army for Washington is its readiness to refrain from threatening western interests, not its respect for human rights and religious pluralism. "Moderate" rebels have religiously cleansed their domains just as thoroughly as the Islamic State.

SUNNI SUPREMACISM AND IDEOLOGY OF JIHAD

The assortment of Sunni rebel forces that control territory in Syria have varying relationships with the United States. The Islamic State's conquest of Mosul in 2014 went nearly unopposed. The United States and its coalition partners began waging war against the Islamic State only after its subsequent efforts to capture Baghdad and Erbil. But the Coalition's current relationship with the Nusra Front, which nominally broke off ties with al-Qaeda in 2016 and rebranded itself as Jabhat Fateh al-Sham (Front for the Conquest of the Levant) is ambiguous. Other so-called moderate groups, such as the

FSA, are shadowy and subject to frequent reformations, name changes and shifting alliances within the rebel movement. They are furthermore overtly or covertly financed, trained and armed by the members of the Coalition. But there is something that virtually all of these "moderate" armed groups have in common with al-Qaeda and the Islamic State. They are driven by a strong sense of Sunni supremacism.

A declassified secret Defense Intelligence Agency (DIA) report, dated August 2012, provides confirmation of this. "The Salafist, the Muslim Brotherhood, and AQI [al-Qaida in Iraq]," it states, "are the major forces driving the insurgency in Syria."[15] Not intended for public consumption, the DIA report made no mention of "moderate" rebels. It made this omission for the obvious reason that non-Islamist Sunni forces are not a significant factor in the armed opposition. Even the Coalition-backed Syrian political opposition-in-exile is dominated by the Muslim Brotherhood.[16]

One of the key conditions for genocide—as noted in CSI's 2011 genocide warning—is the "prevalence of a racially or religiously discriminatory ideology or worldview that upholds a utopian vision of a homogenous society as the foundation of political unity." In his genocide determination, Secretary Kerry rightly observed that the Islamic State embraces and promotes such an ideology. But this ideology is not unique to al-Qaeda and the Islamic State. All of the dominant Islamist groups in Syria share it. Sunni supremacism is one of the fundamental principles on which their common Islamist ideology is based, and is a far more powerful factor in the politics of Syria's Sunni Islamists than grievances regarding particular injustices. This principle encourages and provides legitimization for religious cleansing. It must be noted here that Sunni supremacism is not the only form of religious or ethnic chauvinism on the field. But in Syria it is the most powerful by numbers, history, tradition and resources.

Sunni supremacism is on full display in the writings of the late chief ideologue of the Muslim Brotherhood, Sayeed Qutb. There is no shortage of authorities to cite on this subject. But I choose Qutb for two reasons. On the one hand, his movement is regarded by the United States as a legitimate political actor. Both the Bush and Obama administrations regarded Turkey, under the Muslim Brotherhood-linked the Justice and Development Party of Recep Erdogan, as a model for a democratically transformed Middle East. On the other, as Gilles Keppel noted, Qutb's classic, *Milestones*, is the "royal road to the ideology of the Islamicist movement."[17] Thus Qutb inspires Islamist tendencies ranging from members of the NATO alliance to al-Qaeda and its Islamic State spin-off. While Islamist thinkers certainly do not uncritically accept *Milestones* lock, stock and barrel, the debates that surround Qutb's ideology focus on tactical issues, such as the use of violence as opposed to engaging in the democratic process, not on the principle of Sunni supremacism. On this score, there is near unanimity within the ranks of Sunni Islamists.

In *Milestones*, Qutb left no doubt about the superiority of Sunni Shari'a adherents over the rest of humanity. He says to be a Sunni Muslim means "to be above all the powers of the earth," "to feel superior to others," to have a "sense of superiority," to be "most superior in his values and standards," to be "most superior in his conscience and understanding," and to be "most superior in his law and system of life." In Sunni polities where traditional Shari'a norms prevail, this supremacism is institutionalized, and obstructs notions of common national citizenship based on equality. But even where "the Muslim [has lost] his physical power and is conquered," Qutb writes, "the consciousness does not depart from him that he is the most superior." "If he remains a Believer," Qutb continues, "he looks upon his conquerors from a superior position."[18] Sunni Muslim supremacism could not be expressed more clearly.

Qutb's teaching prescribes *jihad* as a sacred obligation for Sunnis. In *Milestones*, he vehemently rejected the notion that *jihad* was a purely defensive reaction to attack, and wrote:

War should be declared against those from among the People of the Book [i.e., Christians and Jews] who declare open enmity, until they agree to pay *jizya* [i.e., protection money] or accept Islam. Concerning the polytheists [i.e., non-Muslims who do not belong to the People of the Book, like Alawites, Druze and Yezidis] and the hypocrites, it was commanded . . . that *jihad* be declared against them and that they be treated harshly. The Prophet—peace be on him—carried on jihad against the polytheists by fighting.[19]

It must be born in mind that Qutb's references to various groups of non-Sunnis apply to communities as a whole, and not just to individuals, thereby opening the door to legitimizing collective punishments against Christians, Jews and other *kufar*.

It was Qutb's Sunni supremacist ideology of *jihad* that stoked and drove the Muslim Brotherhood's insurrection against the Alawite Hafez al-Assad in the late 1970s and early 1980s—a precursor of the current rebellion, which, in turn, was preceded by a Sunni-dominated independence movement against the French *kufar* during the mandate period. Then as now, Sunni supremacism struck a chord within a strand of Syria's Sunni population. For many centuries, until the end of the First World War, Syria's rulers and its most privileged class came from within Sunni circles. As the historian Ussama Makdisi has acknowledged, under the Ottoman Empire's *millet* system, "Sunni Muslims were treated as socially and culturally superior to the other communities of the Empire."[20] According to the various Sunni schools of Islamic law, Sunnis have a God-given right to rule over non-Sunnis, all of whom should be subject to legal and social disadvantages. There is an old Arabic adage that is in widespread currency in Sunni parts of the Levant and Mesopotamia. It goes: "Sunnis are born to rule, while Shi'ites are born to lash themselves."[21]

When the Alawite "infidel" Hafez al-Assad assumed power and packed the key posts in the security apparatus with fellow Alawites, this was perceived widely within the Sunni political community as an affront against God's law. Robert Kaplan perceptively compared the Assads' ascent to power to "an untouchable becoming maharajah in India or a Jew becoming tsar in Russia." This outrage, Kaplan added, was "an unprecedented development, shocking to the Sunni majority population which had monopolized power for so many centuries."[22] This supremacism is certainly not embraced by all Syrian Sunnis, but it remains perhaps the most potent political force in Syria today. Certainly the spirit, if not the letter, of Qutb's supremacist ideology of jihad inspires all significant sectors of Syria's armed opposition.

MA'ALOULA

The case of the ancient, predominantly Christian town of Ma'aloula, which I visited at the end of 2014, brings to life just how the ideology of jihad is being put into practice today, with religious cleansing as a consequence. This town was attacked by rebels in September 2013. According to the BBC and AFP, the joint perpetrators of the attack were units from the FSA and the al-Qaeda affiliated Nusra Front. AFP reported these details:

> Jihadists who overran Syria's ancient town of Maalula . . . disparaged Christians as "Crusaders" and forced at least one person to convert to Islam at gunpoint, say residents who fled the town. One of them, Marie, was still frightened as she spoke of that day. "They arrived in our town at dawn . . . and shouted 'We are from the al-Nusra Front and have come to make lives miserable for the Crusaders,'" an Islamist term for Christians, Marie said . . . "I saw people wearing al-Nusra headbands who started shooting at crosses," said Nasrallah, a Christian. One of them "put a pistol to the head of my neighbor and forced him to convert to Islam by obliging him to repeat 'there is no God but God . . .'" Another resident, Rasha, recounted how the jihadists had seized her fiancé Atef, who belonged to the town's militia, and brutally murdered him. "I rang his mobile phone and one of them answered," she said. . . . [He said,] "We are from the Free Syrian Army. Do you know your fiancé was a member of the shabiha (pro-regime militia) who was carrying weapons, and we have slit his throat." The man told her Atef had been given the option of converting to Islam, but had refused. "Jesus didn't come to save him," he taunted.[23]

Ma'aloula was emptied of its Christian inhabitants. Only after the town was retaken and secured by the Syrian army half a year later were some of the displaced able to return. Such scenes of the targeting of non-Sunni minorities have been commonplace throughout rebel-conquered areas.

Not only Christians are targeted by Sunni supremacist rebels. A revealing case was reported in 2015 in *The New York Times*, in an article entitled "Caged Hostages from Syrian President's Sect Paraded through Rebel Held Suburb."[24] *The Times* report was based on a video production of the unfortunately named Sham [Levant] News, the media organ of the western-backed "moderate" rebel group called the Army of Islam. The otherwise religiously cleansed rebel-held neighborhood of East Ghouta still had a few Alawite residents. But they seemed to be captives. The video showed Alawite men, women and children being drawn through the streets and placed on rooftops in cages. The confined Alawite women wore Sunni headscarves and long overcoats, suggesting that they had been forced to convert to Sunni Islam. A media representative of the Army of Islam claimed that the captives had collaborated militarily with the Syrian government. This allegation suggests that the collective punishment aspect of the ideology of *jihad* is operative in this case. Today, the leader of the Army of Islam, Mohammed Alloush, leads the Supreme Council for Negotiations at the suspended UN-sponsored peace talks, representing all armed Sunni rebel armies, apart from the al-Nusra Front and the Islamic State.[25] Syria's religious minorities and moderate non-Islamist Sunnis are not oblivious to this grim reality.

THE OBAMA DOCTRINE

So, what is the key factor that created conditions for success for the Sunni insurgency to conquer territory and drive out non-Sunnis? I maintain that it is a campaign of externally driven hybrid warfare. Hafez al-Assad was able to contain and crush the Muslim Brotherhood's insurrection in 1982 mainly because it had no significant external support. His son Bashar has not been so fortunate. Within months of its outbreak, the Arab Spring uprising was transformed into an insurrection for the restoration of Sunni supremacy, not western-style democracy. Mosques became the starting point for anti-government demonstrations that were soon vocalizing incitement to genocide in the form of the slogan: "Alawites to the grave, and Christians to Beirut." (*Alawiyyé bi-taaboot, w Masihiyyé 'a-Bayroot.*)[26]

The Obama administration opted not to remain passive. Already, the Bush administration had imposed economic sanctions against Syria in 2004 following the American invasion of Iraq the previous year. The declared reason for the Bush sanctions was Syria's support for Hamas and Hizbullah, and permitting Sunni insurgents to use its territory to launch attacks against American-occupied Iraq. In 2009, the Obama administration renewed the sanctions. Syria had long been a thorn in Washington's flesh, and when the uprisings of the spring of 2011 shook the regimes of the region to their foundation, the Obama administration believed the time was ripe for revolutionary change. In his address to the American nation on May 12, the President declared, "It will be the policy of the United States to promote reform across the region, and to support transitions to democracy." He furthermore condemned the violent means of repression used by the Syrian authorities against demonstrators, and the close relationship between Damascus and Iran. He then instructed President Assad to lead a "transition to democracy," or "step out of the way," warning that should he disobey, "his regime will continue to be challenged from within and will continue to be isolated abroad."[27]

Bashar al-Assad did not obey. As a result, Secretary of State Hillary Clinton declared in July 2011 that the Syrian President "has lost legitimacy."[28] President Obama followed this with his announcement on August 18 that "for the sake of the Syrian people, the time has come for President Assad to step aside."[29] Obama articulated a clear and simple policy objective. It was regime change. In doing so he cited grave human rights abuses as factors to legitimize his policy. But the American goal in Syria was presented rather differently one year later by the previously cited DIA analyst. The ouster of the Assad was not the real aim of the enterprise. Instead, the anonymous analyst noted in a secret memorandum that the foreign powers that were backing the armed rebellion against the Assad regime sought the establishment of a "declared or undeclared Salafist principality in eastern Syria." The defined function of the envisioned Salafist principality was to "isolate the Syrian regime, which is considered the strategic depth of the Shia [Iranian] expansion." In other words, the purpose of the envisioned Salafist principality was to break the "Shi'ite Crescent." The DIA analyst also dismissed the notion of regime change, stating in no uncertain terms that "the regime will survive and have control over Syrian territory."[30]

From hindsight, we can see that assessment of the DIA analyst was largely correct. Assad still controls much territory, and, not just one, but a host of Salafist principalities have indeed been established in eastern Syria, the principal one being the Islamic State. The severing of the "Shi'ite Crescent" by the establishment of a Sunni polity in eastern Syria is a much more credible geopolitical goal than simply the removal of Bashar al-Assad from power. Assad could, undoubtedly, have been eliminated long ago, and with relatively little loss of life, if that had been Washington's true war goal.

The question the Obama administration had to face in the summer of 2011 was how to achieve its policy goal in Syria. The president's preliminary instinct, according to Jeffrey Goldberg, was to lean back on what White House insiders knew to be the Obama military doctrine: "Don't do stupid shit."[31] White House staff understood this tongue-in-cheek "presidential decree" to mean not making the same fatal political mistake that George W. Bush made when he committed thousands of American boots on the ground for an invasion and occupation of Iraq. President Obama was neither a pacifist nor an isolationist. He was a progressive internationalist who is ideologically convinced that the United States should pursue vigorously the goal of global liberal hegemony in the tradition of all post–Cold War U.S. Presidents. He conducted foreign policy within the framework of the Enlargement Doctrine, which in 1993 replaced George Kennan's famed Containment Doctrine as the paramount National Security guideline in the post–Cold War era.[32] This means the projection of American power to fill vacuums wherever and however they arise. In 2011, President Obama had no doubt about the United States' ability to do so in the case of Syria.

Obama believed that "smart" wars for the development of liberal global hegemony would not be characterized by large scale American invasions, like Operation Iraqi Freedom. Instead they would be fought somewhat along the lines projected by Lt. Col. Frank Hoffman in his influential study *Conflict in the 21st Century: The Rise of Hybrid Wars*. Such wars are designed to combine multiple modes of warfare to produce synergy and greater impact. According to Hoffman, hybrid warfare employs "conventional capabilities, irregular tactics and formations, terrorist acts including indiscriminate violence and coercion, and criminal disorder." Non-attribution of some of the modes of hybrid warfare is one of its key qualities. Such warfare, Hoffman continues, "can be conducted by both states and a variety of non-state actors." He proposes that "these multi-modal activities can be conducted by separate units, or even by the same unit, but are generally operationally and tactically directed and coordinated within the main battlespace to achieve synergistic effects in the physical and psychological dimensions of conflict."[33] The U.S. intervention in Syria appears to correspond to many of Hoffman's conditions.

There are many debates surrounding the concept of "hybrid warfare," a term which has no universally agreed definition. Some deny that it constitutes a new, distinct form of warfare. In an article in *NATO Review*, Damien van Puyvelde asks whether "it even exist[s]," and recommends that NATO policy-makers "forget about everything 'hybrid' and focus on the specificity and the interconnectedness of the threats they face."[34] He might be right. But the fact is that his advice is largely ignored.

The term "hybrid warfare" continues to be used by the highest officials of the western alliance, mainly to brand threats emanating from Russia and the Islamic State. NATO officially defines it in simple terms:

A hybrid threat is one posed by any current or potential adversary, including state, non-state and terrorists, with the ability, whether demonstrated or likely, to simultaneously employ conventional or unconventional means adaptively, in pursuit of their objectives.[35]

NATO's outgoing Supreme Allied Commander Europe, General Philip Breedlove, has put a little meat on this bare bone. He portrays the hybrid warfare undertaken by Russia in Ukraine, and IS in Iraq and Syria, as:

A continuum of threat, including unconventional and conventional methods . . . . These methods exploit non-attributable means like cyber, information warfare, surprise, deception, extensive use of proxy and special forces. On the unconventional side, [there is] the use of political sabotage, economic pressure, intelligence operations and special operations . . . and the posturing of conventional forces for a wide range of options.[36]

Since the term "hybrid warfare" has leapt into the rhetoric of the upper echelons of NATO's leadership, I take the liberty of using it, as opposed to other related concepts such as irregular or asymmetrical warfare, to brand Washington's efforts to achieve its strategic objective in Syria.

THE SYRIA PLAYBOOK

Let us look briefly at the Obama administration's playbook for creating an Islamist Sunnistan in eastern Syria. As President Obama was ramping up pressure against the Assad regime during the spring and summer of 2011, economic sanctions were the principle overt means of coercion. He announced in August the imposition of what he called "unprecedented sanctions to deepen the financial isolation of the Assad regime and further disrupt its ability to finance a campaign of violence against the Syrian people."[37] These sanctions are indeed "unprecedented," and appear to be wreaking enormous death and destruction. While bombs, bullets and beheadings capture media headlines, the sanctions quietly kill and gravely damage whatever economic activity and infrastructure that survives the direct violence. We can see with hindsight that the economic sanctions imposed on Iraq between the Gulf War and the overthrow of Saddam Hussein so weakened the state that it became largely dysfunctional. We can expect similar results in Syria should these draconian sanctions remain in place.

It should be noted here that there is enormous enthusiasm in Washington for the use of sanctions as a coercive instrument for the advancement of American interests abroad. Economic sanctions are a weapon of war that can be employed at low cost in terms of both blood and treasure. Yet they can have powerfully destructive impact. As the globalized banking system develops, with the U.S. dollar dominating international financial transactions, the might and reach of this instrument spreads globally. In a recent report entitled *The New Tools of Economic Warfare: Effects and Effectiveness of Contemporary U.S. Financial Sanctions,* a team at the Center for a New American Security, under the leadership of Michèle Flournoy—a former Deputy Defense Secretary in the Obama administration—highlighted the significance of financial sanctions for the United States' global aspirations:

> Sanctions may become one of the most important instruments of economic competition or hybrid warfare in the future, with undeniable staying power because of their utility in projecting power to achieve desirable policy outcomes.[38]

Syria provides a wonderful but grisly laboratory for examining the destructive effectiveness of this new tool of economic warfare.

Information warfare is another important aspect of Washington's Syria strategy. The U.S. government, using its full range of covert and overt instruments of what used to be called "psychological warfare" during the Eisenhower and Kennedy eras, has largely succeeded in creating a dominant and powerful media narrative designed to delegitimize the Syrian government. Some of the leaked Clinton emails show that Google's Jared Cohen, who seems to personify what we might call today the Digital-Military Complex, has been involved in this process.[39] One of the most advanced aspects of the information war is the establishment and funding of an extensive media network in rebel-held territories. It is made up mainly of so-called citizen reporters, NGOs and activists, purporting to represent civil society. They feed outlets like the opposition-linked Syrian Observatory on Human Rights with information and broadcast quality footage that is then forwarded to the media. Most of the output focuses on the appalling death and destruction caused by Syrian army offensives. But the religious cleansing of territories captured by Islamist rebel armies (quite apart from the Islamic State) scarcely features in the narratives of these information networks.

Finally, lethal and non-lethal military aid to the armed opposition has a direct impact on religious cleansing. The model for Washington's Syria strategy appears to be the Reagan administration's policy of supporting Sunni jihadists in Afghanistan against the "infidel" Soviets. They included the Afghan Arabs, out of which al-Qaeda emerged. Among the American masterminds of both the Afghan and Syrian *jihad* operations was Michael Vickers. He helped engineer the former while serving in the CIA's Special Activities Division, and the latter while serving as Undersecretary of Defense for Intelligence between the outbreak of the Arab Spring uprisings and 2015. General David Petraeus, the advocate of arming moderate elements within al-Qaeda, also played an instrumental role as Director of the CIA from September 2011 until November 2012.

Just what is delivered by whom and to whom is shrouded in mystery. But every now and again the public is able to catch a glimpse of aid for Syrian rebels. By early 2013, American aid alone accounted for a "cataract of weaponry" to them, according to a former U.S. official cited by the *New York Times*.[40] Investigations into the attack against the U.S. Consulate in Benghazi raised the possibility the CIA was sending weapons from the deposed Libyan strongman Mo'ammar Gaddafi's arsenal, including missiles, to unidentified anti-government rebels in Syria via Turkey.[41] The Syrian operations of the Benghazi CIA station were meant to remain secret. But it is open knowledge that the Agency, together with American allies, provides support for Syrian rebels out of facilities in both Turkey and Jordan.[42] As early as October 2012, the *New York Times* reported that "most of the arms" being sent to Syria by Qatar and Saudi Arabia, with the United States support, "are going to hardline jihadists."[43] And "moderate" Syrian rebels openly claimed that they used anti-tank missiles supplied by the CIA to help al-Qaeda and its allies conquer Idlib province in early 2015.[44]

Perhaps the greatest embarrassment for the Obama administration came when Vice President Joe Biden, speaking off-the-cuff, stated that Washington's Sunni regional partners—such as the Turks, the Saudis and the Emiratis—had "poured hundreds of millions of dollars and . . . thousands of tons of weapons into . . . al-Nusra, al-Qaeda and the extremist elements of jihadis coming from other parts of the world." The Vice President furthermore admitted that the United States was not able to provide support for "moderate" forces, because there is no "moderate middle."[45] President Obama himself disparaged the notion of "the moderate opposition" in the spring of 2014, when he stated that "many of these people were farmers or dentists or maybe some radio reporters who didn't have a lot of experience fighting."[46] It is difficult to imagine that Washington and its European and Sunni allies are pumping huge amounts of money and weaponry into the hands of peaceful, moderate Muslims who want no more than to lead tranquil lives and provide a respectable living for their families. All the available evidence strongly suggests this is not the case.

The U.S. armed forces have intervened more directly on the ground in Syria since Washington and its allies opted to wage war against the Islamic State in 2014. The U.S. Air Force regularly bombs Islamic State positions. It has also established its own facility in Rimelan, Hassakeh Province. American and allied special forces are on the ground training opposition forces. Washington acknowledges that there are three hundred American special forces in the country, but there could be many more. Half a dozen or so of these special forces made headlines last September when they were roughly expelled by their FSA hosts, while being threatened with slaughter. On YouTube, the public can watch "moderate" U.S.-backed rebels shouting, "They are crusaders and infidels. Down with America. Get out you pigs. They are coming to Syria to occupy it."[47] These are the same kind of insults that are routinely hurled at religious minorities by Sunni supremacists in Syria.

CONCLUSION

Writing at the beginning of 2016 in *Military Review*, Charles Bartels, an analyst at Fort Leavenworth, summed up the Russian military's perception of how Washington directly, or through its extensive networks of alliances and intelligence relationships, puts hybrid warfare into play. Much of what Bartels had to say was based on Anthony Cordesman's detailed eyewitness account of the Russian Ministry of Defense's 2014 Moscow Conference on International Security. Bartels wrote:

> Instead of an overt military invasion the first volleys of a U.S. attack come from the installment of a political opposition through state propaganda (e.g., CNN, BBC), the Internet and social media, and non-governmental organizations (NGOs). After successfully instilling political dissent, separatism and/or social strife, the legitimate government has increasing difficulty maintaining order. As the security situation deteriorates, separatist movements can be stoked and strengthened, and undercover special operations, conventional, and private military forces (defense contractors) can be introduced to battle the government and cause further havoc. Once the legitimate government is forced to use increasingly aggressive methods to maintain order, the United States gains a pretext for the imposition of economic and political sanctions, and sometimes even military sanctions such as no-fly zones, to tie the hands of the besieged governments and promote further dissent.

The character of the war waged against Syria by the United States and its allies corresponds to a large extent to what the Russian military views as the pattern of contemporary American hybrid warfare. Whether or not we choose to call the kind of violent coercion practiced by Washington and its allies in Syria "hybrid warfare," there is little doubt that this intervention has contributed materially to extensive religious cleansing and other aspects of a man-made catastrophe. President-elect Trump has made sounds suggesting that he might not continue to prosecute his predecessor's war in Syria. Should this come to pass, the dynamic of religious cleansing will be considerably diminished and Syria's remarkable social pluralism will have a chance of survival.[48]

NOTES

1. Based on a talk given as a part of the Changing Character of Warfare Seminar series, Pembroke, Oxford, November 22, 2016.

2. Barack Obama, "Remarks by the President at the United States Military Academy Commencement Ceremony," West Point, May 28, 2014.

3. Joseph Sassoon, *The Iraqi Refugees: The New Crisis in the Middle-East*, London, 2008.

4. The Alawites are often referred to by contemporary scholars and journalists as Shi'ites. However, the Alawites' beliefs and religious rites bear little resemblance to those of either Shi'ite or Sunni Islam. Their faith system contains elements from Shi'ite Islam, Christianity, Gnosticism, and paganism. It was only in the post-Ottoman 20th century that efforts were made, for political reasons, to recognize the Alawite community as a Muslim sect. Beforehand, they often endured severe persecution. Taqiyya—the practice of concealing one's true religious faith by means of deception—was used by Alawites under Sunni rule for centuries as a survival mechanism. See Martin Kramer, "Syria's Alawis and Shi'ism" in *Shi'ism, Resistance, and Revolution*, ed. Martin Kramer (Boulder, Colorado: Westview Press, 1987), pp. 237–54; and Yaron Friedman, The Nusayri-Alawis: An Introduction to the Religion, History, the Identity of the Leading Minority in Syria, (Brill: Leiden, 2010).

5. Stephen Hemsley Longrigg, *Syria and Lebanon under the French Mandate*, London, 1958, p, 184.

6. At the beginning of the "Arab Spring" uprisings, Syria's ancient Jewish community consisted of a remnant of about 50 people. Most of that remnant has since left the country on account of the general insecurity caused by the current war. The Syrian Jewish community has been driven toward destruction since the 19th century by a combination of Judeophobic forces emanating from Christian and Muslim traditions and modern paganism. Judeophobia continues to be a powerful and destructive political force within the country.

7. "Obama: Assad 'protected' Christians in Syria," *al-Akhbar*, September 12, 2014.

8. "Panetta: '30-year war' and a leadership test for Obama," *USA Today*, October 6, 2014.

9. "Death Toll from War in Syria Now 470,000, Group Says," *The New York Times*, February 11, 2016.

10. Justine Walker, "Humanitarian Impact of Syria-Related Unilateral Restrictive Measures," United Nations (UN) Economic & Social Commission for Western Asia, May 16, 2016, p. 6.

11. *Syria: Confronting Fragmentation!*, Syria Center for Policy Research, supported by UNDP, February 2016.

12. "CSI Issues Genocide Warning for Religious Minorities in the Middle East," Christian Solidarity International, Zurich, November 30, 2011.

13. John Kerry, Remarks on Daesh and Genocide, Press Briefing Room, U.S Department of State, March 17, 2017.

14. Shane Harris, Nancy A. Youssef, "Petraeus: Use Al Qaeda Fighters to Beat ISIS," *Daily Beast*, August 31, 2015; "America's ISIS War is Helping Al Qaeda, *Daily Beast*, February 8, 2016.

15. Department of Defense Intelligence Agency, 14-L-0552/DIA/287-293, Syria, August 12, 2012.

16. Hassan Hassan, "How the Muslim Brotherhood Hijacked Syria's Revolution," *Foreign Policy*, March 13, 2013.

17. Gilles Keppel, *Muslim Extremism in Egypt: The Prophet and the Pharaoh*, London: Al Saki, 1985, p. 38.

18. Sayyid Qutb, Milestones, SIME Journal, 2005, pp. 97–99.

19. Sayyid Qutb, *Milestones*, SIME Journal, 2005, p. 33.

20. Ussama Makdisi, *The Culture of Sectarianism: Community, History, and Violence in Nineteenth-Century Ottoman Lebanon*, Berkeley, California: University of California Press, 2000, p. 11.

21. In Arabic, "Al-Sunna wildo lil-hukm wal-Shi'a lil-latim." The adage refers to the Shi'ite custom of self-flagellation on their festival of Ashura, the remembrance of the Shi'ites' first great defeat at the hands of a Sunni caliph.

22. Robert Kaplan, "Syria: Identity Crisis," *The Atlantic*, February 1993.

23. "Battle for Syria Christian Town of Maaloula Continues," *BBC*, September 11, 2013. "Jihadists force Christian to Convert at Gunpoint," *AFP*, published in the *Daily Star* (Beirut), September 11, 2013.

24. "Caged Hostages from Syrian President's Sect Paraded through Rebel Held Suburb," *New York Times*, November 1, 2015.

25. See, for example, Yara Abi Nader and John Irish, "Syria opposition seeks clarity from power-broker Russia at Geneva talks," *Reuters*, February 26, 2017.

26. Peter Galbraith, "A dilemma for Syria's minorities," *Los Angeles Times*, September 8, 2012. I have spoken with Syrians who witnessed such incitement to genocide in mid-2011.

27. "Remarks by the President on North Africa and the Middle East," The White House, May 19, 2011.

28. "Clinton Blasts Syria, its President after attack on Embassy," CNN, July 12, 2011.

29. "President Obama: 'The Future of Syria must be determined by its own People, but President Bashar al-Assad is standing in their way," The White House, August 18, 2011.

30. Department of Defense Intelligence Agency, 14-L-0552/DIA/287-293, Syria, August 12, 2012.

31. Jeffrey Goldberg, "The Obama Doctrine," *The Atlantic*, April 2016.

32. Remarks of Anthony Lake, Assistant to the President for National Security Affairs, "From Containment to Enlargement," Johns Hopkins University, Washington, D.C., September 21, 1993.

33. Frank Hoffman, *Conflict in the 21st Century: The Rise of Hybrid Wars*, Potomac Institute for Policy Studies, Arlington, December 2007, pp. 2–3.

34. Damien van Puyvelde, "Hybrid War—does it even exist?," *NATO Review*, 2015. http://www.nato.int/docu/Review/2015/Also-in-2015/hybrid-modern-future-warfare-russia-ukraine/EN/index.htm

35. This definition was approved by the NATO Military Working Group (Strategic Planning & Concepts), February 2010.

36. General Philip Breedlove, "Forward," *NATO's Response to Hybrid Threats*, edited by Guillaume Lasconjarias and Jeffery A. Larsen, NATO Defense College, Rome, 2015. p. xxii.

37. "President Obama: 'The Future of Syria must be determined by its own People, but President Bashar al-Assad is standing in their way,'" The White House, August 18, 2011.

38. "The New Tools of Economic Warfare: Effects and Effectiveness of Contemporary U.S. Financial Sanctions," Center for a New American Security, Washington, 2016, p. 55.

39. Doug Bolton, "Google planned to help Syrian rebels bring down Assad regime, leaked Hillary Clinton emails claim," *The Independent,* March 22, 2016.

40. C.J. Chivers and Eric Schmitt, "Arms Airlift to Syria Rebels Expands, With Aid from C.I.A," *New York Times*, March 24, 2013.

41. "Exclusive: Dozens of CIA operatives on the ground during Benghazi attack*,"* CNN, August 2, 2013. See also Andrew C. McCarthy, "Hillary Clinton's Benghazi Debacle: Arming Jihadists in Libya . . . and Syria," *National Review*, August 2, 2016

42. See, for example, Mark Hosenball, "Exclusive: Obama authorizes secret U.S. support for Syrian rebels," *Reuters*, August 1, 2012; Ben Hubbard, "Warily, Jordan Assists Rebels in Syrian War," *New York Times*, April 10, 2014.

43. David E. Sanger, "Rebel Arms Flow is Said to Benefit Jihadists in Syria," *New York Times*, October 14, 2012.

44. Nabih Bulos, "A 'kaleidoscopic' of mix of rebel alliances on Syria's battlefield," *Los Angeles Times,* October 12, 2015.

45. Joe Biden, Q & A at Harvard, October 2, 2014.

46. "Transcript and Audio: President Obama's Full NPR Interview, *NPR*, May 29, 2014.

47. "US troops 'forced to flee Syria town' after SFA Rebel Threats," *Middle East Eye*, September 16, 2016.

48. Postscript: In July 2017, the *Washington Post* reported that President Trump ordered the termination of the CIA's program for arming the rebels fighting for the overthrow of the Syrian government, while retaining the program of support for armed non-state actors who are coalition partners of the United States in the military campaign against the Islamic State. Greg Jaffe and Adam Entous, "Trump ends covert CIA program to arm anti-Assad rebels in Syria, a move sought by Moscow," *Washington Post*, July 19, 2017.

Chapter 20

Christians of the Holy Land–Exodus, Disintegration, and Ideological Necrophilia

(Zurich, May 22, 2017)

Franck Salameh

What may be referred to elsewhere in the world as "ethnic" or "national" groups are in the Near East defined in religious terms. This is, after all, how fourteen centuries of Muslim dominance have come to inform, paint—and often taint—the Near East and its mosaics of identities. And so, in speaking of Near Eastern Christians today, and without diminishing the very important "religious" aspects of their identities as "faith communities," I should like the conversation about Holy Land Christians to be framed in terms of "ethnic groups" defined "religiously," rather than "religious denominations" or "faith communities." This is so in order to avoid reducing the individuality of what amount to pre-modern "national churches" to purely religious attributes. And that is the main reason behind the grisly subtitle of this paper, treating the semantics of *Ideological Necrophilia.*

To be clear, the "ideological necrophilia" invoked in this study refers to a certain attraction to "dead ideas" and their semantics, obsolete terminologies that we, in the West, have come to normalize, valorize, and use in reference to the Near East, the peoples of the Near East, and especially the Christians of the Near East. And so, before tackling the topic at hand—the Christians of the Holy Land—it may prove useful to unpack some of those longstanding terminologies, parse them out, get them out of the way, and suggest some discipline in the taxonomy of things, peoples, places, and events Near East.

ARABS, ARAB WORLD, AND ARAB CHRISTIANS

In the context of modern Near and Middle Eastern history, seldom are the varied peoples of the region viewed beyond oversimplified, often reductive,

211

notions of "Arab" and "Muslim," to the neglect of *other*, pre-Arabs and pre-Muslims—Near Eastern "first nations" as it were, otherwise lapsed from the prevalent paradigms *on*, *of*, and *about* the modern Near and Middle East.

Indeed, a century or more of Western academic interest in this region has yielded precious little beyond clichés and assumptions beholden exclusively to "Arabs," "Arab" fears, "Arab" hopes, "Arab" concerns, and "Arab" hang ups—the emblematic "be all end all" of *all* matters Middle Eastern.[1] Yet there exists a vibrant, venerable, *authentic* Near East past these dominant platitudes. To this point, the *Brill Encyclopedia of Arabic Language and Linguistics* notes that the seventh-century Arab conquests and colonization of a heretofore *non-Arab* Near East never wholly Arabized nor Islamized the new colonial chattel: "Some peoples of the [Near and] Middle East resisted Arabization and Islamization," stresses the *Brill Encyclopedia*, noting that,

> even among those who underwent both these processes, this was not always accompanied by a total abandonment of their earlier culture. Thus, there are still pockets across the [so-called] Arab world using languages other than Arabic and practicing religions other than Islam, and there are still [Near Eastern] groups convinced that their ancestors belonged to a people different from [the Arab and Muslim peoples].[2]

Yet traditional Middle East scholarship remains largely mute on this topic—unsuitable as it may be deemed in some quarters to neat, normative Arab models, or more "legitimate" Muslim molds.

It is within this context that this paper suggests the prevalent assumptions about an essentially Arab (or a uniformly Muslim) Near East be confronted, and it is within *this* framework that the Christians of the Holy Land ought to be examined. Historian Joel Carmichael noted in this regard that,

> It was in fact the Western habit of referring to Arabic-speaking Muslims [. . .] as "Arabs" because of their language—on the analogy of German-speakers as Germans, French-speakers as French and so on—that imposed itself on an East that had never regarded language as a basic social classifier. It was natural for Europeans to use the word "Arab" about a Muslim . . . whose native language was Arabic; they were quite indifferent to the principles of classification in the East. The oddity is simply that this European habit became the very germ that the contemporary Arab nationalist movement has sprung from.[3]

Even some of the main avatars of Arab nationalist ideology admitted to this reality. Sati' al-Husri (1880–1968) for one, the spiritual godfather of linguistic Arabism, was intransigent in his advocacy for a compulsory Arabness. One of his most famous nationalist dictums was "you are an Arab if I say so." Yet, in spite of his intransigence, Husri admitted the idea of a uniform unified, coherent Arab nation to have had "its origins in fiction," to have been born from the ambitions of Europeanized "Arabist dreamers."[4] To this point, Husri stressed that,

> fiction *can* be made into reality, for nary a step may be walked toward progress, and scarcely a noble mission may be accomplished, and hardly a renaissance may be triggered without having had their beginnings and early stirrings in fiction, as fantasies in the minds of some, ambitions in the hearts of others, or lofty precepts dwelling on some high altar of some noble soul.[5]

Also most prominently, to this point, Michel Aflaq (1910–1989), the Syrian-Christian founder of the Ba'ath Party, admitted to the contrived nature of the Arabism that he sought to promote among early twentieth-century Levantine and Syrian Arabophones. In his nationalist manifesto, *For the Sake of the Ba'ath* (Beirut: Dar al-Talii'a, 1959), Aflaq stressed that,

> Seldom were the terms "Arab" or "Arab identity" part of the national consciousness or the political lexicon of early twentieth century Syrians, and rarely were such terms ever used. Indeed, Syrian political leaderships during the 1930s made use of the term "Syrian" as a sort of amulet, to evade negotiating the intricacies of their region's ethno-religious and racial mosaics [and to distinguish Syrians from Arabs tout court.] "Syria" was a regional [geographic] term [not unlike, say, "the Alps," or "New England,"] and it was intended to bring together disparate Muslims, Christians, and non-Arab minorities under the banner of a distinct [albeit fabricated "Arab"] national identity.[6]

Bernard Lewis—who is to many the *doyen* of Middle Eastern and Islamic history—stressed the "newness" of the term "Arab" as one lending itself to confusion and anachronisms when dealing with the pre-modern Near East. "Arab" as a national classifier is a modern phenomenon, noted Lewis, the outcome of twentieth-century Arab nationalist doctrine, ascribed willy-nilly and posthumously to pre-Arab Near Eastern peoples defined by other systems of social classification, often anteceding Arabs, Muslims, and modern Arabist, Arab nationalist, and Islamist discourse. In sum, "Ethnic terms are notoriously difficult to define," and "Arab is not among the easiest."[7] If the identifying factor in identity formation is language, stressed Lewis, then one wonders if an "Arabic-speaking Jew from Iraq [. . . or an] Arabic-speaking Christian [from] Egypt or Lebanon [can be deemed] an Arab" without oversimplifying and misleading.[8]

That is why the term "Arab Christian" often causes unease; not because it is problematic—and I suggest that *it is* indeed problematic—but mainly because it lacks accuracy. What one means by "Arab Christian," or for that matter "Arab Jew," ultimately answers to a political rather than an ethnic or a cultural question. It remains the case that not all—nor even most—Arabic-speaking Near Eastern Christians and Jews can be deemed Arab. Indeed most of them reject that label out of hand and take great umbrage at being folded into that category. And so, for the sake of countering the misleading semantics of "ideological necrophilia," I propose the term "Arab Christian" be used with extreme caution—if used at all.

It is worth mentioning in this regard that a Mediaevalist's and a Modernist's view of what an "Arab Christian" is stem from two disparate perspectives: An "Arab Christian" in pre-modern times (that is to say before the emergence of Arab nationalism in the early decades of the twentieth century) was somebody from the Arabian Peninsula who was a Christian. Those Christians of the Arabian Peninsula (or "Arab Christians" if you will) were all but decimated with the advent of Islam—by way of conversion, mass exodus, or simply by succumbing to the sword.

This is mainly the reason why, for instance, there are no indigenous Christians today (and since the seventh century) in places like Yemen, Saudi Arabia, and elsewhere in the Persian Gulf. Indeed, save for some of today's Arabophone Greek Orthodox Middle Easterners—ironically the only Christian community that claims decent from pre-Islamic Arabian tribes (arguably for reasons of political expediency and ideological necrophilia rather than credible historical data)—no such verifiably "Arab Christians" remain.

Certainly, those Arabophone Christians who claim to be "Arab Christians" have every prerogative to do so—no less legitimate a prerogative than that of those who valorize an opposite narrative. Still, "Arab Christians" (to mean "Near Eastern Christians") from a Mediaevalist's perspective is a term that is anachronistic and misleading; a Mediaevalists's tool; a reference to a pre-Islamic Arabian ethnos that no longer exists; the outcome of European (not Arab) systems of social classification, and in that sense, not a judicious classifier when it comes to the mosaics of identities that are the Near and Middle East of today.

And so, I suggest that the common (and ultimately more accurate and ideologically neutral) terms in reference to Near Eastern users of the Arabic language who happen to be Christian be "Oriental Christians," or "Near Eastern Christians," or "Levantine Christians"—*Chrétiens d'Orient* as the deliciously precise Cartesian language of France terms them. Better yet, using those people's own parameters of identification, reflecting the names of their own "pre-modern national Churches," may ultimately be the more appropriate way of dealing with this ethnic and linguistic quandary: Copts, Chaldaeans, Maronites, Syriacs, and the rest, *are* after all the legitimate pre-modern national appellations of these peoples. (French travelers in the eighteenth and nineteenth centuries referred to them as *"la race Copte," "la race Maronite,"* and the like; meaning "the Maronite nation" and "the Coptic nation.")

Otherwise, the term "Arab Christian" remains a modern device, the out-come of Arab nationalist chauvinism, and in that sense a novel phenomenon and a misleading cognomen when applied to Near Eastern Christians *en masse*.

DEMONYMS, TOPONYMS, HOLY LANDS

This brings us to the topic at hand: Palestine, Israel, and the Christians of disputed Holy Lands. Here too, allow me, again, a few words on taxonomy, because, not unlike the terms "Arab" and "Arab Christians," so are the terms "Palestine" and "Palestinians"—to mean (exclusively) the Arabs of British Mandate Palestine—defective and misleading. Even at the outset of the Middle East's nationalist era during the early twentieth century, those terms confounded scholars, travelers, and indigenous Near Easterners alike.

In the late nineteenth century, long before the passions of Arab nationalism had come to dominate historical writing on the Middle East, French anarchist historian Elisée Reclus noted that,

> The populations of Syria and Palestine, alleged to be "Arab" by some, scarcely warrant this appellation; a designation justified only by way of [an abusive labeling of] spoken dialects [as Arabic language]. Otherwise, these populations issue from the ancient inhabitants of the region, and the conquerors erupting from Arabia were never able to stamp out the indigenous cultures of Syria and Palestine; indeed the Syro-Palestinians were largely left to their own devices, to their fields and their homes, with the Arab [conquerors] only demanding tribute from them. . . . The majority of Syrians might have made haste converting to the Muslim faith [in later times], to the same extent that they might have converted to Christianity in earlier periods, under the Byzantine Empire. But their conversion to the religion of Mohammed was hardly more heartfelt or more deeply rooted than their previous switch from Paganism [and Judaism] to Christianity a few centuries earlier.[9]

And so, observers, analysts, historians, and students of the Near East are not on shaky historical ground calling for caution in the use of demonyms and place-names relative to the Holy Land.

The terms "Palestinian" and "Palestine" in reference to Arabs exclusively (just like the term "Arab" itself) are a novel phenomenon. Indeed, prior to the establishment of the British Mandate, what is today Palestine, geographi-cally and conceptually speaking, belonged to the *Vilayets* (which is to say the Ottoman "States") of Beirut and Damascus, and the *Sanjak* (autono-mous Province) of Jerusalem. In that sense, today's term "Palestinian" had no discrete national meaning in the earlier twentieth century distinct from neighboring terms such as "Beiruty," "Damascene," or "Aleppan." In fact, up until 1964–1967, the "national consciousness" of the Arab-defined inhabitants of what are today Israel and the territories of the Palestinian Authority was delineated by way of local, familial, religious, and tribal loyalties—*not* a distinct Palestinian nationhood.

"Palestine" and "Palestinian" certainly refer to a well-defined toponym and demonym today—namely, the Arabs of what was once British Mandate Palestine. However, the term "Palestine" itself is of Western (European, *not* Arab) provenance, and it refers to the Holy Lands from a modern Christian perspective, as a home for Christians and Jews, usurped by Arabs and Muslims in earlier times. Indeed, only twentieth-century Jews and Christians—imbued as they were in Western ideas and languages—referred to themselves as "Palestinians" during the British Mandate period, with Muslims largely shunning the term and opting for earlier Ottoman labels—religious labels in the main.

And so it was only when the Jews of British Mandate Palestine relinquished the term "Palestinian" in favor of "Israeli"—*only* then—did Arabs and Muslims begin warming to the term "Palestinian," eventually espousing it as their new national moniker *only* in the mid-1960s. Note in this regard that the predecessor of today's *Jerusalem Post*—a Jewish daily publication founded in British Mandate Palestine by Jewish intellectuals in 1925—was *The Palestine Bulletin.* It changed its name to *The Palestine Post* in 1933, only to be renamed the *Jerusalem Post* in 1950, at a time when "Palestine" and "Palestinian" were becoming more acceptable in *some* "Arab" quarters.

Otherwise, the term "Palestinian" up until the late 1940s was generic (not national), European (not Arab), and a reference to *all* inhabitants of British Mandate Palestine (Jews and Christians first and foremost, Muslims—or rather *some* Muslims—in later times). Indeed, except among a few members of the Arabophone Christian educated elites of Beirut, Damascus, Haifa, and Jerusalem, there exist *no* Arabic-language documents from the first half of the twentieth century, *no* local Arabic press, *no* local Arabic literature, and *no* Arabic private or consular correspondence referring to the Holy Land as "Palestine," or its Muslim inhabitants as "Palestinians."[10]

A case in point is that the Arab Palestinians' "call to arms" to counter the Zionist project, throughout the Mandate period (1920–1948), issued under the banners of such outfits as the "Higher Arab Committee," the "Muslim Supreme Council," and a variety of likeminded movements driven primarily by Muslim impulses and Islamist zeal. And, incidentally, the most recognizable "Palestinian Arab" names in this struggle included most notably the Mufti of Jerusalem, Hajj Amin al-Husseini, and the Damascene Sunni preacher Izzeddin al-Qassam—neither of whom can be credited with engaging a distinctly Palestinian national discourse.

And therein lies the quandary of the Christians of the Holy Land today, torn as they are between exile, disintegration, integration, and having to pay lip-service to a declining Arabism on the one hand, and a resurgent Islamism on the other.

Unlike other Near Eastern Christians whose fortunes have vacillated between assertiveness (some even say "conceit" as is the case with the Maronites of Lebanon), and utter submissiveness (even *dhimmitude* as is the case of the Copts of Egypt), the Christians of the Holy Land are marginal at best: marginal politically and culturally speaking in their own communities (whether Arab or Israeli), irrelevant numerically speaking and in comparison to other Near Eastern Christian groups, and negligible in the larger context of Christianity and Christendom as a whole. Their importance on the other hand—and they *are* of critical importance—is in the cautionary tale that their saga offers, the "food for thought" as it were, for the rest of the Middle East and Near Eastern Christians, and indeed for Christendom as a whole and what may be lurking in the future of both Near Eastern *and* Western Christendom.

HOLY LAND CHRISTIANS AND THE ROAD TO PERDITION

Even though they might have been the "first nation" of Christendom, rooted in Christianity's birthplace and at the very center of Christian thought, culture, theology, and indeed Christian civilization, the Christians of the Holy Land are today a mere shadow—not to say a pitiful specter—of their pre-Muslim Conquest existence. Barely two percent of the total population of Israel and the Palestinian territories today—which is to say roughly 160,000 strong in Israel proper and 40,000 in the West Bank and Gaza—Holy Land Christians are caught in the crossfire of the Arab–Israeli conflict. Alienated by Arabs for being Israeli citizens, they suffer restrictions as "Arabs" within Israel itself, and prejudice as non-Muslims and therefore as suspects within an overwhelmingly Muslim-Palestinian community.

Beginning in the seventh century, under Muslim rule, Christians of the Holy Land gradually became a minority in their ancestral homeland, suffering the exactions of *dhimmitude*—that is to say the legal restrictions that Islam placed on non-Muslims in the "Abode of Islam"—causing their status and numbers to deteriorate over the course of 14 centuries.

Like other Christians of the Eastern Mediterranean, the position of Holy Land Christians witnessed a slight, albeit tenuous, improvement in the waning days of the Ottoman Empire, as Western missionaries took advantage of the Capitulations (abolished in 1914) to increase their social, pastoral, and cultural presence, establishing new schools, churches, and hospitals tending to the needs of Holy Land Christians and setting into motion a process of modernization, urbanization, and Westernization.

A useful analogy to help us grasp the diverse nature of the Christians of the Holy Land in our time may be the character of Jesus Christ in Mel Gibson's *The Passion of the Christ* motion picture. In the film, Jesus spoke Aramaic, Hebrew, Greek, and Latin, reflecting the mosaic that was Roman Judaea and the Galilee of his day. During that time Hellenistic colonies had been in the Near East for centuries; Greek was the idiom of the masses and some civil servants; Latin had become the language of administration and the Roman legions; Hebrew—as is the case with Arabic today—was the ceremonial cultic language of the Jewish priesthood; and Aramaic was the language of the indigenous Jews and Pagans, and later the early Judaeo-Christians—that is to say the early followers of Jesus. This diversity in the time of Christ is still the same one that defines and distinguishes the Eastern Mediterranean today—the Holy Land in particular. And this diversity has in turn been tolerated and suppressed and celebrated and maligned at different times, with the consequent changing fortunes of Holy Land Christians getting better or worse depending on the hegemon of the day.

As noted earlier, the Arab-Muslim conquests of the seventh century were traumatic to Near Eastern Christians in general, and to Holy Land Christians in particular. Their situation was somewhat "tolerable" during the early Umayyad period, because, as the Umayyads (661–750) were consolidating their hold on the newly conquered Byzantine world, they showed themselves to be more lenient vis-à-vis the Christian majority population. Yet, as they became more secure in their authority and their presence and their numbers, they likewise became less forgiving.

Under Abbassid rule (750–1250), Muslim anti-Christian attitudes became an article of faith, instigating large-scale emigration, conversion, and overall victimization of Holy Land Christians: building of churches and visible displays of Christian symbols were forbidden; crosses that already figured on church rooftops were forcibly removed; Christians were required to wear distinctive garbs in public so as to clearly identify them and segregate them from the Muslim populace; and their homes had to be marked with a "scarlet letter," further ostracizing them and preventing them from coming into contact with the "righteous"—the Muslims—lest they sully them with their presence.

The vaunted "enlightenment" and "humanism" of Abbasid Caliph Harun al-Rashid (786–809), and his alleged friendship with Charlemagne did not change very much with regards to the status of Holy Land Christians. They still suffered molestation, persecution, banishment, and often death under "enlightened" Muslim rule. But by AD 801, Charlemagne was able to obtain a semblance of an amnesty from Harun al-Rashid, palliating Christian suffering to a certain extent. Thus, with the Caliph somewhat easing the pressure,

Charlemagne saw to it that a Benedictine monastery be built near the Basilica of the Holy Sepulcher, soon to be followed by a new church—the *Sancta Maria Latina*—erected nearby, housing a library and a hospice for Christian pilgrims coming from across the Mediterranean.[11]

This positive interlude may indeed be curious in light of Harun al-Rashid's continued molestation of his Christian subjects, and Charlemagne's open hostility toward Muslims and Islam as a whole, and his otherwise ruthless warring against the Muslims of Spain. But "insecurity," and indeed "unpredictability," were at the heart of the Christians' tenuous existence in the East: being "protected subjects" of Islam—*dhimmis*—and having their "protection edicts"—*dhimmi*—removed at the drop of a hat were foundational to the concept of *dhimmitude* and the incertitude, insecurity, and indignity that this entailed under a regime of legalized—and indeed religiously sanctioned—inequality.[12]

But with Harun al-Rashid's death in AD 809, the degraded status of Holy Land Christians would become more degrading, and the *dhimma* would come to be more strictly enforced.[13] In time, all this led to increased forced conversions and a steady exodus of Holy Land Christians to neighboring Christian territories not already under Muslim jurisdiction. But as Abbasid rule waned and passed on to Turkic generals toward the middle of the tenth century, the fortunes of Holy Land Christians deteriorated even further. More of their places of worship were torched and desecrated; more of their dwelling places were destroyed; more demoralization and dread ensued and gripped their societies, and by the end of the tenth century the Holy Land—and indeed the entire Levantine region—would be passed on to the Fatimid Muslim dynasty.

Under the most infamous of the Fatimids, the Caliph al-Hakim (992–1021), Christian pilgrimage to the Holy Land was altogether banned, whatever crosses had been left (or overlooked) on the rooftops of churches were burned, hundreds of places of worship were desecrated, pillaged, and demolished—among them the Church of the Holy Sepulcher—and small mosques began to appear on the rooftops of remaining churches—a curious spectacle, but not a minor nod to Muslim superiority and dominance.[14] This precipitated further the rising waves of Christian conversion and emigration.

Oddly enough—and again speaking to the muddy frightening nature of the *dhimma* system—toward the end of his reign al-Hakim allowed many Christian converts to Islam to return to their earlier Christian faith and worship on the remnants of the Holy Sepulcher—an act otherwise punishable by death under Islamic law. Indeed, Al-Hakim's Fatimid successors allowed the Holy Sepulcher itself to be rebuilt, so that, by the time the first Crusaders arrived in the Holy Land (AD 1099), a new Church of the Holy Sepulcher had already been in place. The Crusades would briefly improve the lot of Holy Land

Christians; but the positive interlude that they might have provided—as with all of those that preceded it—was temporary, tenuous, and costly.

The Crusades, however one wishes to define them, specifically from a post-colonialist perspective deeming them a rapacious Western Christian penetration of an otherwise gentle faultless East, the Crusades were above all else an act of devotion and self-defense; indeed they were a series of delayed Christian defensive wars waged against an intrusive, assertive, offensive Islam already well entrenched on the European continent. They were ultimately an unsuccessful Christian endeavor aiming at taking back by force Christian lands that exogenous Muslim intruders had wrested from native Christians by force, some five centuries earlier.

It was from Lebanon—that is to say from the East, not from Europe— and with the help of Lebanon's indigenous recalcitrant Maronites that the Frankish Crusaders entered the Holy Land. Thus, advancing southward down the ancient Phoenician coastal highway, the Crusaders, guided by Maronite scouts, rode through Acre, bypassed Jaffa (the Port of Jerusalem), and took Ramla and Lydda before heading eastward toward the Jerusalem hills. As they advanced, they encountered many empty towns and smoldering churches, as angry, defeated, retreating Muslims torched most of what they were leaving behind.[15]

From Ramla, Jerusalem was within earshot. Already emptied of its Christian population, the Fatimid defenders held fast onto the Holy City for close to 40 days, so that by the time the Crusaders took it, they invested it in a most dreadful butchery, slaughtering all of its captured Muslim and Jewish residents. Jaffa was taken soon thereafter, as were Nazareth and Bethlehem, with the latter captured with much more ease, due in large part to its sizeable pro-Crusader Christian population. Thus, the Crusaders were able to establish, for the first time in more than 400 years, a Christian principality in the Galilee. But the re-establishment of a Christian foothold in the Holy Land was short-lived; and so was the relief that Crusader presence might have brought to the embattled Christians of the region. Indeed, the Crusaders' departure in 1291 proved disastrous to what had remained of Eastern Christendom.

By the end of the thirteenth century, the Mamluks had become the masters of the Holy Land. As former slaves—composed in the main of Turks, Circassians, and newly Islamized Christians—the Mamluks brought with them a particular brand of fanaticism, chauvinism, and intolerance that perhaps only neophytes can muster, showing themselves to be particularly violent and cruel vis-à-vis their Christian subjects. Mamluks intolerant

The Ottoman Muslim period (ca. 1516–1917) was likewise a period of ebbs and flows for Near Eastern Christians in general, and the Christians of the Holy Land in particular. At different periods of their reign, the Ottomans betrayed some resignation in the polyglot multi-religious nature of their empire, and sought to "manage" that diversity rather than crush it. But by that time, the Christian population of the Holy Land had become so "impover- ished, its numbers . . . so exiguous" that it had lost all significance culturally, socially, and numerically speaking.[16]

Divided into the *Sanjaks* of Jerusalem, Safed, Nablus, and Gaza, the Holy Land had become a dependency of the *Vilayets* of Damascus and Beirut at different times during Ottoman rule, with each *Vilayet* enjoying varying degrees of autonomy often trickling down to Christians and other minori- ties. Still suffering the exactions of *dhimmitude,* Holy Land Christians were legally recognized *Millets* (or "nations"), which meant that their "autonomy" was restricted to personal and religious matters, accorded with some limita- tions and under well-enforced regulations.

With the dismantlement of the Ottoman Empire in 1918, the British, who inherited some of the Ottoman dominions, kept the *millet* system as the governing basis of the Mandate regime, ceding it in 1948 once more to a Muslim—this time, Jordanian—authority. But for 30 years of the Mandate administration, which amounted to a cultural and social "honeymoon" for non-Muslim minorities, Holy Land Christians breathed a sigh of relief. During that period, 80 percent of them had become urbanized, with more than 90 percent of their children receiving formal schooling, rendering the community a veritable conduit between East and West, and contributing to the modernization, secularization, and all-around worldliness of what might have otherwise remained an essentially Muslim culture.

With the 1948 establishment of the State of Israel as a home for the Jewish people—but a state with institutionalized freedom and equality for all citizens regardless of religion, ethnicity, or gender—the Christians took part in the Israeli electoral process, and many served as members of the Israeli Knesset, the Israeli Defense Forces, the Israeli Justice System, and the Israeli Diplo- matic Corps.

Indeed, non-Orthodox Christians took kindly to the new Jewish state, preaching acceptance and allegiance to it. "In Europe," began the explanation of one Maronite observer describing the events of 1948 to his children,

In Europe there is a man called Hitler. A Satan. For a long time he was killing Jewish people. Men and women, grandparents—even boys and girls like you. He killed them just because they were Jews. For no other reason. . . . Now this Hitler is dead. But our Jewish brothers have been badly hurt and frightened. They can't go back to their homes in Europe, and they have not been welcomed by the rest of the world. So they are coming here to look for a home. In a few days, Jewish soldiers will be traveling through Biram.[17] They are called "Zion- ists." A few will stay in each home, and some will stay right here with us for a few days—maybe a week. Then they will move on. They have machine guns, but they don't kill. You have no reason to be afraid. We must be especially kind and make them feel at home. . . . We are going to prepare a feast [for them]. This year we'll celebrate the Resurrection early—[we will celebrate it] for our Jewish brothers who were threatened with death, and are alive.[18]

Then watching the excitement cropping up on his children's faces, the father bowed his head in prayer, asking his family to join him in his extemporaneous rendition of the Lord's Prayer: "Father in heaven," he prayed softly, "help us to show love to our Jewish brothers. Help us to show them peace to quiet their troubled hearts."[19] As described by one of this Maronite villager's sons, the prayer felt as if "rising into the night sky like the smoky tendrils of incense that was burned at church."[20]

Those were clearly the recollections of children yet untainted by the evil of men, untouched by the foul stench of an Arab–Israeli conflict to come. But they were also symptomatic of certain anxieties, representative of the sensitivies of Holy Land Christians—by no means *all* Holy Land Christians, but many of them—distressed at the thought of being faced once more with the prospects of bondage to yet another Muslim government, falling prey to *other*, more modern forms of Muslim strictures that might have emerged out of the smoldering embers of the British Mandate.[21] But the status of Christians, and the state of Jewish–Christian relations in Israel today remain tenuous, crippled by the intransigence and resentments of the Arab–Israeli conflict.

Yet most Israeli Christians persevere in their attempts at bridging differences and acting as conduits. Against great odds, they remain the most enterprising, open-minded, and prosperous Arabophone element in Israeli society. But they also remain a vulnerable community; an infinitesimally small community; easy prey to Muslim resentments, Islamist retributions, and Jewish mistrust.

Ironically, its warts and blemishes notwithstanding, Israel remains the safest haven for Near Eastern Christians today. Indeed, and despite Christian emigration out of the country, Israel has since its founding recorded a sizeable increase in its Christian population even as the numbers of Christians continue to dwindle elsewhere in the Middle East. In fact, Christian "integration" is stronger than emigration" in Israel, and the challenges that Christians may face in the Jewish state are a far cry from the existential dangers staring their coreligionists under the Palestinian Authority, and elsewhere in the Middle East.[22]

Indeed, unlike the situation of Israel's Christians, which is by no measure an enviable one, the indigenous Christians of the Palestinian Authority have since 1993 been stuck in a religious and cultural ghetto, opting to "vote with their feet," and choosing emigration over integration within a Palestinian society they deem increasingly corrupt, inefficient, and intolerant. Their ability to obtain justice in an openly Islamized Palestinian space, bereft of institutional organization, is almost non-extant.

Faced with daily offenses ranging from the wanton defacement of their institutions, to public displays of contempt, to intimidation, extortion, and pressure to abide by Islamic law, Palestinian Authority Christians may indeed be on the verge of perdition. The numbers issuing out of Bethlehem may suffice as an indicator of things yet to come. Approaching 90 percent of the town's population through the 1960s, the Christians of Bethlehem have been reduced to barely 30 percent according to recent estimates. But that figure may indeed be inflated, and indigenous Christians are by no means ready with censuses and expressions of dismay, all for fear of retribution and accusations of treason—a quandary that is already part of their daily bread.[23]

Yet, based on Israeli documentation—naturally *not* corroborated in Palestinian sources—things are grimmer than most Christians may let on. Reportedly, on the heels of the Six-Day War, some 550 Christian elders from Bethlehem lobbied Israeli Prime Minister Levy Eshkol's government to annex Bethlehem to Israel, "so that both Christian holy sites—the Church of the holy Sepulcher [. . .] and the Church of the Nativity [. . .] would be under one nationality."[24] Israel denied the request. No Christian within the Palestinian authority today would dare pull a stunt like that. And the plot thickens.

CONCLUSIONS

A recapitulation by way of conclusion may be in order, if only to serve as a reminder of the fate awaiting the disintegrating Christians of the Holy Land. Christian citizens of the State of Israel although presumed to be "not equal" to their Jewish compatriots, still *are* equal in the eye of the law, still have recourse to the Israeli Justice System, and may even be more privileged than the country's Muslim population. Indeed, Israeli Christians may be the only Near Eastern Christian community *not* facing persecution and exodus, and Israel may be the only Middle Eastern state to have, since its founding, witnessed an increase in its Christian population rather than a decline. This is indeed remarkable in light of the grim prospects for the dwindling Christian communities elsewhere in the Near East, and the continued exodus of Palestinian Christians from the West Bank and Gaza—a nightmare arguably still at its very beginnings.

In the weeks between September 20 and October 12, 2008, fifteen young Christians were murdered in cold blood on the streets of Mosul, Iraq. A manhunt was launched. None of the offenders were ever brought to justice. With impunity, killings and lootings in Christian neighborhoods would continue unabated, in Iraq, in Egypt, and elsewhere, wherever Near Eastern Christians came into view. But there's nothing unusual here—*not* in the *longue durée* of Near Eastern history! long-forgotten & re-used

On July 18, 2014, in a statement reading like a ninth-century religious edict, the Caliphate of the Islamic State of Iraq and Syria (ISIS) delivered a 24-hour ultimatum to the Christians of Mosul, commanding them to "convert to Islam, submit to the [discriminatory] laws of *dhimma*, or meet the sword."[25] Soon thereafter the Arabic letter "nuun" ("N" for *Nasraani* or Nazarene, a demeaning scarlet letter of *dhimmitude* not unlike the yellow star inscribed with the word "*Jude*" that became the symbol of Nazi persecution of Jews) began cropping up on the outer walls and doorways of Christian properties. Private homes, businesses, and places of worship were now slated *halal* (ritually licit) for confiscation and looting as part of the religious spoils of war, designating them future *waqf* (inalienable religious endowments of the Muslim *umma*). The squaring of this circle is at hand; the destruction of Near Eastern Christendom is well under way and making promising headway. Our times' mass exodus of Iraq's "Nazarenes" may be in its last stages today, but it is the ongoing saga of Near Eastern Christians elsewhere, Christians of the Palestinian territories included. story continues

And this had been the order of things in times past. For centuries in the Middle East, the cross has been trampled in the dust of the *other* children of Abraham, descendants of his first son Ishmael. In quiet desperation, millennial Christian quarters have disappeared, old neighborhoods counted their dead, desiccated clergy given last rites, and panic gripped those precious few left behind. But the plight of Near Eastern Christians does not make for catchy headlines. It is not worthy of second, third, nor even last-page news in the mainstream press. International newswires on the topic often get disseminated in perfunctory manner, like the weather, or other miscellany. There is clearly a prevailing hierarchy in some of the media's treatment of Middle East violence; some Middle Eastern victims do merit (and do get) airtime, on primetime, all the time. Others simply do not get that privilege.

Near Eastern Christians, uncouth "cross-wearing" primitives, are not a top priority of the Western world's moral gauge and outrage; their anguish is not telegenically appealing. They are after all "too Christian" in a world plagued by political correctness, cultural relativism, and false conceptions of the Middle East as a homogeneous Arab or Muslim preserve, where *only* Arabs and Muslims can be the righteous victim, and *only* non-Muslims are the perennial offender. And yet, the Middle East's Christians—chief among them the tiny remaining Holy Land Christians—are indigenous remnants of distinct ancient civilizations, their modern day sagas of dispossession and persecution a phenomenon fourteen centuries in the making, their tormentors often proudly brandishing symbols and edicts of Islam. ME Christian experience

An honest recognition of this long legacy may be imperative to a sound understanding of the turmoil plaguing the region in our time. Still, venerable commentators, seasoned Middle East experts, and serious academics continue to deal with the plight of Near Eastern Christians in cursory fashion, many often concluding with mind-numbing claims that the shrinking numbers of Eastern Christians are largely the outcome of modern ills ranging from economic hardships, to American intrusions, to the Arab–Israeli conflict, and sometimes to the putative ancestor of Western colonialism, the eleventh-century Crusades.[26]

Gone from this soothing narrative are the seventh-century Arab-Muslim conquests of the Middle East and the subjugation, expulsions, massacres, and mass population movements that they wrought in their path. Indeed, the destruction of Near Eastern and Holy Land Christians is hardly a modern phenomenon. And so the silent exodus continues disguised, underhanded, unnoticed.

In 2014, the United Nations Security Council convened three times to discharge clear-throated statements of condemnation at the Israeli onslaught against Gaza. Yet, not a single expression of outrage has come out from any official quarters to denounce the ethnic cleansing of the ancient Christian communities of Iraq, Egypt, or the Palestinian territories. But the onus is not on the international community alone. This is a tragedy besetting Muslims and Arabs of good conscience as well, and some Muslims and Arabs *have* indeed summoned their own, pressing for introspection, scrutiny, and accountability. On July 21, 2014, in a searing soul-searching *cri de coeur* in the Kuwaiti daily *Al-Qabas*, Ahmad al-Sarraf issued his own decent man's indictment of the crimes being committed in the name of his faith against the battered Christians of the Near East.

In a combustive tongue-in-cheek editorial titled "Begone, O Christians," Sarraf, facetiously, of course, and in a diatribe lampooning the ISIS playbook, noted that Muslims could not care less that Near Eastern Christians may be the indigenous peoples of Egypt, Syria, Iraq, Lebanon, and Palestine; he demanded that they be expelled regardless, "so that Muslims no longer be put to shame when their eyes meet the searching gaze of Christians wondering what had gone awry with Islam!"[27] "Yes, begone already," concluded Sarraf,

And take with you the mercy of your pacifist creed! Why, because with al-Nusra and ISIS and al-Qaeda and the rest of them on our side—with the gangs of Muslim Brothers and their latest finest products—we are scarcely in need of [the Christians'] mercy and compassion. Let the bloodletting commence! Let the violence reign supreme! Let the hearts get ripped out of their chest-cavities, and let human livers get eaten raw! Let the tongues be torn out! Let the necks get hacked off, and the knees get shattered! For, we shall eagerly return to the medicine of old, to our herbal remedies and our old musty books of alchemy and witchcraft! [. . .] Yes, begone O Christians, and leave us be to our desert creed! For, we crave the glint of our swords, the heat of our sands, and the energy of our mules! We scarcely need you, your civilization, or your scientific and literary contributions; for, we have our own capital in abundance; our own gangs of murderers and bloodthirsty butchers and executioners. Scram, you Christians, and spare us your civilization already! We are replacing your culture with that of the gravediggers![28]

But this was 2014, and the show *does* go on in a series of unending reruns. And so, we have seen that movie before: eighty years ago, the Armenian-American novelist William Saroyan was already assailing our resigned attitudes of today. Eighty years ago, Saroyan was already issuing his indictments of the world's silence before the tragedy of Near Eastern Christians today.

In 1933, Saroyan's short story, *Seventy Thousand Assyrians,* was a decent man's refusal to commit the aggrieved Near Eastern Christians to oblivion. It was, of course, not written with today's events in mind, but it is chillingly premonitory, and it *can* be read like a news item from yesterday's newspaper. But *Seventy Thousand Assyrians* is eighty years old, written on the heels of the Assyrian Genocide, long before the invention of political correctness, at a time when murderers could still be taken to task, and when one could still name names and hand down indictments without the fear of being branded as racist, "Islamophobe," or "Orientalist."

I am reproducing a long excerpt from Saroyan's *Seventy Thousand Assyrians* here because it eloquently captures the essence of the plight of Holy Land Christians today. At times the text may seem too frivolous a depiction of a serious human tragedy. But bear with it. Saroyan's story is a serious one indeed, despite its evident levity; his account is that of a subtle scrupulous compassionate observer; and his sarcasm is a devastating commentary on political apathy—not unlike Martin Niemöller's famous statement on the crimes of Nazi Germany, and the world's apathy then. Niemöller's "First they came for the Communists . . ." might very well have had its origins in Saroyan's *Seventy Thousand Assyrians.* Saroyan's testimony certainly lacks the lapidary brevity of Niemöller's, but its lesson is the same; one equally disturbing and moving.

In this tale, Saroyan begins by telling his readers how it has been ages since he has had a haircut; how he is beginning to look seedy and unkempt, "like several violinists out of work [. . .] and ready to join the Communist Party," as he put it. "We barbarians from Asia Minor" he wrote, "are hairy people; and when we need a haircut, *we need* a haircut." So he goes to the San Francisco Barbers' College for a fifteen-cent haircut, and he lands himself a new apprentice. Here is what happens next:

The young man who gave me the haircut was tall; he had a dark serious face, thick lips, on the verge of smiling but melancholy, thick eyelashes, sad eyes, a large nose. I saw his name on the card that was pasted on the mirror: Theodore Badal. A good name; genuine; a good young man; genuine!! Theodore Badal began to work on my head. A good barber never speaks before he's spoken to, no matter how full his heart may be.

"That name," I said, "Badal. Are you an Armenian?" I'm an Armenian. I've mentioned this before. People look at me and begin to wonder, so I come right out and tell them. "I'm an Armenian," I say. Or they read something I've written and begin to wonder, so I let them know. "I'm an Armenian," I say. It's a meaningless remark, but they expect me to say it, so I do. I have no idea what it's like to be an Armenian or what it's like to be an Englishman or a Japanese or anything else. I have a faint idea what it's like to be alive. This is the only thing that interests me greatly. This, and tennis. I hope some day to write a great philosophical work on tennis, something on the order of "Death in the Afternoon," but I'm aware that I'm not yet ready to undertake such a project. [. . .] (It may seem to some sophisticated people that I'm trying to make fun of Hemingway. I'm not. "Death in the Afternoon" is a pretty sound piece of prose. [. . .] Even when Hemingway is a fool, he's at least an accurate fool.)

"Are you an Armenian?" I asked.

We're a small people, and whenever one of us meets another, it's an event. We're always looking around for someone to talk to in our language. Our most ambitious political party estimates that there are nearly two million of us living on the earth, but most of us don't think so. Most of us sit down and take a pencil and a piece of paper and we take one section of the world at a time and imagine how many Armenians at the most are likely to be living in that section and we put the highest number on the paper, and then we go on to another section, India, Russia, Soviet Armenia, Egypt, Italy, Germany, France, America, South America, Australia, and so on, and after we add up our most hopeful figures the total comes to something a little less than a million. Then we start to think how big our families are, how high our birthrate and how low our death rate (except in times of war, when massacres increase our death rate), and we begin to imagine how rapidly we will increase if we are left alone, [even for] a quarter century, and we feel pretty happy.

I remember the Near East Relief drives in my hometown. My uncle used to be our orator and he used to make a whole auditorium full of Armenians weep. He was an attorney and he was a great orator. Well, at first the trouble was war. Our people were being destroyed by the enemy. Those who hadn't been killed were homeless and they were starving; *"our flesh and blood,"* my uncle said, and we all wept. And we gathered money and sent it out to our people in the old country. Then after the war, when I was a bigger boy, we had another Near East Relief drive and my uncle stood on the stage of the Civic Auditorium of my hometown and he said, "Thank God this time it is not the enemy, but an earthquake. God has made us suffer. We have worshipped Him through trial and tribulation, through suffering and disease and torture and horror and (my uncle began to weep, began to sob), [we've worshiped Him] through the madness of despair, and now he has done this thing, and still we praise Him, still we worship Him. We don't understand the ways of God." And after the drive I went to my uncle and I said, "Did you mean what you said about God?" And he said, "That was oratory. We've got to raise money. What God? God is nonsense!" "And when you cried?" I asked, and my uncle said, "That was real. I could not help it. I had to cry. Why? . . . For God's sake, why must we go through all this Goddamn hell? What have we done to deserve all this torture? Man won't let us alone. God won't let us alone. Have we done something wrong? Aren't we supposed to be pious people? What is our sin? I am disgusted with God. I am sick of man. The only reason I am willing to get up and talk is that I don't dare keep my mouth shut. I can't bear the thought of more of our people dying. Jesus Christ, have we done something wrong?"

I asked Theodore Badal if he was an Armenian.

He said, "I am an Assyrian."

Well, *that* is something. They, the Assyrians, came from our part of the world, they had noses like our noses, eyes like our eyes, hearts like our hearts. They had a different language. When they spoke we couldn't understand them, but they were a lot like us. It wasn't quite as pleasing as it would have been if Badal had been an Armenian, but *that* was really something.

"I am an Armenian," I said. "I used to know some Assyrian boys in my home town, Joseph Sargis, Nito Elia, Tony Saleh. Do you know any of them?"

"Joseph Sargis, I know him," said Badal. "The others I don't know. We lived in New York until five years ago, then we came out West to Turlock. Then we moved up to San Francisco."

[. . .] We began to talk about the Assyrian language and the Armenian language, about the old world, conditions over there, and so on. I was getting a fifteen-cent-haircut and I was doing my best to learn something at the same time, to acquire some new truth, some new appreciation of the wonder of life, the dignity of man. (Man has great dignity; do not imagine that he has not.)

Badal said, "I can't read Assyrian. I was born in the old country, but I want to get over it."

He sounded tired; not physically, but spiritually.

"Why?" I said. "Why do you want to get over it?"

"Well," he laughed, "simply because everything is washed up over there."

I am repeating his words precisely, putting in nothing of my own.

"We were a great people once," he went on. "But that was yesterday, the day before yesterday. Now we are a topic in ancient history. We had a great civilization. They're still admiring it. Now I am in America learning how to cut hair. We're washed up as a race, we're through, it's all over, why should I learn to read the language? We have no writers, we have no news—well, there's a little news: once in a while the English encourage the Arabs to slaughter us, and that's that!! It's an old story, we know it all too well. The news comes over to us through the Associated Press, anyway."

These remarks were very painful to me, an Armenian. I had always felt badly about my own people being destroyed. I had never heard an Assyrian speaking in English about such things. I felt great love for this young fellow. Don't get me wrong. There is a tendency these days to think in terms of pansies whenever a man says that he has affection for a man. I think now that I have affection for all people, even for the enemies of Armenia, whom I have so tactfully not named. Everyone knows who they are! I have nothing against any of them because I think of them as one man living one life at a time, and I know, I am positive, that one man at a time is incapable of the monstrosities performed by mobs. My objection is to mobs only.

"Well," I said, "it is much the same with us. We, too, are old. We still have our church. We still have a few writers, Aharonian, Isahakian, a few others, but it is much the same."

"Yes," said the barber, "I know. We went in for the wrong things. We went in for the simple things, peace and quiet and families. We didn't go in for machinery and conquest and militarism. We didn't go in for diplomacy and deceit and the invention of machineguns and poison gases. Oh well, there is no use in being disappointed. We had our day, I suppose."

"We are hopeful," I said. "There is no Armenian living who doesn't still dream of an independent Armenia."

"Dream?" said Badal. "Well, that is something. Assyrians can't even dream anymore. Why, do you know how many of us are left on earth?"

"Two or three million," I suggested.

"Seventy thousand," said Badal. "That is all. Seventy thousand Assyrians in the world, and the Arabs are still killing us. They killed seventy of us in a little uprising last month. There was a small paragraph in the paper. Seventy more of us destroyed. We'll be wiped out before long. My brother is married to an American girl, and he has a son. There is no more hope. We are trying to forget Assyria. My father still reads [an Assyrian] paper that comes from New York, but he is an old man. He will be dead soon."

Then his voice changed, he ceased speaking as an Assyrian and began to speak as a barber: "Have I taken enough off the top?" he asked.

The rest of the story is pointless. I said "so long" to the young Assyrian and left the shop."

I thought about this whole business: Assyria and the Assyrians, Theodore Badal learning to be a barber, the sadness of his voice, the hopelessness of his attitude. This was months ago, in August, but ever since, I've been thinking about Assyria, and I have been wanting to say something about Theodore Badal, a son of an ancient race, himself youthful and alert, yet hopeless. Seventy thousand Assyrians, a mere seventy thousand of that great people, and all the others quiet in death and all the greatness crumbled and ignored, and a young man in America learning to be a barber, and a young man lamenting bitterly the course of history.

[. . .] I am thinking of seventy thousand Assyrians, one at a time, alive, a great race. I am thinking of Theodore Badal, himself seventy thousand Assyrians and seventy million Assyrians, himself Assyria and man, standing in a barber shop, in San Francisco, in 1933, and being still himself, the whole [Assyrian] race.[29]

This is what is at stake in the Middle East today; Copts, Maronites, Armenians, Assyrians, Holy Land Christians, and others still; dwindling emaciated Christian minorities; remnants of ancient civilizations undergoing a silent exodus, an undercover genocide; precious few remaining specimens of the world's most ancient human civilizations; besieged, abused, brutalized, forgotten endangered species, barely clinging to their dignity, barely clinging to their lives, barely clinging to their homelands, their ancestral homelands; the very first cradles of our human history.

This story of Saroyan's, written some eighty years ago, might as well have been written last night, or eighty hours ago, or eight days ago. But it also might as well have been written eight hundred years ago, because not very much has changed in the shifting fortunes of Holy Land Christians in the past millennium and a half except further etiolation of their numbers and a fading cultural footprint—in their ancestral homelands no less.

Holy Land Christians need serious discussions of their plight; straightforward, honest inquiries into their history of dispossession. And beyond the jeremiads, beyond the platitudes, and beyond the perfunctory expressions of concern and sympathy, they need answers as to whether or not their cultures, their civilizations, their histories, and their ancestral languages are worth saving. Their plight needs to be looked at distinctly and separately from all the other problems plaguing the Middle East. Their troubled present days are not an outgrowth or an outcome or an emanation or a derivation or a reaction to the Arab–Israeli conflict—or at least "not only." Nor is their plight related to the modern rise of Islamism or to shifting economic fortunes. Their problems preceded the Arab–Israeli conflict, the establishment of the State of Israel, the rise of Islamism, or economic tribulations. Their plight is the sequel and the natural continuation of a long process of erasure and annihilation; not only physical annihilation, but also a process of debasement whereby they are rendered dejected, self-effacing, self-loathing, and almost apologetic for their own existence.

The twentieth century has turned out to be a mass grave for many an ancient people. But it has also witnessed the continuation of the silent slow death of the indigenous Christians of the Middle East. These people's ancient quarters on the Eastern shores of the Mediterranean, in the Judean Hills, and further East in the Syrian hinterland and the Mesopotamian highlands—once bustling metropolises—are now destitute ghost towns and vacant "spiritual Disneylands" devoid of spirit and substance; obscene tourist attractions and curious museum artifacts, exploited by their very own despoilers. We do the Middle East and its complexities no favors by engaging the dishonest causalities and apologia of Arab nationalists and Islamists and framing their prejudice and intransigence vis-à-vis their minority peoples within the context—and inside the many injustices that may flow out—of the Arab–Israeli conflict.

Lest it be forgotten and trampled in the dust of "fake news" and "alternative facts," the exodus of Near Eastern and Holy Land Christians *precedes* the Arab–Israeli conflict and is very likely to outlive it. Holy Land Christians and other Christians throughout the Near East—for all intents and purposes the "First Nations," the "Native Americans" of the region, "the ones who were there *first*" as it were—constituted 20 percent of the region's population at the turn of the twentieth century, a decent percentage by any measure given the millennial history of Islam as hegemon in that part of the world. Yet in our second decade of the twenty-first century, the number of Near Eastern Christians has dwindled to a mere 5 percent, and in the past hundred years prejudice against them ceased being the veiled affliction of a bigoted few; it has become the banner of those who allege themselves to speak for Islam.

And so, the questions that beg asking in conclusion are the following: For how long must the Middle East's keepers of cultural, religious, linguistic, and national orthodoxy be allowed to get away with their cruel historical record? The cradle of classical civilizations, the Eastern Mediterranean, had seemed until the seventh-century Muslim conquest a veritable center of the universe; a crucible and a meeting place of cultures, ethnicities, languages, belief systems, and civilizations, where Antioch and Alexandria, high altars of ecumenical Hellenic Christendom rivaled the glories of Rome and Byzantium. Yet precious little of this majestic history remains—that is, precious little remains besides the harshness of denuded landscapes and the anguish of dilapidated neighborhoods; bitter reflections of the intellectual sterility of a world no longer able to produce anything of note.

How, then, can one *not* question the silent exodus of Near Eastern Christians in light of the rigid religious foundations that have, for over a millennium, determined the social and political organization of what is now called "the Arab Middle East"? How can the usual suspects—Israel, economic hardships, Western intrusions, and the twelfth-century Crusades—continue to be indicted when the real villains go on winning acquittal on top of acquittal?

NOTES

1. Elie Kedourie, "Not So Grand Illusions," *New York Review of Books* 9, no. 9 (November 23, 1967): n. p.

2. Kees Versteegh, ed., *Encyclopedia of Arabic Language and Linguistics* (Brill, 2009).

3. Joel Carmichael, *The Shaping of the Arabs: A Study in Ethnic Identity* (New York: The Macmillan Company, 1967), 309.

4. Abu Khaldun Sati' al-Husri, *Al-'Uruuba bayna du'aatiha wa mu'aridiiha* [Arabism Between its Advocates and its Proponents] (Beirut, Lebanon: Markaz dirasaat al-wihda al-'Arabiyya, 1984), 9.

5. Ibid.

6. Michel Aflaq, *Fii Sabiil al-Baath* [For the Sake of the Ba'ath], (Beirut: Dar al-Talii'a, 1959), 93.

7. Bernard Lewis, *Arabs in History* (Oxford: Oxford University Press, e-book edition, 2002), 13.

8. Ibid.

9. Élisée Reclus, *Nouvelle Géographie Universelle: La Terre et les Hommes* (Paris: Librairie Hachette et Cie., 1884), 745.

10. The sole exception to this rule was the Arabic-language newspaper *Falastin* (*Palestine*), which began publication in Jaffa in 1911, under Ottoman rule, and acted mainly as the mouthpiece of Jaffa's Greek Orthodox Christian community. *Falastin* may certainly be credited with having "shaped" Arab "Palestinian" identity over the course of fifty-five years, specially toward the end of the British Mandate period. With the establishment of the State of Israel in 1948, *Falastin* moved its headquarters from the Ajami quarter of Jaffa to East Jerusalem, placing it under the Hashemites' jurisdiction when the West Bank came under Jordanian rule between 1948 and 1967. It ceased publication in 1967. Yet *Falastin* ultimately remained a "Christian"—specifically Greek Orthodox—enterprise, whose audience was largely Arabophone Christian, and whose lodestar was Arab nationalism rather than "Palestinianism" as such, appealing in the main to a Greek Orthodox Christian community.

11. See Saul P. Colbi, *A History of the Christian Presence in the Holy Land* (Lanham: University Press of America, 1988), 30.

12. This may also be understood in light of Harun al-Rashid's enmity toward the Byzantines, who still laid claim to the Holy Land as usurped "Christian land," an enmity shared by Charlemagne himself, who *also* viewed himself as the principal protector of Christendom, thus justifying his cooperation with the Muslim interloper. "My enemy's enemy is my friend" is an old-world adage, and a concept that might very well been at play in this relationship between those most improbable of friends.

13. See Colbi, 32. By this time, the *dhimmis* were required to wear yellow patches on their outer garments, affix images of monkeys and swine on the doors of their dwellings, ride on wooden saddles carved in bead-shaped configurations to make riding painful, dismount from their mules when passing a walking Muslim, and were strictly forbidden from practicing their rites in the open (church bells, clappers, calls to prayer, and outward expressions of religiosity were banned).

14. See Colbi, 34.

15. See ibid., 38.

16. Ibid., 79.

17. Biram is a Maronite village on the 1948 line between Lebanon and Israel.

18. Elias Chaccour, *Blood Brothers* (Michigan: Chosen Books, 2003), 27–29.

19. Ibid., 29.

20. Ibid.

21. See Daphne Tsimhoni, *Christian Communities in Jerusalem and the West Bank Since 1948* (Westport and London: Praeger, 1993), 1.

22. See Allen D. Hertzke and Timothy Samuel Shah, eds., *Christianity and Freedom; Contemporary Perspectives,* vol. 2, (New York: Cambridge University Press, 2016), 428.

23. This is an estimation, as no official data are available, and some experts suggest the real figure may be closer to 20 percent.

24. Nadav Shragai, "Why are Christians Leaving Bethlehem?" *Israel Hayom,* December 26, 2012, http://www.israelhayom.com/site/newsletter_article.php?id= 6865.

25. Le Monde, "En Irak, les djihadistes lancent un uiltimatum aux chrértiens de Mossoul," *Le Monde,* July 18, 2014, http://www.lemonde.fr/proche-orient/article/2014/07/18/irak-l-etat-islamique-force-les-chretiens-a-fuir-mossoul_4459855_3218.html.

26. See Don Belt, "Arab Christians: The Forgotten Faithful," *National Geographic,* June 2009, http://ngm.nationalgeographic.com/2009/06/arab-christians/belt-text.

27. Ahmad Al-Sarraf, "Begone O Christians," *Al-Qabas,* July 21, 2014, http://www.alqabas .com.kw/node/882999.

28. Ibid.

29. William Saroyan, *Seventy Thousand Assyrians* (1933), excerpts, http://www.zindamagazine .com/html/archives/2007/06.03.07/pix/Saroyan.pdf.

WORKS CITED

Aflaq, Michel. *Fii Sabiil al-Baath* [For the Sake of the Ba'ath]. Beirut: Dar al-Talii'a, 1959.

al-Husri, Abu Khaldun Sati'. *Al-'Uruuba bayna du'aatiha wa mu'aridiiha* [Arabism Between its Advocates and its Proponents]. Beirut: Markaz dirasaat al-wihda al-'Arabiyya, 1984.

Al-Sarraf, Ahmad. "Begone O Christians." *Al-Qabas.* July 21, 2014. http://www .alqabas.com.kw/node/882999.

Belt, Don. "Arab Christians: The Forgotten Faithful." *National Geographic.* June 2009. http:// ngm.nationalgeographic.com/2009/06/arab-christians/belt-text.

Carmichael, Joel. *The Shaping of the Arabs: A Study in Ethnic Identity.* New York: The Macmillan Company, 1967.

Chaccour, Elias. *Blood Brothers.* Michigan: Chosen Books, 2003.

Colbi, Saul P. *A History of the Christian Presence in the Holy Land.* Lanham: University Press of America, 1988.

Hertzke, Allen D. and Timothy Samuel Shah, eds. *Christianity and Freedom; Contemporary Perspectives* vol. 2. New York: Cambridge University Press, 2016.

Kedourie, Elie. "Not So Grand Illusions." *New York Review of Books* 9 no. 9 (November 23, 1967): n.p.

Le Monde. "En Irak, les djihadistes lancent un uiltimatum aux chrértiens de Mossoul." *Le Monde.* July 18, 2014. http://www.lemonde.fr/proche-orient/article/2014/07/18/irak-l-etat-islamique-force-les-chretiens-a-fuir-mossoul_4459855_3218.html.

Lewis, Bernard. *Arabs in History.* Oxford: Oxford University Press, e-book edition, 2002.

Reclus, Élisée. *Nouvelle Géographie Universelle: La Terre et les Hommes.* Paris: Librairie Hachette et Cie., 1884.

Saroyan, William. *Seventy Thousand Assyrians* (1933). Excerpts. http://www.zin-damagazine .com/html/archives/2007/06.03.07/pix/Saroyan.pdf.

Shragai, Nadav. "Why are Christians Leaving Bethlehem?" *Israel Hayom.* December 26, 2012. http://www.israelhayom.com/site/newsletter_article.php?id=6865.

Tsimhoni, Daphne. *Christian Communities in Jerusalem and the West Bank Since 1948.* Westport and London: Praeger, 1993.

Versteegh, Kees, ed. *Encyclopedia of Arabic Language and Linguistics.* Leiden: Brill, 2009.

Index

About the Contributors

Dr. Taner Akçam is a professor at the Department of History at Clark University in Worcester, MA, where he holds the chair of Armenian Genocide studies. He was one of the first Turkish intellectuals to acknowledge and openly discuss the Armenian Genocide. Born in the province of Ardahan, Akçam graduated from Middle East Technical University in Ankara and emigrated to Germany, where he worked as a research scientist in the sociology department at the Hamburg Institute for Social Research. He received his PhD from the University of Hannover with a dissertation entitled *Turkish Nationalism and the Armenian Genocide: On the Background of the Military Tribunals in Istanbul between 1919 and 1922*. He moved to the United States in 2000 and served as a visiting scholar at the University of Michigan for a year, and as a visiting associate professor of history at the University of Minnesota from 2002 to 2008.

Dr. Cengiz Aktar is a leading voice in Turkey for democratic reform, including respect for the rights of religious and ethnic minorities, in accordance with EU standards. Born in Istanbul, he graduated from the Lycée de Galatasaray and completed his tertiary education at Panthéon-Sorbonne, where he received his PhD in economic epistemology. During his time at the UN, Aktar held seminars in the universities where he was working. He has played a major role in promoting an online campaign calling for apology-based reconciliation with the descendants of the Armenian Genocide of 1915–1918.

Dr. Madawi Al-Rasheed is a visiting professor at the Middle East Centre at the London School of Economics and Political Science and a research fellow at the Open Society Foundation. Her research interests include gender, religion, and politics, with a focus on the Arab Gulf and especially Saudi Arabia, as well as Islamist movements and the anthropology of Muslim societies.

Dr. Fabrice Balanche is an associate professor and research director at the University of Lyon 2 and a visiting fellow at The Washington Institute. He holds a doctorate in geography from the University of Tours. Balanche, who also directs the Research Group on the Mediterranean and the Middle East (GREMMO), has spent 10 years in Lebanon and Syria, his main areas of study, since first engaging in fieldwork in the region in 1990. Today, he is frequently called upon as an expert consultant on Middle East development issues and the Syrian crisis.

Bat Ye'or was born in Egypt and later became a British citizen. She dedicates her work to documenting the situation of religious minorities living in the Muslim world. Bat Ye'or is well-known for using the term *dhimmitude* as a description of the status of non-Muslims living in an Islamic state. In 1997 and 2002, she spoke to the US Senate Foreign Relations Committee and at US Congressional Human Rights Caucus (CHRC) Briefings.

Award-winning Irish journalist **Patrick Cockburn** has been reporting from war zones in the Middle East since 1978. He is currently the Middle East correspondent for the British daily newspaper *The Independent,* and has previously reported from the Middle East for *Financial Times*. Cockburn has been awarded multiple prizes for his work, among them the International Media Award in 2010.

Dr. Marius Deeb, who received his doctorate from Oxford University, teaches Middle East politics at the School of Advanced International Studies at Johns Hopkins University. Previously, he taught at Indiana University, the American University of Beirut, and Georgetown University. He is a leading authority on Middle Eastern politics.

Dr. John Eibner is the CEO of Christian Solidarity International (USA), member of CSI's International Management, and director of CSI's Middle East program. For over 25 years, he has directed field-based research and human rights advocacy campaigns on behalf of endangered religious communities in Sudan and the broader Middle East. He has served as CSI's representative at the United Nations in Geneva, and has appeared before the US House of Representatives. He received his PhD in history from the University of London. From 1986 to 1990, Eibner was on the research staff of Keston College, a UK-based research institute for the study of religion in Marxist-Leninist countries.

Born into a Maronite-Christian family of politicians, His Excellency **Amine Gemayel** also became a member of the Lebanese Al-Kataeb Party, and was elected into parliament after finishing his law degree in the 1970s. Following the assassination of his brother and president-elect Bachir, Amine Gemayel was elected as the president of Lebanon in 1982. After the end of this administration period, during which he survived several assassination attempts, Gemayel went into exile in 1988. He returned in 2000 and resumed his political activities. In 2005 he became chairman of the Al-Kataeb Party. His son Pierre, who was also politically active, was assassinated in 2006. Amine Gemayel lectured at the universities of Maryland and Paris and Harvard University.

Dr. Joshua Landis is director of the Center for Middle East Studies and an associate professor at the University of Oklahoma's College of International Studies. His website "Syria Comment," attracts over 100,000 readers a month. Dr. Landis travels frequently to Washington, DC, to consult with government agencies and speak at think tanks. He was educated at Swarthmore (BA), Harvard (MA), and Princeton (PhD). He has lived over 14 years in the Middle East and speaks Arabic and French fluently. He has lived 4 years in Syria, and spent most summers in Damascus until the revolution began.

Dr. Habib C. Malik is an associate professor of history and cultural studies at LAU Byblos. He has lectured and written widely in both English and Arabic on topics that include the history of ideas, Kierkegaard, existentialism, human rights, the plight of native Middle Eastern Christian communities, Lebanon, democracy in the Arab world, interreligious dialogue, America and the Middle East, and Christian faith in a secular world.

Bishop Michael Nazir-Ali was the first non-white diocesan bishop in the Church of England, and for 15 years was the 106th Bishop of Rochester. Before then, he was the Bishop of Raiwind in Pakistan. By virtue of his seniority as an Anglican bishop, Pakistan-born Nazir-Ali served as a parliamentarian in the British House of Lords. He has long been a pioneer in Christian-Muslim dialogue, having headed his Church's dialogue with Al-Azhar University. Nazir-Ali's secondary education was in Pakistan. He read economics, sociology, and Islamic history at the University of Karachi, and theology at Fitzwilliam College and Ridley Hall, Cambridge.

Dr. Daniel Pipes is president of the Middle East Forum and was Taube Distinguished Visiting Fellow at the Hoover Institution of Stanford University. He is a former official in the US Department of State and the US Department of Defense, and has taught history at Harvard and Pepperdine universities and the University of Chicago, as well as the United States Naval War College. His biweekly column appears regularly in the *National Review* and in newspapers around the globe, including the *Jerusalem Post* and *Yisrael ha-Yom* (Israel), *Al-Akhbar* (Iraq), *Die Welt* (Germany), *La Razón* (Spain), *Liberal* (Italy), *National Post* (Canada), and the *Australian* (Australia).

Dr. Franck Salameh is an associate professor in Near Eastern Studies and the chairman of the Department of Slavic and Eastern Languages and Literatures at Boston College, Massachusetts. Salameh also serves as the senior editor-in-chief at *The Levantine Review*. His publications include *Language, Memory, and Identity in the Middle East: The Case for Lebanon* (Lanham: Lexington Books, 2010), and *Charles Corm: An Intellectual Biography of a Twentieth-Century Lebanese "Young Phoenician"* (Lanham: Lexington Books, 2015).

Dr. Mariz Tadros, an Egyptian scholar, is a fellow at the Institute of Development Studies, University of Sussex (UK), specializing in democratization, Islamist politics, gender, sectarianism, human security, and religion and development in Egypt and throughout the Middle East. She taught development studies for many years as an assistant professor of political science at the American University in Cairo. For almost 10 years, she worked as a journalist for the newspaper *Al-Ahram Weekly*.

Dr. Bassam Tibi taught at the University of Göttingen, Germany, from 1973 until his retirement in 2009, and was AD White Professor-at-Large at Cornell University until 2010. He is a native Syrian, born in Damascus, and since 1974, a German citizen. Pursuant to his retirement 2009, he served as the Resnick Scholar for the study of antisemitism at the Center for Advanced Holocaust Studies/CAHS at the United States Holocaust Memorial Museum in Washington, DC. Between 1982 and 2000, Dr. Tibi worked—in addition to serving at the University of Göttingen—at Harvard University in various functions, inter alia as a Bosch Fellow. His work has been translated into 16 languages. The former president of Germany, Roman Herzog, decorated him in 1995 with the highest Medal/State Decoration for his "bridging between Islam and the West."

Dr. Hannibal Travis received his doctorate from Harvard Law School and currently teaches as an associate professor of law at Florida International University. Travis has taught internet law, intellectual property, antitrust law, and international and comparative law. In his research, he specializes in religious freedom and religious genocide under international law. He has published widely on genocide and human rights.

William Warda is chairman of the Alliance of Iraqi Minorities, and cofounder of the Hammurabi Human Rights Organization (HHRO). He is the former CEO of Ashur Satellite TV, and a former leader of political and military affairs of the Assyrian Democratic Movement in Nineveh (2003).

Daniel Williams was for 30 years a correspondent for the *Washington Post*, *Los Angeles Times*, and *Bloomberg News* in the Middle East, Europe, Russia, and Latin America. Most recently, he served as a senior researcher with the Emergencies Division at Human Rights Watch, focusing on human rights abuses during the "Arab Spring."